The Early Modern Englishwoman:
A Facsimile Library of Essential Works

Series I

Printed Writings, 1500–1640: Part 3

Volume 4

Pudentiana Deacon

The Early Modern Englishwoman: A Facsimile Library of Essential Works

Series I

Printed Writings, 1500–1640: Part 3

Volume 4

Pudentiana Deacon

Selected and Introduced by
Frans Blom and Jos Blom

General Editors
Betty S. Travitsky and Anne Lake Prescott

ASHGATE

Published by
Ashgate Publishing Limited
Wey Court East
Union Road
Farnham
Surrey, GU9 7PT
England

Ashgate Publishing Company
110 Cherry Street
Suite 3-1
Burlington
VT 05401-3818
USA

Ashgate website: http://www.ashgate.com

British Library Cataloguing-in-Publication Data
Deacon, Pudentiana
Pudentiana Deacon. – (The early modern Englishwoman : a facsimile library of essential works. Printed writings 1500–1640, series 1 ; pt. 3, vol. 4)
1.Francis, of Sales, Saint, 1567–1622 – Teachings 2.Nuns – Religious life – Belgium
I.Title II.Blom, Jos III.Blom, Frans, 1945–
248.8'943

Library of Congress Cataloging-in-Publication Data
The early modern englishwoman: a facsimile library of essential works. Part 3. Printed Writings, 1500–1640 / general editors, Betty S. Travitsky and Anne Lake Prescott.

See page vi for complete CIP Block 2002025880

The woodcut reproduced on the title page and on the case is from the title page of Margaret Roper's trans. of [Desiderius Erasmus] *A Devout Treatise upon the Pater Noster* (circa 1524).

ISBN 978-0-7546-0443-3

Transfered to Digital Printing in 2010

MIX
Paper from responsible sources
FSC® C004959

Printed and bound in Great Britain
by Printondemand-worldwide.com

CONTENTS

Library of Congress Cataloging-in-Publication Data
Francis de Sales, Saint, 1567–1622
[Vrays entretiens spirituels. English]
Pudentiana Deacon / [selected and introduced by] Frans Blom and Jos Blom.
p. cm. – (The early modern Englishwoman. Printed writings, 1500–1640, Series 1, Part 3 ; v. 4)
Translated by Pudentiana Deacon.
"Delicious entertainments of the soule is a translation of a collection of conferences which Francis de Sales held for the Order of the Sisters of the Visitation"–P. 4.
Includes bibliographical references.
ISBN 0-7546-0443-8 (alk. paper)
1. Virtues–Early works to 1800. 2. Spirituality–Catholic Church–History–17th century. 3. Spiritual life–Catholic Church–Early works to 1800. I. Deacon, Pudentiana, 1576–1645. II. Blom, Frans. III. Blom, Jos. IV. Francis de Sales, Saint, 1567–1622. Deliciovs entertainments of the sovle. V. Title. VI. Series.

BX2179.F8 V7413 2002
248.8'943--dc21

2002025880

PREFACE
BY THE GENERAL EDITORS

Until very recently, scholars of the early modern period have assumed that there were no Judith Shakespeares in early modern England. Much of the energy of the current generation of scholars has been devoted to constructing a history of early modern England that takes into account what women actually wrote, what women actually read, and what women actually did. In so doing the masculinist representation of early modern women, both in their own time and ours, has been deconstructed. The study of early modern women has thus become one of the most important—indeed perhaps the most important—means for the rewriting of early modern history.

The Early Modern Englishwoman: A Facsimile Library of Essential Works is one of the developments of this energetic reappraisal of the period. As the names on our advisory board and our list of editors testify, it has been the beneficiary of scholarship in the field, and we hope it will also be an essential part of that scholarship's continuing momentum.

The Early Modern Englishwoman is designed to make available a comprehensive and focused collection of writings in English from 1500 to 1750, both by women and for and about them. The three series of *Printed Writings* (1500–1640, 1641–1700, and 1701–1750), provide a comprehensive if not entirely complete collection of the separately published writings by women. In reprinting these writings we intend to remedy one of the major obstacles to the advancement of feminist criticism of the early modern period, namely the limited availability of the very texts upon which the field is based. The volumes in the facsimile library reproduce carefully chosen copies of these texts, incorporating significant variants (usually in appendices). Each text is preceded by a short introduction providing an overview of the life and work of a writer along with a survey of important scholarship. These works, we strongly believe, deserve a large readership—of historians, literary critics, feminist critics, and non-specialist readers.

The Early Modern Englishwoman also includes separate facsimile series of *Essential Works for the Study of Early Modern Women* and of *Manuscript Writings*. These facsimile series are complemented by *The Early Modern Englishwoman 1500–1750: Contemporary Editions*. Also under our general editorship, this series will include both old-spelling and modernized editions of works by and about women and gender in early modern England.

New York City
2002

INTRODUCTORY NOTE

Dame Pudentiana Deacon

Delicious entertainments is a translation of a French work called *Les vrays entretiens spirituels* ['The authentic spiritual conferences'] by Francis de Sales. The translator is a Benedictine nun, Dame Pudentiana Deacon, whose name, however, does not appear in the book itself. The evidence identifying her is contained in a 17th century MS Catalogue of the library of the English Benedictine Convent at Cambrai, now Osborn Collection Yale MS b 268, 237–246bis (see Allison and Rogers 1994, Vol. II, no. 165). Earlier, Allison and Rogers (1956, no. 337) conjecturally attributed the translation to Agnes More, who was of the same house, and who is known to have translated other works from French into English (Gillow, 1913), but the identification in the Catalogue seems unequivocal and decisive: the Catalogue appears to be a transcript of an original compiled by the English Benedictine Augustine Baker (1575–1641) who lived at Cambrai and knew the people involved (see below).

Facts about Pudentiana Deacon's life are scanty and the two main sources of biographical data concerning her, both records of religious communities to which she belonged, contain discrepancies. In the following account it seemed most logical to take the dates of birth and profession from the 'Brussels' source (printed in Hansom), where she was professed, and the date of death from the 'Cambrai' one (printed in Gillow, 1913), where she died. She was born in 1576 as the daughter of Jhon Deacon at a place given in the original source as 'Argaston' (possibly Haggerston) in Middlesex. Presumably after the death of his wife, Jhon Deacon became a Carthusian monk and died on 27 March 1618 in the house of the order at Malines (Bellenger; de Grauwe *Prosopographia*). His decision to enter the religious life may have been inspired by his daughter's earlier decision to undertake the hazardous and illegal journey to Flanders in order to join the Benedictines. In spite of the risks, a surprisingly large number of Pudentiana's contemporaries shared her vocation as is, for example, illustrated by the fate of four girls who in the early 1620s intended to travel to Flanders for the same reason and who were captured by the English authorities, imprisoned and released only after payment of heavy fines (Lunn, 189). On 11 July 1606 Pudentiana Deacon was received into the house for Benedictine nuns that had been founded at Brussels in 1598 by Lady Mary Percy (1570–1642). The Brussels foundation was the first of more than 20 houses for English nuns to be established in the course of the 17th century. Pudentiana was clothed on 23 April 1607 in the presence of the Infanta Isabella, one of the most important patrons of the English religious communities (Arblaster), and was professed on 29 April the following year.

In 1623 she moved on to Cambrai where a new Benedictine community for English nuns was being established; among its nine original members were Gertrude More (1606–1633), the great-great granddaughter of Sir Thomas More, and two of her nieces, Agnes and Anne. Since Gertrude More and her companions lacked any experience of the monastic life, Pudentiana Deacon and two other nuns from Brussels (Frances Gawen and Viviana Yaxley) were lent to the new community in order to provide practical and religious guidance.

The transfer of these three women to Cambrai may not have been inspired by purely altruistic motives on the part of the Brussels abbess, Mary Percy. The Brussels house was internally divided by a conflict between a pro- and an anti-Jesuit faction. The problems that were to surface again later in several other convents concerned both the choice of a confessor and the kind of spirituality that was to dominate the religious life of the nuns. With regard to the latter, the pro-Jesuit party argued for the Ignatian method as laid down in the *Spiritual Exercises*, while a less methodical, more contemplative and mystical spirituality was advocated by the anti-Jesuits. In 1624 tensions in the Brussels house ran so high that the pro-Jesuit party moved out in order to found a house of their own at Ghent. However, as Lunn (202) suggests, the decision to send three nuns to Cambrai might also have been part of an attempt to get rid of three potential trouble makers.

The early history of Cambrai is closely bound up with the role played by the most prominent 17th century English mystic, Augustine Baker. Immediately after the foundation of the community at Cambrai, problems arose about the kind of spiritual guidance to be given to the sisters (with the three nuns from Brussels advocating Jesuit methods). The president of the English Benedictine Congregation, Rudesind Barlow (1584–1656), decided to appoint a Benedictine director and, although Augustine Baker did not have any experience in directing a convent, the choice fell on him. Initially the appointment created more difficulties than it solved, since the majority of the nuns, led by Gertrude More, refused to be guided by him. However, their attitude gradually changed and Baker even succeeded in winning over Gertrude More, who subsequently became his 'star disciple'. After her death in 1633 Baker compiled *The Life and Death of Dame Gertrude More* (Weld-Blundell) partly as a tribute to her, but also partly in order to demonstrate his views on mysticism.

For the rest of her life Pudentiana Deacon lived and worked at Cambrai. In view of the interest in mysticism of Deacon's spiritual director, it is noteworthy that the book by De Sales that she translated strikes one as the opposite of a mystical treatise (see below). Gillow (II, 35) mentions the fact that, apart from *Delicious Entertainments*, she also translated a book entitled 'The Mantle of the Spouse', but no copy has been found, and it is unlikely that the work was ever published. We assume that this was an English version of one of the 16th or early 17th century editions of *Bruygoms mantelken* by Frans Vervoort OFM, which – supposing that Pudentiana Deacon did not have any Dutch – may have reached her through a French translation, e.g. *Mantelet de l'espoux* (Atrecht, 1596). In her obituary notice in the 'Records of the Abbey of Our Lady of Consolation at Cambray, 1620–1793' (Gillow, 1913) one gets a glimpse of her other activities as cellarer, novice mistress and prioress. She died on 21 December 1645.

Delicious entertainments of the soule

Delicious entertainments of the soule is a translation of a collection of conferences which Francis de Sales held for the Order of the Sisters of the Visitation. Francis de Sales (1567–1622), religious author, famous preacher and saint, was Bishop of Geneva at the time when Geneva was a Calvinist stronghold, so that in fact he lived and worked at Annecy in the Savoy. In 1604, two years after his appointment to the bishopric of Geneva, he met Jane Frances de Chantal (1572–1641), the widow of Christoph Baron de Rabutin-Chantal, who had been killed in a hunting accident a few years earlier, after a marriage that had lasted for seven years. Inspired by the spirituality of Francis de Sales, Jane de Chantal felt attracted to a religious life, but decided first to devote another six years to the education of her children. After this period she, together with Francis de Sales, founded the Institute of the Visitation of the Blessed Virgin and established the first convent in March 1610. The Institute was intended for young girls and widows who wanted to enter a convent but lacked the strength or the inclination for the physical austerities of the great orders. The new Institute, officially recognized by Pope Paul V in 1618, turned out to be a great success. By the time of Francis de Sales's death in 1622 there were 13 houses and when Jane de Chantal died the order had expanded to 80 establishments.

It was for these sisters that Francis held conferences or 'familiar conversations' on religious topics at regular intervals both at Annecy and also at the other houses founded by the rapidly expanding order. These conversations were not written out by Francis himself but were noted down and collected by the sisters. Francis did not intend to have his talks, his 'entretiens' published, but the copied manuscripts of the entretiens were very popular among the sisters. They were not meant for and not shown to outsiders. However, after the death of Francis de Sales in 1622 publication was no longer ruled out. In September 1624, in a letter to an unnamed Jesuit priest (MacKay, xvii), Jane de Chantal mentioned for the first time the possibility of having the 'entretiens' published. The reaction was positive, but for some years nothing much happened until suddenly, in 1628, an unauthorized edition appeared. Someone had got hold of the manuscript and had published the 'entretiens' against the wishes of the sisters but with the permission of the civil authorities (the Parliament of Grenoble). The book was entitled *Les Entretiens et Colloques Spirituels du Bienheureux François de Sales Evesque et Prince de Genève, Fondateur des Dames de la Visitation. Tournon, A. de la Clostre. Pour Pierre Dobret, Marchand Libraire à Lyon.* ['The spiritual conferences and conversations of the blessed Francis de Sales Bishop and Prince of Geneva, founder of the Ladies of the Visitation']. This work is often referred to as 'Les Colloques'.

Jane de Chantal immediately protested and tried to get this version suppressed. She also started work on an edition of her own entitled 'Les Vrays Entretiens'. On 8 May 1628 she obtained a Royal Privilege and began assembling and comparing the several manuscript texts. The 'authorized' edition appeared in the summer of 1629 under the title *Les Vrays Entretiens Spirituels du Bien-Heureux François de Sales, Evesque et Prince de Genève, Instituteur, et Fondateur de l'Ordre des Religieuses de la Visitation St. Marie. A Lyon, par Vincent de Coeurssilly, Marchand Libraire, en Rue Turpin à l'Enseigne de la Fleur de Lys, MDCXXIX avec Privilege du Roy.* The sisters reprinted the book in 1630, 1631 and 1632, and this last edition was the one incorporated in the first edition of the complete works (Toulouse 1637). A whole series of pirated editions (not respecting the Royal Privilege) and a range of translations testify to the book's popularity (Mackay xv–xvi; see also the catalogue of the Bibliothèque Nationale).

As a matter of fact the very first of these translations is our present edition, *Delicious entertainments* (Douai 1632). As was said above, the book consists of more or less verbatim transcripts of talks by Francis De Sales on topics quite often suggested by the nuns themselves. This form enables the reader to get an idea of the personality of the speaker, and De Sales's personal charm must have been one of the reasons why his work has been so popular. He comes across as a humane, commonsensical, practical man with an occasional sense of humour and a pretty shrewd idea of the specific worries and temptations of the audience in front of him. Thus he tells the sisters that if they want to fast more than the Rule commands them to, they can ask for permission to do so, but

> Lett not those that shall fast, dispise them that eate, nor those that eat them who doe fast, and euen so in all other things, which are not commanded nor forbidden. Let euerie one abound in her sence, that is to say, let euerie one inioy, and vse her libertie, without iudging and controlling others, that doe not as she doth; desiring to haue her manner held to be the best: since it may bee, that one eateth with as much renunciation of her own will, as another would fast … (page 13 of the present edition).

Instead of promises of 'extasies, or rauishments, and visions' (p.45), characterized by De Sales as 'childish fopperies', he gives his audience a number of simple rules: be proud of your convent; don't be too upset about your own imperfections or those of your superiors ('Alas, my deare daughters, if wee should make none Superiors vnless they were perfect, wee must pray to God to send vs Saincts or Angells' [251–2]); find out what the will of God is by being obedient to those appointed to lead you; don't worry too much about the fruit of your labours since you will only be judged on the basis of effort, not on effect. 'Simple' is one of the keywords of the text: even in difficult matters such as the choice of novices or the decision whether a novice shall be professed ('The Seaventeenth Entertainement', 260ff) one's course of action can be based on relatively uncomplicated considerations.

In trying to make Francis de Sales's text available to an English readership Pudentiana Deacon faced a problem that must have been familiar to other exiled writers, editors and translators: the first point in her translator's address to the 'Christian and religious reader' concerns the fact that the printer (Gheerart Pinchon or Pinson) was a 'Wallon' who did not have English. She asks her readers to forgive the imperfections caused by a foreign typesetter, and indeed a forgiving attitude on the part of the reader is necessary since the text is quite literally riddled with mistakes. Word-division, punctuation, page-numbering and spelling are a nightmare and – even less excusable – Mr Pinchon did a very poor job on the actual printing. In some cases words are hardly legible because of lack of proper inking, while in other cases massive amounts of ink have bled through the page, again causing illegibility. (It is noteworthy that other English publications by Pinchon show a much higher level of workmanship.) Apart from excuses for the printer and also for the translator ('a woman, that had not much skille in French'), the address to the reader, not suprisingly, recommends the book highly not only for religious but also for laymen. In the latter case readers are asked, in the true practical spirit of Francis de Sales, to change for themselves the things that are 'peculiar to Religious persons', since 'all meats are not for all stomakes'. Deacon also hopes that the book may fall into the hands of 'illwillers of the Catholike religion' because the insight that they will get into the religious way of life will prevent them from detracting and deriding 'that which they cannot comprehend, much less imitate'.

The final paragraph of the address demonstrates convincingly that Pudentiana Deacon might have made a writer in her own right:

> For conclusion, I dare boldly say, that whosoeuer will follow really & cordially the spirit of this Author & booke, hee shall liue in peace with God, with his neighbour, & with himselfe: he shall taste upon earth how sweet God is in heauen, he shall lead a true Euangelicall or rather Angelicall life, he shall begin his heauen upon earth, & sayle secure, immoueable, quiet, & content through all the chaunges & chaunces, stormes & tempestes of this wauering world, Iesus being his Pilot, hope his ancre, faith his light, solitude his cabinet, prayer his prouision, humility his heauen, heauen his home: farewell.

There is only one edition of *Delicious entertainments*, printed by Gerard Pinchon (Pinson) at Douai in 1632 (*STC* 11316). Pinchon (1609–1636) was active during the years 1629–1636. His major output was in French, but he published besides *Delicious Entertainments* eight other works in English. Douai was one of the centres of the English Roman Catholic exiles abroad. The book was never reprinted. Allison and Rogers (1994) mention seventeen extant copies. Reproduced here is the copy from the Bodleian Library (Mason F1, text block 65 × 120 mm) with pages 170–191 substituted from the Ampleforth copy (the bleeding through of ink makes these pages of the Bodley copy almost illegible). Apart from the many printing errors and the poor quality of the actual printing referred to above, all copies show many mistakes with regard to page numbering. A complete list of all the printing errors would occupy a great many pages and would probably only add to the confusion. The Bodleian copy was selected because, apart from pages 170–191, it tends to be more legible than the other extant copies and, moreover, it shows a number of in-press corrections, marginally diminishing the number of printing errors.

In the following list we give the correct page number followed by the incorrect number in square brackets ('40 [38]' means 'page 40 is wrongly numbered 38'): 40 [38], 48 [24], 52 [25], 68 [70], 69 [51], 128 [116], 129 [117], 150 [120], 176 [178], 177 [179], 180 [181], 181 [180], 200 [211], 201 [212], 269 [265], 280 [180], 282 [288], 288 [188], 299 [331], 304 [430].

Catchwords are lacking on pages 14, 15, 19, 41–46, 68, 104, 185, 186, 294 and 301.

References

STC 11316

Allison, A.F. and D.M. Rogers (1956), *A Catalogue of Catholic Books in English Printed Abroad or Secretly in England 1558–1640*, Bognor Regis

Allison, A.F. and D.M. Rogers (1989–1994), *The Contemporary Printed Literature of the English Counter-Reformation between 1558 and 1640*, 2 vols, Aldershot

Arblaster, Paul (1997), 'The Infanta and the English Benedictine Nuns', in *Recusant History*, Vol. 23, no. 4, pp. 508–27

Bellenger, D.A. (1984), *English and Welsh Priests 1558–1800*, Bath

De Grauwe, Jan (1984), *Histoire de la Chartreuse Sheen Anglorum au Continent*, Salzburg

De Grauwe, Jan (1984), *Prosopographia Cartusiana Belgica (1314–1796)*, Gent

Gillow, J. (1885–1902), *A Literary and Biographical History or Bibliographical Dictionary of the English Catholics*, 5 vols, London and New York

Gillow, J. (ed.) (1913), 'Records of the Abbey of Our Lady of Consolation at Cambrai, 1620–1793' in *Publications of the Catholic Record Society*, Vol. XIII, pp. 77–8

Hansom, J.S. (ed.) (1914), 'The Register Book of Profession ... of the English Benedictine Nuns at Brussels and Winchester, now at East Bergholt 1598–1865' in *Publications of the Catholic Record Society*, Vol. XIV, p. 179

Lunn, David (1980), *The English Benedictines, 1540–1688*, London/New York

Mackay O.S.B., Dom B. (1895), 'Introduction' to Volume 6 of *Oeuvres de Saint François de Sales*, 'Les Vrays Entretiens Spirituel', Annecy, pp. vi–lxii

New Catholic Encyclopaedia, s.v. Francis de Sales; Jane de Chantal

Plomer, Henry R. (1977), *Dictionaries of the Printers and Booksellers who were at work in England, Scotland and Ireland 1557–1775*, Reprint London

Weld-Blundell, Benedict (ed.) (1910) *The Inner Life of Dame Gertrude More* (an abridged edition of Augustine Baker's *The Life and Death of Dame Gertrude More*; a scholarly edition of Baker's text will be published at Salzburg in the near future, edited by B. Wekking), London

FRANS BLOM AND JOS BLOM

Delicious entertainments of the soule (*STC* 11316) is reproduced, by permission, from the copy at the Bodleian Library Oxford, with pages 170–191 substituted, by permission, from the Ampleforth Abbey copy. The text block of the copy measures 65 × 120 mm.

On 18 pages damage to the copy has led to loss of text and occasionally the poor printing quality makes for illegibility.

11.35:	and
11.36:	them
12.33:	assembly
12.34:	Religious
12.35:	perfect
12.36:	them
13.32:	ner
13.33:	eateth
13.34:	will as
13.35:	leth not his
14.33:	obserued
14.34:	and
14.35:	Martha be
14.36:	Magdalene; Lett
82.36:	a hundred
92.18–20:	but that he should aduertise them, that the king that they should haue, should take such dominion ouer them, that he should take
108.10:	turmoyle
117.37:	much
118.37:	myselfe
174.25:	Therefore
180.36:	citye that they practice
180.37:	nie that they yeald
181.36:	I goe to praise
181.37:	hower rather then at another?
210.14:	wee shall render ourselues exact
210.22–3:	that is to say by loue: they loue the commaundements and observe them louinglye,
211.21:	weake and infirme
234.19:	in all that
234.22:	foreseene
319.20:	and God will that you feele them vntill death, for
320.20:	and annihilate your passions, and she who shall
323.2:	did aske
323.3:	oftner
323.4:	it of the
323.13:	haircloth

18/6 [illegible]

[illegible]

Mason

F. 1.

No 8vo Shelf

DELICIOVS ENTERTAINMENTS OF THE SOVLE:

WRITTEN BY

THE HOLY AND MOST REVEREND LORD FRANCIS DE SALES, BISHOP AND PRINCE OF GENEVA.

Translated by a Dame of our Ladies of comfort of the order of S. Bennet in Cambray.

Imprinted at DOVAY,
By GHEERART PINSON, vnder the signe of Cuelen. 1632.

CHRISTIAN AND RELIGIOVS READER.

IF in peruseing this translated treatese of sound doctrine and solide documents, thou meet vvith some faults (as thou vvill doe, vvith many, both in the translation & impression) knovv that the printer vvas a VVallon, vvho understood nothing at all English; and the translatresse a vvoman, that had not much skille in the Frenche, but vvhy did shee then undertake it ? vvilt thou say, truely for her priuate imployment & instruction ; neuer intending more then the vse of a particular cloister ; though God and her superiours haue othervvise disposed of it, & exposed it to the publierk vievv of the vvorld,

as thou

As thou seest.

§. Sure I am, and can assure the of three things. First, that if thou haue the spirit of the authour or the matter, thou vvill interprete & pardon all frindly, freely, & fully. Next, That if thou finde as much profit in the pervsall of it, as she did that translated it, thou vvilt blesse God, & pray for her.

Thirdly, that if it could bee as vvelcome & vvelliked in English, as it vvas and is still in Frenche, the printer vvill not loose his pains in printing it, nor you in pervsing it: for since the late death of this famous Prelat & pillar in Gods Church (vvho vvas one of the most clear, discreet, svveet & deuout spirits of our age;) it hath been published in diuerse editions; and is still exceedingly praised, prized, & practiced; not onely by Religious persons, but also by the best seculars, especially of the deuout sexe:

For although all bee not religious, nor bound to bee so perfect as religious are; yett all are bound to labour for the perfection of christian & solide vertues, such as are humility of heart, poverty of spiritt, purity of

intention

intention, simplicity of affection, conformity of vvill, custodie of heart, naked charity, & filiall confidence, together vvith a generosity of resolution to please and loue God aboue all, to all vvich and much more this little booke leadeth thee by a short, svveet, & secure vvay.

If thou like & loue not the INTRODVCTION TO A DEVOVT LIFE, composed by the same Byshop, I should call thy deuotion into question; if thou approoue and applaud it (as all truely deuout doe) thou shall find that this after-borne fruict is but as it vvere a supplement, or explication thereof in a most plaine & perfect manner, descending to particulars in the obtaiming of vertues, and mortification of vices: If some things bee peculiar to Religious persons, either leaue such for them; or apply to thy self vvith some little chaunge: all meats are not for all stomakes, nor all Doctrines for all dispositions; peruse all, pratize some, pray for the translatresse, & praise God in all.

If any ill vvillers of Catholike religion, & ill-vvishers of a religious vocation come to the vievv of this booke, they may see the liues, Rules, vertues, & customes, of Religious fa-

 milies

milies discipherered vvithout passion or partiality, & admire vvith vvhat charity, discretion, deuotion, & humility they passe ouer the pilgrimage of this mortall & miserable life, sighing after, and suffernig for eternity: & so leaue to detract & deride at that vvhich they cannot comprehend, much lesse imitate; And if perchaunce some scandals arriue amongst them by the meanes of some vvolues or foxes in sheep-skins, I meane by some false brethren & Apostates, it is not to be attributed to the Orders & ordination of holy Church or Religious institution, but to the malice of satan & humane frailtie, for neuer yett since the Church began, vvas it free from scandals, and false brethren & Apostats, nor neuer vvill it be untill the vvorlds end; yett cursed are they that voluntarily blovv & kindle the fire of faction or diuision in the house of God, or that adde fevvell unto it to continevv it, & blessed are the peaceable, humble and innocent spirits that are prooued & purified ther-in.

§. For conclusion, I dare boldly say, that vvhosoeuer vvill follovv really & cordially the spirit of this Author & booke, hee shall liue in peace vvith God, vvith his neighbour,

&

& vvith himselfe: he shall tast vpon earth hovv svveet God is in heauen, he shall lead a true Euangelicall or rather Angelicall life, he shall begin his heauen vpon earth, & sayle secure, immoueable, quiet, & content through all the chaunges & chaunces, stormes & tempestes of this vvauering vvorld, Iesus being his Pilot, hope his ancre, faith his light, solitude his cabinet, prayer his prouision, humility his hauen, heauen his home: farevvell.

LIVE LORD IESVS IN OVR SOVLES.

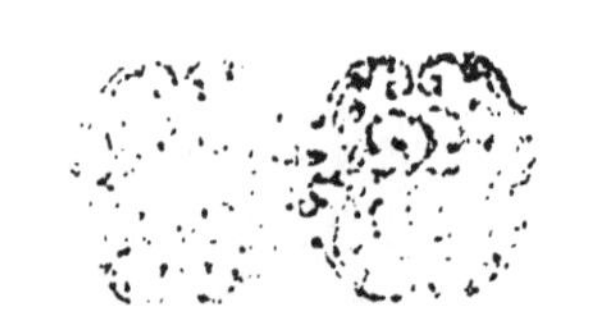

THE BISHOP OF GENEVA HIS SPIRITVALL ENTERTAINMENTS.

THE FIRST ENTERTAINMENT

VVHERIN IS DECLARED THE OBLIgation of the constitutions of the visitation of Our Blessed Ladie, & of the qualities of deuotion, vvhich the Religious of the sayd order oughto haue.

1. These cōstitutions, of themselues doe in no sorte oblige any one vnder sinne, either mortall or veniall: but they are giuen onely for direction & guide to those of the congregation; yet not with standing, if any should violate them willingly, of purpose, with contempt, or with scandall, aswell to the sisters as to strangers: she should with out doubt committ à great offence; for such a person cannot be exempt from fault, who debaseth and deshonoreth the things of God, belieth her profession,

ouer-

ouerthroweth the congregation, and dissipateth the fruites of good example & sweet sauour, wich she ought to produce towardes her neighbour: so that such a voluntarie contempt shall in the ende be poursued with some great chastisment from heauen, & especially with depriuation of the graces and guifts of the holy Ghost, wich are ordinarily taken from them, who abandon their good designes, & quitt the way into which Almighty God hath introduced thẽ.

2. Now the contempt of Constitutions, as also of all other good workes, is knowne by these considerations following.

That person failleth therein, which through contempt violateth, or omitteth to execute any ordinance, not only voluntarily, but of deliberate purpose; for if he violate it in consideratly, by obliuion, or surprise of some passion; that is another thing: for contempt contayneth in it a deliberate will, and a determinate purpose to doe that, wich it doeth; where of it followeth, that the person, who violateth the ordinance, or disobeyeth through contempt, he not onely disobeyeth, but he will disobey; he doth not onely cõmitt an act of disobedience, but he doth it with intention to disobey: as for example, It is forbiddden to eate out of the times of meales, a sister eateth plummes, Apricokes, or other fruites; she violateth the Rule and committeth an act of disobedience: now if she eate being allured with the delighte, which she thinketh to receaue in it; then she disobeyeth but not through disobedience, but through *Liquorousnes*; or else she eateth, beccause she hath the Rule in little esteme, neither will regard

gard it, nor submitt her selfe there vnto, & then she disobeyeth through contẽpt & disobediẽce.

More ouer hẽce it followeth, that the party that disobeyeth, by some alluremẽt, inticing, or sodayne passion, would gladly be able to cõtent her passion and not disobey, euen at the same time that she taketh pleasure in matter of eating: for exãple, she is sorrie that it is with disobedience; in which case, disobedience followeth or accompanieth the worke: but in the former, disobedience precedeth or goes before the actiõ, and serueth for the cause and motiue of it, euen although it be for delicacye; for whosoeuer eateth against a commaundement, consequently, or together, committeth an act of disobedience; although if it could be auoyded in eatting he would not commit it: euen as he that drinketh very much, would not willingly become drunke, although in drinking he maketh himselfe drunke. But they who sinn through neglect or disesteeme of the Rule, and by disobedience, they will and intend the same disobedience, in such sorte that they doe not the worke, nor would doe it, if they weare not moued to doe it by the will and pourpose they haue to disobey. The one then disobeyeth, willing and intending that to the which disobedience is ioyned, the other disobeyeth willing and pourposing the same thing because disobedience is conioyned therunto: The one encountereth and disobedience, in the thing she willeth, and would be glad not to edcounter it: the other seeketh after disobedience and would not doe the thing, but with intention to find disobediẽce therein. The one sayeth, I disobey because, I entend to eate

 this

this apricoke, which I cannot doe but with disobedience: the other sayeth, I eate it, because I will disobey, wihch I shall doe in eating: disobedience and contempt followeth the one, and it conducteth the other:

Now this formall disobediēce and contempt of good and holy things, is neuer with out some sinne at least veniall, no not in things which are onely conunsells. Althoughe one is not bound to followe the councells of perfectiō, by the election of other things vnder any offēce: yet may she not therefore by disesteeme, and contēpt refuse them, with out offence. For though we are not obliged to follow all that is good, yet we ought to honnour and esteeme it, and cōsequētly we haue much more reason not to contemne or sett little by it.

More-ouer it followeth that she who by cōtempt violateth the Rule and constitutions, esteemeth it vnprofitable and vile, which is a very grear presumption & pride: or else peraduenture, if she esteeme it profitable, yet for all that, will not submitt her selfe there-vnto: then she breaketh her purpose, with great dōmage of her neighbour, to whome she giueth scandall, and euill example, & she doeth contrarie to her promise made to the companie, and disordereth a deuout house; vhich are three greeuous faults.

But to the end, it may in some sorte be discerned When a person violateth the Rules of Obediēce by contempt, behould here some signes.

1. When as being corrected, she mocketh at it, and hath not any repentance.

2. When she perseuereth with out demonstra-

stration of any desire or will to amẽd her selfe.

3. when she contesteth, that the Rule or commaundement, is not to the purpose.

4 when she endeuoreth to draw others into the same breach, and taketh the feare thereof from them, saying, that it is nothing, & there is no danger, therein. Yet these signes are not so certayne, but they may happen sometimes for other causes, aswell as that of contempt: for it may happen that a person, derideth the party, who reprehendeth her; for the little estimation she hath of her; That she perseuereth through infirmity; or that she contesteth out of despite and choler; or to haue cõpanions she debaucheth others, the better to excuse her disordered behauiour Neuerthelesse, it is easye to iudge by the circumstances, when these things are done by contẽpt: for in the ende shamelessnes, impudẽcie, and manifest liberty ordinarilie follow contẽpt; and those who haue it in their hart, in fine powre it forth at their mouth, saying (as Dauid noteth) *vvho shall controll vs?*

4. I must needs add a worde concerning a tentation, which may arriue vpon this point: that is this, somtimes a person esteemeth not her selfe to de disobedient and a libertine whẽ shee neglecteth but one or two Rules, which seeme to her of smal importance, prouided that she obserue all the others; But O good God, who seeth not this deceipte considering that what one shall esteeme little, an other will much regarde; and contrary. Likwise when in a companye one maketh no accompt of one Rule, the second dispiseth another, the third another, so the whole frame of Religious disci-

pline; is put out of order. For whilest that the spirit of man is no otherwise conducted then according to his inclinations and auersiōs, what hapneth vnto him, but a perpetuall inconstancie, with varietie of defects and offences? yesterday I was ioyfull & silence did dislike me; and a tentation did suggest to me that I was Idle; perchance I am melancholie this day, & it will tell me that recreatiō and intertaynment are yet far more vnprofitable; I was yesterday in consolation, then it did please me to sing: this day I am in desolation and it will displease me, & so of other such like accidents.

So that whosoeuer will liue perfectly a happy life, of necessitie he must accustome himselfe to liue according to reason, to his Rules, and Obedience; and not according to his inclinatiōs or auersions; and much to esteeme all the Rules, and to honour them. and cherish them, at least in his Superior will; for if he neglect one now, to morrow he shall cōtemne another, & further more the next day another, and thē incontinētly the bond of duty being brok n, in an instant all whatsoeuer vas bound there with, by little and little wilbe dispersed and scatterred abroad.

God forbid that any of the daughters of the visitation should straye so farr out of the way of the Loue of God, that she loose her selfe in the contempt of the Rules by disobedience, hardnesse and obstinacie of hart. For what greatter mischeife or disaster could happen vnto her? especially since there are few particular and proper Rules of the congregation, the most part, and almost all of them being

being either generall good Rules, which they ought and should obserue in their houses, were they in the world, if they will liue with any honour, reputation and feare of God; or else they regard the apparent comelines (or) decencie of a deuoute house, or the officers them selues in particular.

5. If so be somtimes there arriue vnto them some disgust or auersion from the constitutions, and Rules of the Congregation: they shal comport themselues in the same manner, as they are to doe about other temptations, correcting the auersion by reason, and by a good and strong resolution, framed in the superiour part of the soule; attendig till God sende them consolation in their way, and make them to see, (as another Iacob, when he was wearie and tired in his voiage,) that the Rules and method of Life which they haue embraced, are the true ladder, by which they ought, in guise of the Angell, to mount vnto God by Charitie, and to descend into themselues by humilitie.

But if, without auersion, it happen vnto them to violate the Rules through infirmity: then they are instantly to humble themselues before God, demaund pardon of him; and renewing their resolution of obseruing the same Rule, they shall take care, and wach aboue all, that they enter not into discouragement of spirit and vnquietnesse; but with new confidence in God, haue recourse to his holie Loue.

6. And in regard of violating of the Rule, (which is not done, but by pure disobedience or by contempt) if they doe it by carelesnes,

 infir-

infirmity tentation, or negligence: then they may & ought to confesse it as a veniall sinne; or otherwise as a thing, wherin there might haue bene a veniall sinne; for although there be not any kind of sinne there in, in vertu of obligation to the Rule; there may be neuerthelessin respect of their negligēce carelessnes, sodaynesse, or other such defects; since it rarelie arriueth, that seeing some good proper for our aduance-ment (and especiallie if we be called and inuited to doe the same) we voluntarilie giue it ouer & omitt it with out offence; in so much as such an omission, proceedeth no otherwise thē, of neglicence, and deprayed affectiō, or want of feruour. And if we must render an account of those wordes which are trulie idle, how much more for hauing rendred vnfruitfull and vn profitable the call which our Rule giueth vs for the practice there of? I haue sayed, *It hapneth rarely not to offend god whē we Leaue undone a good, fitt for our adduancement*; because it may so fall out, that we omitt it not willingly, or deliberatly; but by obliuion, vnwarinesse, and subreption; and thē there is no sinne therein, neither little nor great; vnlesse the thing, which we forget, weare of so great importance that we weare obliged to hould our selues so attentiue, that we doe not fall into obliuion and vnwarinesse; as for exemple, if a sister break silence, because she is not attentiue, that it is time of silence, & therefore she remembreth not her selfe; for somuch as she thinketh of other things or else she is suprised with some motion to speake, in the wich occasiō she shall haue sayed some thing, before she hath well thought to represse

presse it; with out doubt she sinneth not: for the obseruance of silence is not of so great importance, that they be obliged to haue such an attention, that they forgett it not: rather contrariewise it is a very good thing in the time of silence to imploy themselues in other pious and holy thoughts, and if being attentiue to them, one forgett her selfe to be in time of silence, this obliuion proceding from so good a cause can neuer be euill, nor consequently, the wante of silence, which proceedeth there of.

But if she should forgett to serue a sicke person, which weare in danger for want of seruice, and that this office had bene enioyned her, for the wich all reposed on her care: it should be no good excuse for her to say, I thought not of it, I did not remember my selfe; no: for the thing was of so great importāce, that she ought to bee attentiue there vnto, not to faile there in; and the want of this attention may not be excused, in regard of the quallitie of the thing which doeth deserue and require due attention.

7. It ought to be beleeued, that according to the measure which diuine Loue shall make progresse in the soules of the daughters of the Congregation, it will alwaies render them more exact, and carefull in the obseruance of their Constitutions, although they of them selues oblige not vnder payne of sinne neither mortall nor veniall; for if they did oblige vnder payne of death, how much more straitly, should they obserue them? Now *Loue is strong as death*; then the attractions of Loue are also as powerfull to execute a resolution, as the threatnings of death: *zeale*

 sayeth

sayeth the sacred Canticle) *is hard and strong as hell*: the Soules then which haue zeale, will doe as much and more in vertu of the same, thẽ they would doe for feare of hell. So likwise by the sweet violence of Loue, the daughters of the Congregatiō wil obserue so much more exactly their Rules, God assisting thẽ, then if they weare obliged vnder payne of eternall damnation In summe, they shall haue perpetuall memorie of that which Salomon sayeth in the Prouerbs 19. *he which keepeth the commaundement, gardeth his soule, and he who neglecteth his way shall die*: now your way is that manner of Life, in the which God hath placed you. I speake nothing heere of the obligatiō which we haue to the obseruance of vowes: for it is most euident, that whosceuer absolutely trãsgresseth the Rule, in the essentiall vowes of Pouertie, Chastitie, and obedience, sinneth mortally, and he shoulde doe as much breaking inclosure.

8. Lett the sisters make a particuler Profession to nourish in their hartes an interiour, strōg and generous deuotiō; I say *interiour* that they haue their wills cōforme to the good *exteriour* actiōs they shall doe, whether they be little or great; Lett nothing be done out of custome: but by electiō and applicatiō of the will; & if somtimes the exteriour action preuent the interiour affection because of the cōtinuall vse there of: at least lets affection immediatlie follow; if before that I incline my selfe to my Superiour, I haue not the interiour inclination by an humble electiō to be subiect vnto her: at least lett this electiō accōpanie, or follow neere the exteriour inclinatiō. The sisters of the Congregatiō haue very few

Rules

Rules for the exteriour; fewa usterities, few ceremonies, short seruice: let thē therefore willinglie and louinglie accommodate their hartes to them, making the exteriour to proceede from the interiour, and nourishing the interiour by the exteriour, euen so as fire produceth ashes, and ashes nourish the fire.

More ouer this deuotion must be *strong*,

First to support tentations which are neuer wanting to them, wich will with an entire hart serue God.

Secōdly *strōg* to support the varietie of spirits which they shall find in the congregatiō, which is so great a triall for weake spirits that they shall scarcely encounter any thing more difficult.

Thirdly *strong* to support each one her owne imperfections, and not to be disquieted to see her selfe subiect to them: for euen as she must haue a strōg humilitie, not to loose courage, but to lift vp her confidence in God in the midst of her imbecillities; so must she haue a powerfull courage to entreprise the correction and amēdment of them.

Fourthly, *strōg* to fight again her imperfectiōs

Fifily *strong* to contēne the worlde and iudgemēts of the world, which are neuer wāting to cōtroll pious institutes, espetially in the beginning.

Sixtly, *strong* to hould her selfe independant of affections, frindships or particuler inclinations, to the end she liue not according to them; but according to the light of true pietie.

Seuenthly, *strong* to hould her selfe independēt of tēdernesse, sweetnesses, and cōsolatiōs which come vnto vs aswell from God, as frō creatures, [illegible]d not to permitt our selues to be ingaged to [illegible]em.

Again

Again, strong to enterprise a continuall warre against our euill inclinations humours, habitts, and propensions.

In fine it must be *generous*, not to be astonished or daunted with difficulties; but rather contrarie wise increassing her courage by them. For (as S. Bernard sayeth) he is not very valiant whose courage groweth not in midst of paynes and contradictions. *Generous* to pretend the most high point of perfection, notwithstanding all imperfections, and weaknes or frailty; sustayning her selfe by a perfect confidence vpon the diuine mercye, following the example of that soule who sayed to her beloued: *Drawe me We will rune after thee in the odour of thy oyntmēts*: as if she would haue sayed: of my selfe I am immouable; but when thou shalt drawe me, I will rune The diuine Louer of our soules leaueth vs often as it weare sticking in our miseries, to the end we may know our deliurance commeth from him; and when we haue it, we hould it deare, as a most pretions gift of his bountie. For this cause as generous deuotiō neuer ceaseth to cry vnto God, *drawe me*; so she neuer ceaseth from aspiring, frō hoping, and from promising her selfe couragiously to *runne* one, and sayeth, *we will runne after thee*; And we ought neuer to be troubled, if at the first onsett we runne not after our Sauiour, prouided that we allwaies say, *drawmee*, & that we haw the courage for to say: *we will runne*; for although we rūne not, it sufficeth that God assisting *we will runne*. This congregation not being an assembl[ie] of perfect persons, no more then other Relig[ions] are, but of persons who pretend to perf[ection]

th

themselues: not of persons *running*, but of persons who *pretend to runne*; and, who for this cause learne first to walke a slow pace, then to hasten themselues, after to walke more roūdly, and in fine to runne.

9. This *generous* deuotion contēneth not any thing: and causeth that with out trouble or vnquietnesse we see euery one to walke, to runne, to fly diuerslie, according to the diuersities of inspirations, and variety of measures of the diuine grace, which euerie one receaueth. This is an aduertisement which the great Apostle S. paule made to the Romains. 14. *one* (sayeth he) *beleeueth he may eate of all things, the other, vvhich is vveake, eateth hearbs; Lett not hym that eateth, despise him vvhich eateth not, & he that eateth not, lett him not iudge him that eateth. Lett euerie one abound in his sence: he that eateth, eateth to our* Lord, *and he that eateth not, eateth not to our* Lord, *and asvvell the one as the other rendreth thankes to God.* Your Rule doeth not commaund many fastes, neuerthelesse some for particuler necessities may obtayne licence to faste more. Lett not those that shall fast, dispise them that eate, nor those that eat them who doe fast, and euen so in all other things, which are not cōmāded nor forbidden. Lett euerie one abound in her sence, that is to say, let euerie one enioy, and vse her libertie, with out iudging and controlling others, that doe not as she doth; desiring to haue her ma-[illegible]er held to be the best: since it may bee, that one [illegible]eth with as much renunciation of her owne [illegible] as another would fast; & that one tel-[illegible] faultes by the same renunciation, by

tho

the which another telleth thē. Generous deuotiō will not haue cōpanions in *all* that she doth; but only in her *pretentiō*, which is thē Glorie of God and aduancement of her neighbour in the diuine Loue; and, prouided they walke rightly to that end, she careth not by what way it is; on cōditiō that he which *fasteth*, fast for God; and he who fasteth not, also *fast not* for God, she is wholie satisfied, as well with the one, as with the other. She will not then drawe others to her course, but followeth simply, humbly, and peaceably on her way Yea if it should happen that one should eate not for God, but by inclinatiō; or that she should not take a disclpline, not for God, but by à naturall auersion; yet for all that, those who doe the cōtrarie exercises shall not iudg her; but with out censuring shall gentlie and sweetlie follow on their way, with out dispising, to the preiudice of the weake; remēbring them selues, that if in these occasiōs, some incline perchance to nicenes: their owne inclinations and auershōs also in other occurrences doe perhapps the same; but also those who haue such inclinations and auersions, ought to take great heede, not to vtter any wordes, nor to giue any manner of signe of disgust, that others doe better: for it should be a great impertinēce in them: but rather cōsidering their imbecillity they ought to regard the better doers with a holy sweete and cordiall reuerence; for thereby they may be able to drawe as much profitt frō their weaknes by the humility that proceedeth there of, as the others doe gaine by their exercises. If that this point be well vnderstood and wel obseru[illegible] it will conserue a meruelous tranquilly[illegible] sweetnes in the Congregation. Lett M[illegible] actiue, but lett her not controll M[illegible]

Magdalene contemplate, but so that she dispise not Martha; for our Lord will take the cause of her that shalbe censured.

But neuerthelesse if some sisters should haue auersiōs from pious, good and approoued things, or inclinations to things lesse pious; if they will beleeue me, they shall vse violence, and shall resist their auersions, and inclinatiōs, as much as they shalbe able, the better to render thēselues true mistrisses of thē selues, and to serue God by an excellēt mortification, repugning euen this their repugnāce, contradicting their contradictiō declining from their inclinations, diuerting thē selues from their auersions, and in all and by all making the authoritie of reason to reigne, principallie in things, in which they haue time to take their resolution: and for conclusion, they shall endeuour to haue a gentle and tractable hart, submisse and easie to condescend in all lawfull things, and to shew in euerie enterprise, Obedience and Charitie; for to resemble the doue, who receaueth, all the brightness and shinings the sunne giueth her; Blessed are the pliable harts, for they will neuer breake.

10. The daughters of the visitation shall allwaies speake very hūbly of their little congregation, and they shall preferr all others before it, (as touching honour and precedence) yet neuerthelesse they shall preferr it before al other, as touching Loue; willinglie witnessing, when occasion shall present it selfe, how contentdllie they liue in this vocation, euen so as women ought to preferr their husbands before all others, not as more honourable, but in affection; so euerie one preferrs his country before others in Loue, not in esteeme: and each

Pilot cherisheth more the vessell wher in he saylleth, thẽ others, although they be more rich, and better furnished. Lett vs freelie auouch that other Congregations are better, more rich, and more excellent; but therefore not more amiable, or more desirable, or more conuenient, for vs; since our Lord hath willed this should be our countrie, our barke; and that our hart should be maried to this institute, following the speach of him, who being demaunded which was the most delightfull resting place, and the best foode for the Child, the breast (sayed he) and the milke of his mother; for although there are many more beautifull breasts and better milke, yet for him there is not any more proper, nor more amiable.

THE SECOND ENTERTAINEMENT.

VVherin is demaunded, whether we may appeare before God whith great confidence, hauing whith in our selues the feeling of our miserie, and hovv; and of the perfect abnegation of our seues.

YOv demauded of mee, most Deare daughters, whether a soule, that hath the feeling of her miserie, may present her selfe before God with a great cõfidence? now I aunswere, that not onelie the soule, which hath the knowledg of her miserie, may haue great confidence in God; but also she cannot haue true confidẽce, vnlesse she haue the kenowledg of her miserie; for this kenowledg and confession of our miserie introduceth vs before God; euen so all the great saints as Iob, Dauid, and others, did begin all their prayers by the confession of their miserie and indignitie; therfore it is a very good thing for a person to acknouledg her selfe poore, vile, abiect and vnworthy to appeare in the presence of God. This saying, *knovve thy selfe*, so much celebrated by the antients of former times; although that it extendeth it selfe to the knowledg of the greatnesse, and excellencie of the soule, that it doe not abase and prophane it selfe in things vnworthy of its nobilitie: it also extendeth to the knowledg of our indignity, imperfection, and miserie. For looke how much more wee shall acknowledg our selues to be miserable; so much more shall we confide in the bounty and mercy of God: for betweene mercie and miserie there is a certayne connexion so great, that the one cannot be exercised with out the other. yf God had not created mā, he had bene truely totally good; but he had not bene actuallie mercifull; for so much as mercie exerciseth not it selfe but to the miserable. You see then, that how much more wee acknowledg our selues miserable, so much more we haue occasion to put our trust in God, since we haue nothing wher of to confide in our selues Disttust of our selues proceedeth from the knowledg of our imperfections: It is good then to distrust our selues. But to what purpose will it serue vs, vnlesse we cast our whole confidence vppon God, and relie vppon his mercie? the faults and infidelities that wee cōmitt euerie day, ought indeed to bring vs shame and

and confusion, when we will approch neere our Lord; and so we read, that there haue bene holy soules (S Katherin of Siēne, and S. Theresa) who whē they weare fallē into any fault, felt exceeding great confusiō; It is truelie very reasonable that hauing offēded God, we should retire out selues a little by humilitie. and remayne confounded; for hauing offēded a freind onely, we are ashamed to approch to him; but wee must not remayne there; for these vertues of humilitie, of abiection & confusion, are mediate vertues by the which we ought to mount to the vnion of our soule with God. It would be no great matter, to be annihilated and left naked of our selues (the which is donne by acts of cōfusion) if it weare not to giue our selues wholie to God: euen as S. Paule taught vs, when he sayed, *vncloth your selues of the ould man, and put on you the new*, for you must not remayne naked, but cloth your selue with God; This little recoyle is not made but to the end the soule may thereby leape forward into God by an act of Loue and confidence; for wee must not be confounded with sadnes or vnquietness; it is self Loue that giueth these confusions, by which we are sorrie for not being perfect, not so much for the Loue of God, as for the Loue of our selues.

Yea although you feele not any such confidence, yet may you not ommitt to make acts therof, and say vnto our Lord, although, my Lord I haue not any confidence in thee, yet I know thou art my God, that I am wholie thine, and haue no other hope then in thy goodnes: and therefore I giue my selfe ouer quite into thy hāds It is allwaies in our power to make these acts;

and

and albeit we haue difficultie in it, it is not therefore impossible: and it is in these occasions, and theses difficulties, that we ough to giue testimonie of our fidelitie to our Lord: for although we make such acts with our gust and with out any satisfaction, we must not be troubled; since our Lord loueth them better so; And doe not say, as you are wont: alas it is no otherwise then from the mouth: for if the hart would it not, the mouth would not speake a worde; Hauing done this, remayne in peac with out reflecting vppon your trouble; speake to our Lord of some other thing Cōsider then for conclusiō of this first point, that it is very good to haue confusion, when we haue the knowlegd and feeling of our miserie, and imperfection: but we must not there in nor for it fall into into discouragemēt. but raise vp our hart vnto God by a holie Confidence, the foundation where of ought to be in him; and not in vs: For so much as we change, and he neuer changeth, but remayneth allwais as good and as mercifull, whē we are weake and imperfect, as when we are strōg and perfect. I am wōt to say, that the throne of the mercie of God is our miserie: it followeth thē that how much greater our miserie shalbe, so much greatther Confidence must we haue.

3. Lett vs pass now to the other question, of *forsaking ones selfe*, and what ought to be the exercise of the soule abandoned; It must then be vnderstood that to abādon our soule and to leaue our selues, is no other thing, then to quitt, & break vs of our selfe will, to giue it vnto God: for it should serue vs but little (as I haue alreadie sayed) to renounce and leaue our selues, if it weare not to vnite vs more perfectlie to the diuine goodnes: it is this then for which

this *giuing ouer ones selfe* ought to be made, which otherwise would be vnprofitable, and should resẽble those of the antiẽt philosophers who made admirable renuntiations of them selues and of all thinges, for a vaine pretext to giue them selues to philosophy, as *Epictet* a most renowned philosopher, who being a slaue by condition, by reason of his great wisdome they weare content to haue giuen hem his freedome; but he out of an extreame renuntiation would not haue his liberty, and so voluntarilie remayned in slauerie with so great pouertie, that after his death they found no other houshold stuffe of his but a Lampe, which was sould very deare, because it had bene the Lãpe of so great à man; But we must not abandon our selues, vnles it weare to leaue our selues to the mercie of the will of God. There are many who say to our Lord: I giue my selfe wholie to thee with out any reseruation; bnt there are verie few, which imbrace the practice of this renuntiation, which is no other thing, then a perfect indifferencie to receaue all sortes of euents according as they arriue by the order of the diuine prouidence: aswell affliction, as cõsolatiõ; sicknes as health; pouertie, as riches, contẽpt as honour, & infamy as glorie, the which I meane according to the Superiour part of our soule; for there is not any doubt, but that the inferiour and naturall inclination will allwaies bend and tend to the side of honour, rather then that of contempt: of riches, then that of pouertie although there are not any that can be ignorant; that contempt, abiection, and pouerty, are more pleasing to God, then honour, and abundance

dance of great riches.

§.4. Now to gett this relinquishing of all what soeuer, we ought to obey the wil of God *signified*, and that of his *good pleausure*, the one is done by may of resignation, the other by way of indifferencie. The will of God *signified* comprehendeth his commaudements, his councells his inspirations, our Rules, and the ordinances of our Superiours. The will of his *good pleausure*, regardeth the euents of things, which wee connot foresee (or) preuent: as for example; I knowe not if I shall die to morrow, I doe see that this is the good pleausure of God, and therefore I render my selfe to his holy will, and will die willinglie, In like sort I know not if the next yeare, all the fruites of the earth shalbe blasted; if it happen they be, or there be plague or other like euents, it is euident that this is the good pleasure of God, and therefore I cõforme my selfe there vnto. It may happen that you shall not haue consolation in your exercises; it is certayne that then this is the good pleasure of God, wher-fore you must remayne with an extreame indifferencie betweene desolation, & consolation. The same ought to be done in all things, which shall arriue vnto vs, in the cloathes that are giuen vs, and in the meates that are presented vs.

§.5. It ought moreouer to be noted, that there are things in which the will of God *signified* is ioined to that of his *good pleasure*: as if I fall sicke of a greeuous feauer, I see that the *good pleasure* of God in this euent is, that I remayne indifferẽt either for health or sicknes; but the will of God *signified* is, that I who am not vnder obedience, call

call for the phisition, and that I apply all the remedies I can; I doe not say the most exquisite, but the common and ordinarie; and that the Religious, who are vnder a Superiour, receaue the remedies, and vsage which are presented them in simplicity and submission: for God hath signified it vnto vs, in this that he hath giuen vertu vnto remedies, the holy Scripture teacheth it in many places, & the church ordayneth it: now this being done, lett the sicknes surmount the remedie, or the remedie surmount the maladie, we ought to be perfectlie indifferēt in such sort, that if sicknes and health weare presēt before vs, and that our Lord did say vnto vs: if thou chose health, I will not take from thee one graine of my grace: and if thou make choise of sicknes, I will not augment it one iott at all: but to make choise of sicknes would be more agreable to my will; the soule then, that intirely abandoneth, and comitteth it selfe into the hāds of our Lord, will with out doubt choose sicknes, for this cause onelie, that there is in it some what more of the good pleasure of God: yea though she weare to remayne all her life in a bedd, not being able to doe any other thing, thē to suffer, yet would not she for any thing in the world desire any other estate then that. Euen the saints which are in heauē, haue such an vniō with the will of God, that if there weare to be had a little more of the good pleasure of God in hell, thy would quitt paradice to goe thither. This estate of *forsaking of ones selfe* comprehendeth also the entire resignation to the good pleasure of God in all temptations, as drinesses, auersions, and repugnances, which may arriue in a

spirituall

spirituall life; for in all these things we see the good pleasure of God; when they arriue not by our default, and that on our part there be no sinne. In fine this renuntiation of our selues, is the verta of vertues: it is, the creame of Charitie, the sweete sauour of humilitie, the meritt (as it seemeth) of patience, and the fruite of perseuerance. O great is this vertue, and onlie worthy to be practiced by the most deare Children of God. *My father;* sayed our most Sweet Sauiour vppon the crosse *I committ my spiritt into thy handes* as yf he would Saye: its true that all is consummate, and that I haue accomplished all that thou hast commaunded me: but more ouer If such be thy will, that I remayne yet on this Croß, to suffer more, I am content, and committ my spirit into thy handes, thou mayest do therewith, euen as it shall please thee We ought to doe the same, my most deare daughters, in euerie occasion, be it that we doe suffer, or that wee doe enioy some contentment; Leauing our selues to be conducted by the diuine will, according to his good pleasure, with out euer permitting our selues to be preoccupated by our particuler will. Our Lord loueth with an extreeme tender loue those, who are so happie, as to abandon themselues totally to his paternall care, leauing themselues to be gouerned by his diuine prouidence, with out musing (or) considering whether the effects of this prouidedce, shabe beneficiall, profitable, or dommagable to them, being most assured, that nothing shall be sent

sent vnto them from his paternall and amiable hart; nor that he will permitt any thing to arriue vnto them, aut of which he will not cause them to drawe good and profit; prouided that they put theyr whole confidence in him, and that thy say with a good hart: I remitt my spiritt my soule, my bodie, and all that I haue into thy blessed hands, to doe according as it shall please thee: For we are neuer reduced to such extremitye, that we may not allwaies powre before his diuine maiestie perfumes of holy submission to his most blessed will, and a continuall promise neuer willinglie to offend him.

§. 2. Somtimes our Lord will that the soules, chosen for the seruice of his diuine maiesty should nourish them selues wih a firme and inuariable resolution to follow him, among the disgusts, drinesses repugnãces, and asperities of a spirituall life, with out consolation, sweetnesse tendernesse and gusts; & that they beleeue them selues, not to be worthy of other treating: following our diuine Sauiour with the pure point (or) quintessence of the spiritt, hauing no other prop or stay, then that of the diuine will, which would haue it so. Behould then how I desire you should walke my Deare daughters.

But now you demaund of me, wherin this soule ought interioulie to imploy her selfe, which is totally abãdoned into the hãds of God? she shall doe nothing but remayne neere vnto our Lord with out care of any thing, no not of her owne bodie nor of her soule; for since she is imbarked vnder the prouidence of God, what hath she to doe to thinke of that which is to come? our Lord, to whome she hath totallie left her selfe,

will

will prouide sufficietlie for her. Yet my meaning is not, that she think not of those things, to which she is obliged, according to her charge; For a Superiour ought not vnder colour of abandoning her selfe to God, and reposing in his care, neglect to read, and learne the documents, which are proper for the exercise of her charge. It is most true that she ought to haue great confidence, to forsake her selfe in such manner, without any reseruation to, the diuine prouidence; Moreouer that when wee abandon our selues wholie, our Lord taketh care of all, and conducteth all: but if we reserue any thing of the which we confide not in him, he leaueth vs; as it he sayed, You thinke to be wise enough with out mee, I leaue you to gouerne, you shall see how you will find your selues there-in Those who are dedicated to God in Religion, ought to abandon all with out any reseruation. Sainct Marye Magdalene, who was totallie giuen ouer to the will of our Lord, remayned at his feete, and did hearken whilst he spake; and when he ceased to speake, she also ceased to hearken; but she did not therefore remoue from being neere him: euen so the soule, which is so giuen ouer, hath noe other thing to doe, then to remayne beweene the armes of our Lord, as a child in the bosome of his Mother, who when she setteth him on the ground for to goe, he goeth, vntill such time as she taketh him vp againe; and when she will carrie him he permitteth it; for he knoweth not, nor thinketh whether he goeth; but leaueth himselfe to be carryed, or lead, whether it pleaseth his Mother; in the same sort, this Soule louing the will of the good pleasure of God, in all things, that arriue vnto her, leaueth her selfe to be carried, and walketh neuerthelesse, performing with great diligence the will of God, as farre forth as it is signified vnto her.

§. 3. You aske now, if it be possible, that our will may be so dead in our Lord that we may come in a sort to know no more what we will, or what we will not? I say in the first place, that it neuer hapneth so to abandon our freedome and the libertie of our free will, that it remaynes not with vs; so that allwaies we haue some desire, and some will; but these are not *absolute* wills, and *formed* desires; for so soone as a soule, which hath plunged it selfe into the good pleasure of God, perceaueth in it selfe any will, she incontinently maketh it to dye in the good will of God.

§. 4. You would also know, if a soule which is yet vnperfect, may be able to remayne profitably before God, with this simple attention to his holy presence in prayer; I tell you, if that God place you there, you may well remayne there; for it hapneth very often, that our Lord giueth these quietnesses, & tranquillities to some soules, that are not well purged; but whiles it is expedient that they purifie them selues more perfectlie, they ought out of prayer to consider what is necessarie for their amendment; For although God would allwaies hould them throughly recollect, yet haue they sufficient libertie besides to discourse with the vnderstanding vppon diuers indifferent things: wherefore then may they not consider and make resolutions for their amend-

ment

ment and the practice of vertues ? There are verye perfect persons, to whom our lord neuer giueth such sweetnes, nor this quietnes; who doe all with the Superiour parte of their soule, and make their will to die with in the will of God by a sweet and liuelie force, and with edge of reason: this death I speake of, is the death of the spouse the which is much more excellent and generous then the other, and ought rather to be called a sleeping, then a death; for this soule which is imbarked in the ship of the prouidence of God, permitteth her selfe to saile sweetlie; as a person who sleeepth with in a shipp vpon a calme sea, yet doeth not cease therefore to goe forward; this manner of death so sweet, is giuen by way of grace; the other is giuen by way of merit.

§. 5. You would further know, what foundation our confidence ought to haue? It must be founded vppon the infinite Goodnes of God, and vppon the meritts of the death and passions of our lord IESVS-CHRIST, with this condition on our part; that we haue and know in our selues an entire and firme resolution to be wholie Gods, and to abandon our selues totallye with out any reseruation, to his prouidence; I desire allwaies that you marke that I say not, that we *must feele* this resolution of being totallie Gods, but only that it *must be had and knowen* in vs: for so much as we must not studie (or) muse on that wee feele or on that wee feele not, because the most part of our feelings and *satisfactions* are no other then delayes of going forward,

 instigated

instigated by selfe loue. Also it must not be vnderstood, that in all these things heere spoken of renuntiation, and of indifferencie, we neuer haue desires contrarie to the will of God, and that nature doe not repugne at the euents of his good pleasure: for this may often happẽ: these vertues are those which make their residence in the *Superiour* part of the soule; the *inferior* ordinarilie knoweth nothing of it; and no account must be made of what that inferiour part feeleth: but not regarding what it willeth, or willeth not, wee ought to imbrace this diuine will; & vnite our selues there vnto whether it will or no; There are few persons that arriue to this degree of perfect forsaking themselues; but wee all of vs neuerthelesse ought to pretend it; each one according to her abillitie and capacitie.

LIVE IESVS LIVE.

THE THIRD ENTERTAINEMENT.

Vppon the flight of our Lord, into Egipt: where in is treated of the Constancie which we ought to haue, in the middest of the accidents, of this World.

1. WEE Celebrate the octaue of the feast of the Holy Innocents, on which day the holie Church causeth to be read the Gospell, tha[t]

that treateth, how the Angell of our Lord, spake to the glorius S. Ioseph in a dreame; that is to say, in sleepe, that he should take the Child and his mother, and fly into Egipt, for so much as Herod being iealous of his Royaltie, did search after our Lord to put him to death, for feare least he should depriue him of it; and being filled with choller, because the wise men did not retourne to him into Ierusalem as he expected, he commaunded that they should kill all the children from two yeares ould and vnder, beleeuing our Lord should be found among them, and that by this meanes he should be assured of the possession of his kingdome: This Gospell is full of diuers excellent considerations. I will content my selfe with such as shall serue vs for an entertaynment, aswell pleasing as profitable.

§. 2. I begin with the first remarkable note which the great S Ihon Chrysostome maketh; which is, of the inconstancie varietie, and instabilitye, of the accidents of this mortall life. O how profitable is this consideration; for the want there of, is that, wich carrieth vs into discouragment, and fantasticallnesse of spirit, vnquietnesse, varietie of humours, inconstancie, and instabilitye in our resolutions; for we would not encounter in our way with any difficulty, or contradiction, nor any payne. we would alwaies haue consolations, and be free from ariditics and drinesse of spirit; we would allwaies haue good things with out mixture of any euill; health with out sicknes; repose with out labour, & peace with out trouble; Alas who seeth not our follie? for we will that which cannot be: Vnmingled puritie is to be found in no other place, then in heauen, and in hell: in heauen, goodnes, pleasure, rest, and consolation are in there puritie, with out mixture of any euill, trouble, or affliction; on the contrarie there is found in hell, euill, dispayre, trouble and vnquietnesse, in their puritie with out mixture of any good, hope, tranquillitie, or peace. But in this decaying life of ours good is neuer found with out euill; riches with out vnquietnesse, rest with out labour, consolation with out affliction, health with out sicknes: in breife all is mixed and mingled, the good with the badd; there being a continuall variety of diuers accidents. Euen so would God diuersifie the times of the yeare; that Sommer should be followed by the autumne: and winter by the spring; to shew vnto vs that temporall things are perpetuallie mutable, inconstant and subiect to change, and that nothing is permanent in this life. And the defect of the knowledg of this truth is, as I haue sayed, that which maketh vs mutable, and changing in our humours: for so much as we doe not serue our selues, with the reason that God hath giuen vs, the which reason causeth vs to become immutable, firme and solide, and therefore like to God. When God sayed; *Let vs make man to our liknes* he immediatly gaue vnto him reason, and the vse there of, to discourse, consider, and discerne good from euill, and those things which deserue to be elected or reiected. It is reason that maketh vs Superiours and lords ouer all creatures. Whē God had created our first parentes, he gaue thē entire dominion, ouer the fishes of the sea and beastes

beastes of the earth, and consequentlie gaue them the knowledg of their diuers kindes, and meanes to rule them, and become their maister and lord: God hath not onely done this grace to mã to make him lord of creatures, by meanes of the gift of reason giuen vnto him, by the which he becommeth like vnto himselfe; but furthermore he hath giuen him full power ouer all sortes of accidents and euents. It is sayed that a wise man, that is to say, a man that is guided by reason, shall cause himselfe to be absolute maister of the planetts: what is the meaning of this, but that by the vse of reason he shall remayne firme and constant, in the diuersitie of accidents and euẽts of this mortall life? whether the time be fayre, or that it rayne; whether the ayre be calme, or the wind blowe; the wise man taketh no thought therfore, knowing very well that nothing is stable, and permanent in this life, this not being the place of rest. In affliction he dispayreth not, but expecteth consolation: in sicknnes he doeth not vex himselfe, but expecteth health; or if he perceaue the euill to be such, that death is to follow, he blesseth God expecting the repose of an immortall life to follow this; yf he encounter pouertie, he is not afflicted: for he knoweth well, that riches are not in this life with out pouertie; if he be despised, he knoweth well that honour heere, hath not any perpetuitie, but is ordinarilie poursewed with dishonour, or contempt. In breife in all sortes of euents, be it prosperitie or aduersity he remayneth firme, stable and constant in his resolution of pretending, and tending to the enioyng of eternall goods.

§. 3. But we must not onelie consider this varietie change and mutation in materiall and transitorie thinges of this mortall life: no; but we ought to cōsider them also in the successe of our spirituall life where stabilitie and constācie are so much the more necessarie, by how much the spirituall life is raysed farre aboue the corporall and mortall life. It is a very great abuse, not to haue a will to suffer, or feele mutations and changes in our humours, whiles we doe not gouerne our selues by reason, neither will be gouerned by others: we say commolie, behould this Child, he is very young, but yet for all that he hath allreadie the vse of reason: euen so many haue the vse of reason, who yet for all that, euen as Children, doe not gouerne themselues by the commaundement of reason. God hath giuen man reason for his guide: but notwithstanding there are verie few which permitt it to rule in them; contrariwise they giue ouer themselues to be gouerned by their passions, which should be subiect and obedient to reason, according to the order which god requireth of vs. I will make it more easy to be vnderstood; for the most part persons of the world yeald them selues to be gouerned and guided according to their passions, and not according to reason; they are also ordinarilye iarring, varying, and changing in their humors; if they haue a desire to goe to bed earlie or late, they doe it; and if they haue a mind to walke in the feeldes, they rise betimes in the morning: and if to sleepe, they effect it; when they will, they breake their fast, sooner or latter, as they please; and they are not onely iarring and vnconstant

constant in this, but they are the same likewise in their conuersation; they will that euerie one should accommodate them selues to their humours, but they will not be accommodated to those of others: they giue themselues ouer to be carryed by their inclinations, particular affections and passions, and this is not esteemed vitious among worldlie people, & prouided they doe not much disturbe the minds of their neigbour, they are not esteemed fleeting and vnconstant: and wherfore is this? For no other thing, but for so much as this is an ordinarie euill among seculars. But in Religion, they cannot permitt themselues, in such sort to be transported by their passions, considering that for exteriour things, our Rules are to keepe vs in order to pray to eate, and to sleepe (and the like of other exercises) allwaies at the same houre when obedience, or the bell signifieth it vnto vs; furthermore we allwaies haue one manner of conuersation, we cannot seperate our selues; in what then may vnsetlednes, and inconstancie be exercised? it is in the diuersitie of humours of wills, and of desires: now I am ioyfull, because all things succeed according to my will, with in a while I am sorrowfull, because there shalbe some little contradiction, which I did not expect. But do you not know, that this is not the place, where pure pleasure is to be foũd, with out mixture of displeasure? and that this life is interlaced with the like accidents? this day you are encouraged, because you find consolation in prayer, and you resolue to serue God verie well: but to morrow you shalbe in drinesse, and you will haue no hart for the seruice of God, Good God, say you, how I am decayed in vigour, and violentlie borne downe! Tell me now, I pray you; if you gouerned your selfe by reasō, should you not see, that if it were good to serue God yesterday, that it is yet more good to serue him this day, and that it shall be much better to serue him to morrow? for he is allwaies the same God, as worthy to be loued when you are in drinesse, as whē you are in cōsolatiō. Now will I one thing, to morrow I would haue another: that I see such a one to doe at the presēt, pleaseth me, and with in a while displeaseth me; in such sort that it wilbe capable to make me conceaue an auersion from her; at the presēt I loue a person verie much, and her conuersatiō is gratfull and pleasing to mee, and to morrow I shalbe scarce able to support it; and what meaneth this? is she not as capable to be loued this day, as she was yesterday? if we did regard what reason doeth dictate to vs,, we should see, that this person ought to be loued, because it is a creature, which beareth the Image of the diuine maiestie; so we should haue as much content in her cōuersatiō now as heretofore we had; therefore this proceedeth of noe other cause, thē that we giue our selues ouer to be guided according to our inclinations, passions, and affections; so peruerting the order that God hath placed in vs, that all should be subiect to reason: for if reason raigne not ouer all our powers, ouer our faculties our passions, inclinations and affectiōs, and in fine ouer all our proceedings: what will happen of it? but a continuall vicissitude, inconstancye, variety, changing, and iarring, which wlle make vs at the present to be feruēt

and

and little after remisse, negligent, and slothfull; one while ioyfull, and by & by melancholie: we shalbe peacefull and tranquill one houre, and after vnquiet two dayes together. In breife our life shall passe away in sloth and losse of time. Then by this first note wee are incited, and summoned, to consider the inconstancy, and varietie of successes, aswell in tẽporall things as in spirituall; to the end that by the euents that occurre, which may be able to affright our spirits (as being new things, and not preuẽted) wee loose not our courage, nor permitt our selues to be carried into inequalitie of humours in the midst of the inequalitye of accidents that arriue vnto vs; but rather submitt our selues to be guided by the reasõ that God hath placed in vs, and resigne our selues to his prouidence, and so remaine firme constant and inuariable, in the resolution we haue mode to serue God, constantlie, couragiouslie, and orderlie, with out any discontinuation what soeuer.

§ 5. If I did speake before persons that did not vnderstand me, I would endeuour to inculcate it vnto them, in the best manner that were possible for mee; but you knowe that I haue allwaies endeuored throughly to ingraue in your memorie, this most holie equallitie of spiritt, as being the most neccessarie and peculier vertu of Religion. All the ancient Fathers of Religious orders haue had particuler care and prouidence for it, that this equallie and stabilitie of humours, and of spiritt should raigne in their Monasteries: for this they haue established statutes, constitutions and Rules, to the end the Religious might serue themselues of thẽ as of a bridge

bridge to passe from the equallitie of exercises which are there appointed, and to which they are to be subiect; to this so amiable, and desirable equallitie of spiritt, in the midst of the inequalitie of accidents they meete with all, aswell in the way of our mortall life, as in the way of our spirituall life. The great S. Chrysostome sayeth. O man, wherefore doest thou disquiet thy selfe, because euerie thing succedeth not as thou wouldest haue it? art thou not ashamed to see, that this that thou wilt haue, was not to be found, euen in the familie of our Lord? Cōsider I pray thee, the change, the alteration, the diuersitie of subiects, that are there to be seene: Our blessed ladie hauing receaued the message, that she should cōceaue by the holie Ghost a sonne, who should be Lord and Sauiour of the World, what ioy, what iubilation did she feele in that sacred houre of the incarnation of the eternall Worde? a while after Sainct Ioseph perceauing her to be with child, and knowing well, that it was not by him; good God, in what affliction and distresse was he? what did he not endure? and Bl. Ladie, what extreamitie of greefe and afflictiō did she not feele in her soule, seeing her deare spouse at the point to leaue her: her modestye not permitting her to discouer to Sainct Ioseph the honour and grace where with God had magnified her? A little after this tempest was passed, the Angell hauing discouered to S. Ioseph the secreat of that mysterie, what content and ioy was wanting vnto them? truely none? when our Bl Ladie brought forth her sōne the Angell declared his byrth to the shepheardes. and the Wisemen came to adore him: I leaue to your consi-

consideration, what Iubilation, and consolation they had in this occasion; But attend, for this is not all: immediatlie after the Angell of our Lord came to S. Ioseph in his sleepe saying: Take the child and his mother, and fly into Egypt, for Herod will seek meanes that the child be slayne. O, with out doubt this was a subiect of most great greife vnto our Bl. Ladie, and S. Ioseph. O how the Angell treateth *S.* Ioseph like a true Religions person: Take the child, sayeth he, and his mother, and flye into Egypt, and remayne there vntill such time as I shall tell thee; what is this? might not the poore S. Ioseph haue sayed: you bid me to goe, will there not be time enough to depart earelie in the morning! or will you haue me to goe in the night? my furniture is not readie; how will you haue me carrye the child? shall I haue armes strong enough to carrye him continuallie in so long a iorney? or would you haue his mother to carry him in her turne? alas! doe you not see that she is young, & very tender? I neyther haue horse nor monye, for the voyage: and doe you not knowe that the Egyptians are enimies to the Israelites? who shall receaue vs? and the like difficulties which surely we had alleaged to the Angell, if we had beene in the place of S. Ioseph, who sayed not so much as one word to excuse himselfe from performing the obediēce; but departed at the same hower, and accomplished all that the Angell had commaunded him. There are many profitable documents in this commaundement: first we are taught, that we must in no sort delay and be remisse in that which concerneth obedience: it is the fashiō of the

the slothfull to linger and say, (as S. Augustine sayed of him selfe) By and by, yet a little, and then I will conuert my selfe. The Holy Ghost will brooke no delay, but desireth a great prõptitude in following of his inspiratiõs. Our losse cõmes of our negligẽce, which maketh vs to say I will begin by and by; and why not in this houre which he inspireth and exciteth vs forward? truly because we are so tender ouer our selues, that we feare euerie thing that may seeme to take away our rest and repose: which is no other thing then our backwardnes, and lasines, from which we will not be with drawne by the solicitatiõ of any obiects, which inuite vs to goe out of our selues: and we say in a manner as the slothfull man, who cõplayning of those, that would haue him come forth of his house: how shall I come forth sayed he, for there *is a liõ in the high way, and a Beare in the passages*; and with out doubt they will deuoure mee? O how much are wee to blame, to permitt God our Lord, to send and resende, to knocke and strike at the gate of our harts so many times, before that we will open it vnto him, and permitt him to dwelle therein; for it is to be feared that we doe prouoke and constraine him to abandon & forsake vs Moreouer the great peace and equalitie of spiritt of the most Holie virgin, and S. Ioseph ought to be cõsidered: and their cõstancye in the thickest of so great inequalitie of diuers accidẽts, which happned vnto them as we haue sayed. Now cõsider if we haue reasõ to trouble our selues and be astonished, if we find the like encoũters in the house of God, which is Religion, since that this was in the same famylie of our Lord, where stabilitie & solidite soliditie it selfe made his residence, which was our lord Iesus? This ought to be spoken and repeated of vs many times, to the ende to engraue it the better in our soules; to witt, that the inequallity of accidents ought neuer to carrye our soules and spirits into the inequallity of humours; for the inequallitie of humours proceedeth from no other source or spring, then of our passions, inclinations, or immortified affections; and they ought not to haue power ouer vs, whiles they incite vs to doe, to leaue vndone, or desire any thing, how little soeuer it may be, which is cõtrarie to that, which reason doth dictate vnto vs to be done, or left vndone for to please God.

I will passe to the second consideration, that I note vppon this word of the Angell of our lord, who sayed to S. Ioseph, Take the child, and that which followeth; but I will insist vppon this worde, *The Angell of our lord*: vppõ which I desire we would marke well, what estimation wee ought to make of the care, helpe assistãce & directiõ of those, whõ God hath placed round aboud vs, to assist vs the more securely to goe forward in the way of perfection. First it must be vnderstood that whẽ it is sayed: *The Angell of our lord*: it may not be thought to be spoken as if it weare sayed of one of vs: the Angell of such a one; or the Angell of such a one: for this weare as much as so say our Angell gardiã, who hath care of vs by Gods appointment: but *our lord*, who is the king and guide of Angells thẽselues, had no neede during the course of his mortall life of an Angell gardien. Therfore when it is sayed, *The Angell of our lord*, it ought thus to be vnderstood, to witt the Angell appointed to guide and conduct the

familie

familie of our Lord, and more spetiallie dedicated for his seruice, and that of his holie Mother the B. Virgin. Now to explicate this more familiarlie, we changed Officers and *aydes* some dayes past; what signifieth these *aydes* that are giuen you? wherefore doe we giue you them? S. Gregorie sayeth; that in this miserable world we ought to doe, as those, who walke vpõ the ice if we will keepe our selues stedye and solide in the enterprise of sauing our soules, or perfitting our selues: for sayeth he, they take one the other by the hand, or vnder the arme, to the ende that if any one among them slipp, he may be held vp by the other, and that the other may be stayed by him, when he shalbe in danger to fall in his turne. We are in this life as vppon the ice, finding in euerie designe occasions apt to make vs stũble and fall; sõtimes into anxietie now into murmors a little after into ficklenes and inconstancy of spiritt; which will cause, that nothing that is done, shalbe to giue vs contentment, and we will begin to be disgusted with our vocation: melancholy suggesting vnto vs, that we shall neuer doe any thing of worth; and the like things and accidents, that encounter vs in our little spirituall world: for man is an abrigmẽt of the world; or, to say better, a little world in the which he meeteth with all that is seene in the great vniuersall world: our passiõs represẽt the beastes and liuing creatures, which are with out reason, our sences, inclinations, affections, powers, and the faculties of our soule, all these haue their particular signification: but I will not stay on this. but will follow on my discourse begun: These aydes then, who are giuen vs, are to assist vs, and to keepe vs firmelie in our way, to the end to hinder vs frō falling; or if we fall, to helpe vs to rise againe. O God! with what freedome, hartinesse, sincerity, simplicity, and faythfull confidēce ought we to treat with these assistants, which are giuen vs of God for our spirituall aduancement? certanlie no otherwise, then as with our good Angells: and wee ought to respect them with the like reuerence; for our good Angells are called our Angells gardians, because they haue charge to assist vs with their inspirations; to defend vs in our dangers; to reprehend vs for our faultes; to incite vs to the porsute of vertue: it is their charge, to carrye our prayers before the throne of the bountie and mercie of our Lord, and to bring vnto vs the full grant of our requests; and the fauours which God will doe vs, he doeth them by the mediation, or intercession of our good Angells. Our assistants are our visible good Angells, euē as our holy Angells gardians are our inuisible: they ayde vs visibly, in that which our good Angells doe interiorlye; for they aduertise vs of defects, they encourage vs in our weaknes and faynt hartednesse they excite vs to the porsute of our intēded course for to attayne vnto perfectiō they hinder vs by their good councell frō falling and helpe vs to rise agayne, whē we are throwne downe into some steepe, & deepe downefall of imperfections or fault; yf we be ouerwhelmed with irksomnes and disgusts, they assist vs to beare our paynes patiently, and they praye to God to giue vs strēgh to support it as we ought to doe, and not to be subdued in tēptation. Now you see the account we ought to make of their assistance, and of the care they haue for vs.

I consider next, wherfore our Lord IESVS CHRIST who is the eternall wisdome, did not take care of his familie, I would say did not aduertise S. Ioseph, or his most shweete Mother, of all that was to arriue vnto them; might not he very well haue layed to his foster father S. Ioseph: Let vs goe into Egipt, we shalbe there some time since it is a most assured case, that he had the vse of reason, from the instant of his conception with in the intrails of the most Holie virgin Mother? but he would not doe a miracle, to speake before the time was come; might not he very well haue inspired it into the hart of his most holy Mother, or of his welbeloued supposed Father S Ioseph, the spouse of the most sacred virgin? wherefore then did he not this, but rather left it to the commission of the Angell, which was much inferiour to our Blessed Ladie? this was not with out mysterie. Our Lord would not take vppon him the office of the Angell Gabriell, who hauing bene deputed to announce the mysterie of the incarnation to the glorious virgin, from the eternall father; was thenceforth as it were high steward & gouerner of the house & familie of our Lord to haue care there-of in the diuers accidēts, and occurences, which they should encounter with all; and to hinder that nothing might happen, which should be able to shorten the life of our little infant new borne: this was the cause, wherefore he aduertissed S. Ioseph, to carry him speedily into Egipt, to auoyd the tirãnye of Herod who had determined to murther him: Our Lord would not be gouerner of himselfe, but permitted himselfe to be carryed where they would, and by whom they would: it seemeth that he did not esteeme himselfe wise enough to guide himselfe nor his famylie; but leaued the Angell to gouerne, euen so as pleased him; although he neither had the knowledg nor the wisdome, to enter comparison with his diuine Maiestie. And now shall we be so daring for to say, that we will gouerne our selues, as hauing no more necessitie of directiō, nor of the assistāce of those, that God hath giuen vs for guides; not esteeming them of capacitye sufficient for vs? tell me, was the Angell greatter then our Lord, or our Ladie? had he a better spirit and more judgmēt? in no case; was he indued with any speciall or particuler grace, or more quallified? this cānot be, seeing, that our Lord is God, and man both together: aud that our Bl: Ladie being his Mother, by cōsequēce hath more grace and perfectiō thē all the Angells together haue; not withstāding all this, the Angell cōmaunded, and he is obeyed. Moreouer behould the order, that is kept in this holy familye, there is no doubt it was the same of the sparrowhauke where the femalts are mistrisses and are more worth then the males: who can doubt that our Bl. Lady was much more worthy then S. Ioseph, and that she had more discretiō and quallities proper for gouermēt then her spouse? Neuerthelesse the Angell addressed not himselfe to her, for euerie thing that was requisite to be done, whether it weare to goe or to come, nor in fine for whatseouer it weare that the angell commanded. Doth it not seeme to you great indiscretiō to addresse himselfe rather to S. Ioseph then to our Bl: Ladie, who is the cheife of the house, carrying with her the treasure of the eternall father? had not she reasō to be offēded with this māner of proceeding and vsage? with out doubt she might haue sayed to her spouse: Werefore shall I goe into Egipt, since my sone hath not reuealed to me that I should doe it: neither hath the Angell spoken vnto mee of it? But our Bl. Lady sayed nothing of all this, she was not offended, because the Angell addressed himselfe to St. Ioseph; but rather she simply obeyed in all: because she knewe, that God had so ordayned it; she informed not her selfe wherefore, but it was sufficient for her that God would haue it so, and with out consideration she tooke, delight to submitt her selfe. But I am greatter then the Angell or S. Ioseph, might she haue sayed; but she spake not one such word. Doe you not see that Allmightie God taketh pleasure to treat with men in this manner, to teach them most holy and amourous submission? Saint Peter was an ould man, ignorant and rusticall: and S. Ihon on the contrarie, was young, sweete and pleasing; neuerthelesse it was the will of God that S. Peter should gouerne others, and be the vniuersall Superiour, and S. Ihon be one of them that weare guided by hym, and obedient vnto him. It is a strange case of mans spiritt that will not be brought to adore the secrett mysteries of God, and his most holy will, if it haue not some kind of knowlege, wherefore this or wherefore that. I haue a better spiritt, (say they, in praise of themselues,) more experience, and the like goodlie reasons, that are proper for nothing else then to produce vnquietnesse, inconstant humours; and murmours? what reason had they to giue this Office? wherefore haue they sayed this? to what ende doe they such a thing to this partie, rather then to another?

These spirits truely are greatly to be pittied. Assoone as we giue our selues ouer to search narrowlye into euerie thing that we see done; Alas what doe we not, for to loose the tranquillitie of our harts? wee ought not to seeke any other reason, but that God will haue it so, and that must suffice; but who shall, or will assure me, that this is the will of God, say they? would we that God should reueale all things, by secreat inspirations? would we expect, vntill he should send his Angells to declare vnto vs what is his will? he did not so to our Ladie, her selfe (at the least in this subiect) but he would haue her know his will by S. Ioseph, to whom she was subiect as to her Superiour; we would peraduenture be taught and instructed by God hymselfe, by way of extasies, or rauishments, and visions, and I know not what like childish fopperies, that we frame in our spiritts, rather then submitt our selues, to the assured and most amiable way of true & holy submission, to the gouernment of those, whome God hath placed to direct vs, and the obseruãce and direction aswell of our Rules as of our superiours. Lett it suffice then for vs to know, that it is the will of God, that we obey: and and Lett vs not muse, nor enter into consideration of the capacitie of those we ought to obey: and then we shall submitt our spiritts to walke simply on in the way of most holy humilitie, which will make vs infinitlye pleasing to God.

§.7. I must now passe to the third consideration, which is a note that I haue taken, vppon the cõmaundement the Angell gaue to S. Ioseph: to take the Child, and his mother, and to goe into Egipt, to remayne there vntill such time as he did aduertise him for to retourne Truly the Angell did speake verie brefly, and did treat S. Ioseph like a good Religious mã; sayng, Goe, and returne not, vntill I tell thee; by this manner of proceeding betweene the Angell and S. Ioseph, we are taught in the third place, how we ought to embarke our selues vppõ the sea of diuine prouidence, with our biskitt, with our Rowers, with out oars, with out sailes, and in fine wi h out any kind of prouisiõ: and euen so to leaue all the care of our selues, and successe of our affayres to our lord with out recours or replyes, or any feares whatsoeuer of that which may arriue vnto vs: For the Angell sayed simply; take the child and his mother and flye into Egipt; not telling him, neither by whay way they should goe, nor what prouisiõ they should haue to passe the iourney, nor into what part of Eg ipt rhe should goe; much lesse who should receane thẽ, or of whome they should be maintayned being there. Had not the poore S. Ioseph some reasõ to make reply saying, why bidd you me to leane this country, and that so speedilie, euẽ in an instãt? But this was to shew vnto vs the promptitude that the Holie spiritt requireth of vs, when he sayeth vnto vs, raise thy selfe aboue thy selfe, goe out of such an imperfection Oh the holy spiritt is a great enimie of remissnes, negligence and delayes! Consider, I beesech you, the great Patrõ and modell of perfect Religious, holy Abrahã, behould how God dealt with him; Abraham saith he *goe forth of thy country and frõ thy kindred, and goe to the mountayne that I shall shew thee*; what sayest thou, lord? that I goe forth of the towne? but tell me thẽ, if I shall goe towardes the East or the west? he made no such reply, but departed thence promplie, and went whether the spirit of God condu-cted him, euen vnto the mountayne, which hath euer since bene called *the vision of God*; for so-much as he receaued great and notable graces in this mountayne: to demonstrate vnto vs how gratfull and pleasing promptitude in obediēce is vnto him Might not S. Ioseph haue sayed vnto the Angell, you commaund mee to conduct the child and his mother, tell me then if you please, where with shall I nourish them in the way? for you knowe well, my lord, I haue no monye to beare our charges; But he alleaged no excuse, fully confiding, that God would prouide what should be requisite for them; which he did although meanely: causing thē to find where with to intertayne thēselues simply, either by the trade & labour of S. Ioseph; or otherwise by the almes that good poeple did bestowe on thē. Truelie all the anciēt Religious of former times haue bene admirable in the confidēce they haue had, that God would allwaies prouide sufficient of that they had neede of, for the sustayning of their life; leauing all care of themselues to his diuine prouidence.

§. 8. But I consider that it is not onely requisite for vs to repose in the diuine prouidence for that which regardeth temporall things, but much more for that which appertayneth to our spirituall life, and the perfectiō there of It is no other thing, truely, then the ouer much care we haue of our selues, which maketh vs loose the trā-quillitie of our spirit, and carryeth vs into cōtra-riety, ād inequallitie of humours: for that as soone as any cōtradictiōs happē to vs, yea whē we doe perceaue but onlie a little act of our immortifi-

cation

cation or when we cōmitt some fault how little soeuer, it seemeth to vs all is lost; and is that so great a meruaile, to see vs (poore creatures) somtimes to fall? but I am so miserable, so full of imperfections? knowe you it well? Blesse God, who hath giuē you this knowledge and, doe not lament so much; you are very happie to knowe, that you are no other then miserie it selfe After you haue thāked God for the knowledge which he hath giuen you, cutt of this vnprofitable tendernesse ouer your selues, which causeth you to complayne of your infirmities. Wee haue diuers delicacies concerning our bodies, which are exceeding contrarie to perfection: but they are more without comparison, which we haue ouer our soules. My God! sayeth one, I am not faythfull to our lord, and therefore I haue not any consolation in prayer; great pittie truelie! But I am so often in drinesse, that it maketh me beleeue, that things stand not well betweene God and my soule, he being so full of consolatiō; is not this wiselie spokē? as it God did allwaies giue consolation to his freinds: hath there euer bene a pure creature, so worthy to be beloued of God, & which hath bene more beloued of him, then our Lady, and S. Ioseph? Behould if they weare allwaies in cōsolation; Can there be imagined a more extreame affliction, then that, which S. Ioseph did feele, when he perceaued that the Glorious virgin was great with child, knowing well, it was not his fact? his affliction and anguish of mind being so much the greater as the passion of loue is more vehement, thē the other passions of the soule; and furthermore, in loue Ielousie is the extremitye of payne: the spouse

spouse in the canticles declareth in to be so, Loue, sayeth she, is strong as death; for loue worketh the same effects in the soule, that death doth in the bodye. But Ielousie, sayeth she, is as hard as hell: I leaue then to your consideration, what anxiety and greife the Bl. S. Ioseph did indure: and our Bl. Lady also, when she perceaued what opinion he, who loued her so dearlye, might haue of her; and knowing her selfe to be so dearely beloued of him; Ielousye made him to languish, and not knowing what way to take, he resolued rather then to blame her whome he had allwaies so much honoured and loued, to leaue her, and depart secretlie. But you will say, I am very sensible of the payne that this tentation, or my imperfection, causeth mee. I beleeue it, but is it any way comparable to that, where of we speake? it cannot be; and if it be, consider, I praye you, if we haue any reason to cōplayne and lament since S. Ioseph did not complayne, nor witnesse any disgust in his exteriour: he was not any whitt more harsh in his conuersation, neither did he alter his countenāce towards our Bl. Ladye, nor treat her ill; but simply suffered this vexation, and meant no other thing, then quit her companye. God knoweth what he might doe in this subiect. My auersion, sayeth some one, is so great from that person, that I doe not almost know how to speake vnto her, but with great difficultye; her actiō displeaseth me greuouslie; that is all one, you must not therefore enter into dislike against her, as if she could hinder it. But rather you ought to comport your selfe as our Blessed ladye and S. Ioseph: we must be quiet in our payne, and leaue the care to our lord, to take it from vs when he shall please. Our Blessed Ladye might verie well haue appeased this storme, not with standing she would not doe it, but left the issue of this affayre fully to the diuine

 prouidence;

prouidence; these are two discording cords, but equally necessarie to be accorded, that is to say, the treble string and the base, if one meane to play well vppon the lute; there is nothing more discording then the high with the lowe: notwithstanding with out the accorde of these twoe strings the harmonye of the lute cannot be delightfull. Likewise in our spirituall lute, two things are equallie discordant, & necessarie to be accorded, to witt, to haue a great care to perfect our selues; and not to haue care of our perfection, but to leaue it entirelie vnto god: I would say, that we must haue that care, that God would we should haue to perfect our selues; yet neuerthelesse must leaue the care of our perfection to him. God willeth that we haue quiet and peacefull care, which may cause vs to doe that, which is iudged proper for vs, by those who direct vs; and allwaies walke faythfully forward in the way, which is marked by the Rules, and directions that are giuen vs; and for the rest, that we repose our selues in his Paternall care, endeuoring as much as shalbe possible for vs, to keepe our selues in peace, for the habitation of God is made in peace, and in a peaceable & well reposed hart. You know, when a lake or poole is very calme, and the windes doe not moue the waters, in a bright cleare night, the skye or firmament with the starres are so well represented therein, that looking downeward, we see aswell the beautie of the heauens, as if we did looke vpwards. Likewise when our soule is well pacified, and the windes of superfluous cares, inequallitie of spiritt, and incōstācie, doe not trouble and disquiett it, she is very capable to beare with in her the Image of our Lord Iesvs; but when she is troubled vnquiet, and moued with diuers tempests of passiōs and permitteth her selfe to be gouerned by them, and not by reason (which only maketh vs become like

like to God) then is she nothing capable to represent the fayre and most amiable Image of our Lord IESVS crucified, nor the diuersitye of his excellent vertues, neither can she be capable to serue him, for his nuptiall bedd. Therefore we must leaue the care of our selues to his diuine mercie and prouidence; neuerthelesse orderlie and simply doing what is in our power, to amend and perfect our selues allwaies taking especiall heed, not to permitt our spiritts to be troubled and disquieted.

§. I note in fine, that the Angell sayed to S. Ioseph, that he should remayne in Egypt, vntill such time as he did aduertise him to returne, and the holy Sainct made him noe reply, saying, But when shall it be, O Lord, that thou will tell mee? To teach vs, that when we are commaunded to embrace any exercise, we ought not to say, shall this be for a long time? But rather wee ought to imbrace it with simplicitye, imitating the perfect obedience of Abraham who when God commaunded him to sacrifice his sonne, alleaged not any excuse, he complayned not, neither delayed to execute the commaundement of God: therfore God did fauour him so much, as he caused him to find a ramme there, the which he sacrificed vppō the mountayne in place of his sonne, God being satisfied with the promptnes of his will.

§. I conclude with the simplicitie that S. Ioseph did practice, in taking his iourney vppon the commaundement of the Angell into Egipt, where he was assured to find so many enimies, as there weare inhabitants in that country. Might he not haue sayd very well to the Angell, thou makest me to carrye the child into Egypt, and so we fly from one enimye, and expose our selues into the hands of a thousand thousand others, which we shall find in Egipt, for so much as we are of Israel? But he made

no reflection vppon the cōmaundement and therefore went his way full of peace and of confidence in God. In like manner, my daughters, when any imployment is imposed vppon you, doe not say, Good God! I am so rash and hasty, if they impose this office vppon mee, I shall haue a thousand cares and feares, and be extreemly put to my plunges, I am allreadie so distracted, if they giue me such a charge, I shalbe much more: but if they would leaue me to my cell, I should be modest, peacefull, and recollected; Goe simply into Egipt, in the midest of the great multitude of enimyes, that you shall haue there; for God who maketh you to goe thither, will conserue you there, neither shall you dye there; whereas contrariwise; if you remayne in Israell, where is your great enimye your proper will, with out doubt it will kill you there: it should not be well done to take offices, and charges by our proper election, for feare least we performe not our duty there-in: but when it is by obedience, neuer bring any excuse; for God is for vs, and we shall profitt more in perfectiō, then if wee had nothing to doe. Doe you not know what I haue sayed to you at other times? and it is not amisse to repeate it agayne formitt: that vertu requireth not that the occasions of falling into imperfections be taken away it suffireth not, (sayeth Cassian) to be depriued of the conuersation of men, for to be patient, sweet and gentle in our selues; for it hath happned to me, being in my cell all alone, to be angry with my selfe, when my mater did not take fire, that I haue cast it away in a chotay. I must end, and in the meane time leaue you to goe into Egipt with our Lord, who (as I beleeue and also others doe hould) began then to make little Gosses, when he had vacant time, after he had ayded S. Ioseph in some little things; demonstrating euen then the
desire

desire he had of the worke of our Redemption.

THE FOVRTH ENTER-TAINEMENT.

Of Cordiality, where-in it is demaunded, How the sisters ought to loue each other with a Cordiall loue, yet vsing no indecent familiaritye.

1. TO satisfie your demaund, and to make it well vnderstood wher-in Cordiall loue consisteth, wher with the Sisters ought to loue one an other: you must know that Cordiallnesse is no other thing, then the essence of true and sincere freindship: which cannot be, but betweene persons, that haue reasō, who cherish & nourish their freindships by the mediation reason. For otherwise it cannot be frindship, but onlie loue. Euen beastes haue loue, but they cannot haue frindship, since they are with out reason: they haue loue amongst them, because of some naturall correspondence, yea likewise they beare loue towardes man, as it appeareth by experience euerie day, and diuers Authours haue written of admirable things in this kinde: as that they relate of a Dolphin, that did loue a young child which he had seene many times vppon the sea shore so exceeissitly that this child being dead, the Dolphin himselfe died with greife, But this ought not to be called freindship, for as much as necessarilie the correspōdence of freindship, is to be found betweene two that loue each other, and that this freindshipe be contracted by the meanes of reason: so as the greatter part of freindships that men make not hauing a good end, nor being guided by reason

doe not in any sort deserue the name of freindship. More-ouer, besides the mediation of reason, there must be a certayne correspondence, either of vocation, or of pretence, or of quallitie betweene them that contract freindship. Experience doth clearly teach vs this; for is it not true, that there is not more true freindship, nor more strong, then that which is betweene brethren? we doe not call the loue of fathers toward their childrē freindship, nor that the childrē beare towards their parēts, because it hath not this correspōdēcē, whereof we speake, but are different: the loue of Fathers being maiesticall loue, and full of authoritie; and that of children towardes their parents, a respectiue and submissiue loue; but betweene Brothers, because of the resemblance of their condition, the correspondence of their loue, maketh a firme, strong and solid freindshipe. For this cause the ancient christians of the primitiue church, did all call themselues brethren: and this first feruour waxing could among the common multitude of Christians, Religions weare instituted, where they did ordayne that Religious should call themselues Brethren and Sisters to declare the true cordiall and sincere freinship that they did beare, or which they ought to beare, one towardes an other: as there is not any freindship comparable to that of Brethren, all other freindship being either vnequall, or artificiall (as that which maried persons haue the one with the other the which they haue by contracts, written & pronūced by notaries, or otherwise by simple promises. Also these freindships, which worldly poeple contract together, are either for some particular interest, or for some friuolous subiect, and are most ordinarilie very subiect to perish and to be dissolued: But that which is betweene Brethren, is cleane contrarie; For it is naturall, not artificiall; and therefore very recom-

recommendable: This then beiug so, I say that this is the cause, wherefore the Religious call each other Brethren, and therefore they haue loue which truely meriteth the name of freindship, not common, but cordiall freindship, that is to saye, frindship that hath his foundation within the hart. VVe must thẽ vnderstand, that loue hath his seate within the hart, and that we can neuer loue our neighbour too much, nor exceed the termes of reason in this loue, prouided that it reside in the hart: but touching the testimonie of this loue, we may well faile, and exceede therin, passing beyond the rules of reason. The Glorious S. Bernarde sayeth that the measure to loue God, is to loue him with our measure, and that our loue to him should not haue any limitte; but it must be free to spreed his branches so farr as possible may be. That which is sayed of God, ought also to be vnderstood of the loue towardes our neighbour, prouided allwaies that the loue of God doe euen swimme aloft, and hould the first ranke: next vnto which we ought to loue our sisters with all the dilatation of our hart, not contenting our selues to loue them as our selues, (as the commaundements of God doe oblige vs) but we ought to loue thẽ more then our selues (as to our tẽporall life) to obserue the rules of Euangelicall perfection which requireth this of vs. Our Lord hath sayed this himselfe: Loue you one another, euen as I haue loued you: that is to say, more then your selues: & euen as our Lord hath allwaies preferred vs before himselfe; and furthermore doth the same euerie time, that we receaue him in the most Blessed Sacrament making himselfe our foode; likewise his will is, that we haue such a loue one to another, that wee euer preferr our neighbours before our selues; and euen as he did all he could for vs, except the damning of himselfe (for he neither ought, nor could doe it because he could not sinne, which is of it selfe the onely thing that leadeth to damnation) he willeth, and the rule of perfection requireth it, that we doe all that we are able one for another, except that which may cause vs to be damned; but this excepted, our freindshipe ought to be so constant, cordiall and solid, that we neuer refuse to doe, or suffer whatsoeuer it be for our neighbour and sisters.

§. 2. Now this cordiall loue ought to be accōpanied with two vertues, the one is called affabilitye, the other, good Conuersation: Affabilitye, is a vertu that powreth forth a certayne sweetnesse into the serious communications and affayres we haue one with another; Good conuersation, is that, which rendreth vs gracious, and pleasing in recreations, and lesse serious communications, that we haue with our neighbour. All vertues, as you know haue twoe contrarye vices, which are the extremityes of vertue; the vertu of Affabilitye is in the midst of two vices; to witt Statelinesse, or ouergreat seriositye, and toogreat tendernesse, to make too much of, and to speake frequent wordes that tend to flaterie; now the vertu Affabilitye houldeth her selfe betweene too much, and too little, vsing kindnesses according to the necessities of those with whom wee treat, neuerthelesse cōseruing a sweete grauitie, according as the persons and affayres, where-of wee treat, doe require. I say, that cherishings (or) making much of, are to bee vsed at proper times: for it would bee very indiscreet to vse about a sicke person so much grauity, as they should doe with others, not being willing to cherish her more, then if she weere in good health. Also we should not so frequently vse kindnesses, and vppon euerie occasion speake honye wordes, casting whole handfulls of them vppon the first we

meete

meete with all: for euen as, if you put too much su-
gar vppon any meate, it will bee distastfull, because
it wilbe too sweete and vnsauorie; in like mãner too
frequent tendernesse and kindnesses will become
disgustfull, and not be esteemed, knowing they are
done but for fashion sake. Likewise meates vppon
which are put great hãdfulls of salte, are displeasing,
because of their sharpnes; but those whereon the
salte, and suger are put by measure, are made pleasing to the tast, in like sort courtiseys, which are vsed
by measure and discretion, are pleasing and profitable to them, to whom they be exhibited. The
vertu of Good Cõuersation requireth that we cõtri-
bute and condescend to holy & moderate ioy, and
to gracious entertaynments, which may serue for
consolation or recreation of our neighbour: that
in no sort we cause any vexation to him or her,
by our frowning and mellancholie countenances,
or by refusing to recreate in the time ordayned for
it. VVe haue allreadie treated of this vertu in the
discourse of modestie; wherefore I passe further
and say, that it is a very difficult thing to hitt
allwaies the marke we ayme at: it is true indeed,
that vve ought all to haue this pretence, to attayne and ayme iust vvith in the vvhite marke of
vertu, the vvhite vve ought ardentlye to desire:
but notvvithstanding vve ought not to lease courage vvhen vve doe not rightly encounter the
essence of vertu, nor be astonished therat, prouided that vvee keepe our selues vvith in the round,
that is to say, the neerest that vve may to true
vertu, for it is a thing vvhich the Saints themselues
haue not knovven hovv to doe in all vertues, there
hauing not bene any (but our Bl. Lord and Ladye)
vvho haue bene able to doe it. The Saints haue
practiced them with a very great difference: what
[illegible] C 5 [illegible] difference

difference I pray you is there betweene the spiritt of Saint Augustine, and that of Saint Ierome? as may bee noted in their writings: there is nothing more sweete then S. Augustine, his writings are swetnes and hony it selfe; contrariwise S. Ierome was extreeme austere: the better to knowe it, consider him in his Episteles, he is as it weere allwaies angrie: neuerthelesse both of thẽ were exceedingly vertuous: but the one had more sweetnes, the other much more austeritie of life, and both of them (although not equallye either sweete or rigorous) haue bene great Saints. So as we see, that we ought not to be astonished, if we be not equallie gentle and sweete, prouided we loue our neighbour according to the loue of the hart wholie extent; and as our Lord hath loued vs, (that is to say) more thẽ our selues, preferring him allwaies before our selues in all things with in the Order of holy Charitie, and refusing him nothing that we may be able to contribute for his profitt, except our damnation as I haue alreadye sayed: VVe must there-fore endeuour as much as we shalbe able to render exteriour testimonie of our affection, conformable to reason; to laugh with them that laugh, and weepe with those that weepe.

§. 3. I say we ought to manifest that we loue ours sisters (this is the second part of the question) without vsing indecent familiaritie: the rule declareth it, but let vs see what we ought to doe heerin: nothing, but that sãctitie appeare in our familiaritie and manifest our freindship, as S. Paul sayeth in one of his epistles: Salute, sayeth he, one another with a holy kisse; it was the custome, when the christians did meete together, to kisse each other. Our Lord IESVS did also vse towards his Apostles this forme of salutation, as we learne in the traitour

Iudas;

Iudas; and holie Religious therefore did vse to saye when they encountred each other, Deo gratias, to declare the great contentment they did receaue in beoulding one the other, as if they had sayed or would say, I thanke God, my Deare Brother, for the consolation he hath vouchsafed mee by your presence. Euen so my Deare daughters we must demonstrate how much we loue our sisters, and that we are pleased with them; prouided allwaies, that sanctitie accompanie the signes we giue of our affection; that God may not onely not be offended but that he may be praised and Glorified. Likewise S. Paul (who teacheth vs so to behaue our selues, that our affections may be witnessed by our sanctitie) willeth and teacheth vs to behaue our selues graciously, giuing vs his example: *Salute* (sayeth he) *such a one who knoweth well that I loue him with my hart, and such a one, who must be assured that I loue him as my Brother, and in particular his mother who knoweth also that she is myne.*

§. 4. You demaund vppon this subiect, if we may or should aduenture to shewe more affection to one sister whom we esteeme more vertuous, thē we doe to another. I aunswere to this, that although we are obliged to loue those more that are more vertuous, with the loue of delight, and content: yet ought we not therefore to loue them more with the loue of good will; nor ought we to shewe them more signes of freindship: and this for two reasons. The first is, because our Lord Iesvs did not practice it; but rather it seemeth he shewed more affection to the imperfect then to the perfect: since he hath sayed, that he was not come for the iust, but for sinners; that is to say, for those that haue more neede of vs, to whom we are to witnesse our loue more

more particularlye: for heere it is, vvhē vve shevve best, that vve loue for charitie, and not in louing those that giue vs more consolation, then payne or trouble. And in this vve ought to proceede as the profitt of our neighbour doth require; but further then this, vve must endeuour so to behaue our selues, that vve loue all equallie, since our Lord IESVS did not say: loue those that are more vertuous; but indifferentlie, loue one vvith another, euen as I haue loued you, vvith out excluding any one hovv imperfect soeuer he bee. The second reason vvherefore vve ovve not signes of freindship to one, more then another; and ought not to permitt our selues to be carryed to loue them more, is, that vve cannot iudge vvho are the more vertuous, and vvho haue more perfection: for exteriour apparences are very deceatfull, and very often those, that seeme to you to be the most vertuous, (as I haue sayed in another part) are not so before God; vvho is onelie he that can knovve them. It may be that a sister vvhom you shall see to faile very often, and committ a multitude of imperfections; vvilbe more vertuous & more pleasing to Almightye God, either for the greatnesse of the courage vvhere vvithe she vpholdeth her selfe in the midst of her imperfections, not giuing her selfe ouer to be troubled, nor disquieted to see her selfe subiect to fall, or because she dravveth out of it Humilitie, or for the loue she hath of her abiection: then another vvho shall haue a dozen vertues, either naturall or acquired but hath lesse exercise and labour; and consequently, it may be lesse courage, and Humilitie, then hath the other, vvhom vve see subiect to frailties. Sainct Peter vvas chosen to be the head of the Apostles, although he vveere subiect to many imperfections, in such sort that he did commit them, euen after he had receaued the holy Ghost, but for so much as, not vvith staning these his defects, he allvvaies had a great courage, and vvas not astonished at himselfe; our Lord made him his leiftenaunt, and fauored him aboue all the rest: so as none had reason to say, he did not deserue to haue the priuiledg and to be aduanced before Sainct Ihon, or the other Apostles. VVe must then behaue our selues in the affection vve are to beare our sisters the most equallie, that possibly vve may, for the aforesayed reasons; and all ought to knovve, that vve loue them vvith this loue of the hart; and therefore there is no necessitie to vse so many vvordes, that vve loue them dearly, that vve haue an inclination to loue them in particular, and the like: considering the loue vve beare a partie, is not the more perfect, for hauing an inclination for her more then for others: rather it may be more subiect to change, for the very least thing, that she shall doe to vs: Yf it be so, that it bee true, that vve haue an inclination to loue one rather then another, vve ought not to muse or thinke thereon, much lesse to declare it in vvordes to the partie, for vve ought not to loue by inclination, but to loue our neghbour, either because he is vertuous, or for the hope that vve haue that he vvill become so: but principally, because it is the vvill of God. Novv to giue true testimony that vve loue him, we must procure him all the good that vve can, aswell for soule as bodie; praying for him, and seruing him cordially, vvhen occasion shall present it selfe: for the freindship that endeth in fayre speeches, is no great matter; and it is not to loue, as our Lord IESVS hath loued vs, vvho vvas not content to assure vs, that he did loue vs, but vvould passe further, in doing all that he hath done; for

proofe

proofe of his loue. Saint Paule speaking to his most Deare children: I am most readie (sayed he) to giue my life for you, and to imploye my selfe so absolutelie for you, that I will not make any reseruation for to witnesse how dearely and tenderlie I loue you: yea, would he say, I am readie to leaue vndone, or to doe for you, or by you, all that you will haue of mee; wherin he teacheth vs, that to imploy himselfe, yea to giue his life for his neighbour, is not so much as to leaue himselfe to be imployed at the will of others, eithers by them or for them. And this was that which he had learned of our sweete Sauiour vppon the crosse. This is that soueraigne degree of loue of our neighbour, that Religious men and Religious weemen, and we who are consecrated to the seruice of God, are called vnto: for it is not enough to assist our neighbours with our temporall commodities; it is not enough (sayeth S. Bernard) to imploye our proper person to suffer for this loue; but it must passe further, leauing our selues to be imployed for him, in most holy obedience, and by him, euen so as he will, with out euer resisting ther-in: for when we imploy our selues for our selues, and by choise of our owne will, or proper election, this alwaies giueth very much satisfaction to selfe loue; but to permitt our selues to be imployed in things that others will, and which we our selues would not, that is to say, in businesses, which are not of our election, this is it, wher-in the soueraigne degree of abnegation doth consist. As when we would preach, they send vs to serue the sicke; when we would pray for our neighbour, they send vs to serue him. O how much better and with out cōparison more worth, is that which they will haue vs to doe (I meane in things not contrarie to God, and

and such as are not displeasing to him then that wich we performe or make choise of our selues!
Lett vs then Loue one another well, and serue our selues therefore with this motiue, which is so pregnant, for to incite vs to this holy Loue, which our Lord Iesvs vppō the crosse powred forth vnto the last drop of his most holy bloud vppon the earth, for to make it as it weare a sacred morter wherewith he would soder, vnite, conioyne, and fasten together all the stones of his church (which are faythfull) the one with the other: to the end that this vnion should be so strong that there might neuer be found there-in any diuision, so much did he feare, least this diuision should cause eternall damnation.
The supporting of the imperfections of our neighbour, is one of the most principall points of this loue: Our Lord Iesvs hath shewed it vs vppon the crosse, whose hart was so sweete towards vs, and did loue vs so dearely, vs I say, & euen those which there did cause his death, and who weare in the act of the most enormious sinne, which euer mā could committ: (for the sinne which the Iewes did committ, was a monster of wickednes) and neuerthelesse our sweete sauiour Iesvs had considerations of loue towards them, giuing an exāple aboue all imagination, in that he excused them, who did crucifie him, and did iniurie him with most barbarous rage: for these I say, did he seeke out inuentions to make his father to pardon them, in the very act it selfe of sinne and iniurye. O how miserable are we worldlings! for scarcely can we forgett an iniurye, that hath bene done vs, a long time after that we haue receaued it! therefore he, that will preuent his neighbour in benedictions of sweetnes, shalbe the most perfect imitatour of our Lord Iesvs.
§. 5. Furthermore we ought to marke, that cordiall

cordiall loue, is fastned to a vertu, which is as a dependance of this loue, to witt a simple confidence as children haue. Children when they haue a fine feather or some other thing, that they esteeme braue, they are neuer in quiet, if they haue not mett with their little companions to shew their feather, & to make them partakers of their ioy, as also they will haue them, to haue part of their greefe: for when they haue a little hurt vppon their fingers end, they ceale not to speake of it to all they meete with, to the end they may bemoane them, and may blowe a little vppon their sore, now I doe not say, that they must be iust as children: although I say that this confidence ought to cause Sisters not to be sparing to communicate their little contents and consolatiōs to their sisters, also not to fear their imperfections to be noted by thē. I doe not say, if they haue had any extraordinarie gift from God, that they must declare it to all the world, noe: but touching their ordinarie consolations I would that they should not be too reserued in them, but (when occasiō shall present it selfe) not by way of boasting or vanting, but with simple confidence, they may communicate them, freely and truelie one to an other. Likewise lett vs not put our selues into vnquietnesse to couer our defects, that they appeare not: for not to permitt them outwardly to shewe themselues, doth not make them any whit the better: for the sisters will not beleeue, that you haue non imperfections, because they see none: and our imperfections it may be wilbe more dangerous, then if they weare discouered, and that they did cause vs confusion: euen as they doe to those who are more facill to lett them appeare exteriourlie. VVe must not then be amased, nor discouraged when we committ defects, and imperfectiōs before our sisters, but contrarie wise we should be glad, that vve are knowne to be such as inded we are. You haue peraduenture committed a fault, some inciuillity, or impertinencie; it is true; but this is before your Sisters which loue you dearelie, and therefore know very well how to support you in your faultes, and will haue more compassion of you, thē passion against you; and by this meanes confidence would exceedinglie increase cordiallitie, and the tranquillitie of our spiritts, which are subiect to be troubled, whē we are knowne to faile in any thing. how little soeuer, as if it weere a great meruaile to see vs vnperfect. In fine, for conclusion of this discourse, it must alwaies be remembred, that for some want of gentlenesse, and suauitie that sōtimes is omitted by mistake, we ought not to be angry, nor to iugd that they haue not a good will towards vs: for they leaue not to haue it: for that an act done heere or there (prouided that it be not frequent) maketh not men vitious, especiallie when they haue a good will to amend.

THE SECOND DEMAVND.

VVhat it is, to doe all things vvith the Spiritt of Humilitie, as the Constitutions doe ordayne?

§. 6. THe better to vnderstand this, we must know, that euen as there is difference betwen pride, the custome of pride, and the spritt of pride (for if you cōmitt an act of pride, behould pride: if you committ acts at euerie turne, & vppō euerie encounter, this is the custome of pride: if you bee pleased in these acts, and seeke after them, it is the spiritt of pride) so likevvise there is a difference betweene

betweene humilitye, the habitt of humilitie, and the spiritt of humilitie. Humilitie is that, which executeth some act for to hūble her selfe, the habite thereof, is to doe so, at euerie encounter, and vppō all occasions that present themselues; but the spiritt of Humilitie is to delight her selfe in humiliation to search after abiection, and humilitie in all things: that is to say, that in all we doe, speake or desire, our principall end be to humble and abase our selues; and that it is pleasing to vs to encounter with our owne abiection in all occasions, louing dearely the very thought ther of. Behould this is that which maketh vs to doe all things in the spiritt of Humilitie, that is as much as who would say, to search and loue Humilitie and abiection in all things. It is a good practice of Humilitie, not to looke after the actions of another, otherwise then to marke their vertues, but neuer their imperfectiōs for, whiles we haue no charge, we must neuer turne our eyes on that side, much lesse our consideratiō, we must allwaies interpret in the best manner that can bee, what we see done to or by our neighbours, and in doubtfull things we must perswade our selues, tha, tthat which we perceaue, is not euill, but rather that it is our imperfection which causeth such a thought in vs; to the end wee may auoyde rash iudgements of the actions of others, which is a most dangerous euill, an which we ought singularlie to detest. In things euidentlye wicked, we must haue compassion, and humble our selues for the faultes of our neighbour as for our owne; and praye vnto God for their amendment with the same hart and good will, as we would doe for our selues, if we weare subiect to the same defects.

But what shall we be able to doe, (say you) for to gett this spiritt of such Humilitie as you haue declared vnto vs? O: there is no other meanes to attayne

attayne to it, then to all other vertues, which are not obteyned, but by reiterating of their acts. Humilitie maketh vs to annihilate our selues in all things, which are not necessarie for our aduancement in grace; as to speake well, to haue a gracious behauiour, great talēts for menaging of exteriour things, a great spiritt of eloquence, and the like; for these exteriour things, we ought to desire, that others should doe them better then vve our selues.

THE FIFT ENTERTAINMENT.

OF GENEROSITIE.

THe better to vnderstand what it is, and wherein consisteth this strength and Generositie of spiritt, which you demaund of mee, first a question that you haue made to me very often, must be aunswered: to witt, in what true Humilitie consisteth? for so much as resoluing this point, I shall make my selfe the better to be vnderstood, speaking of the second, that is, of the Generositie of which you now desire that I treate.

1. Humilitie is not any other thing, then a perfect knowledg that we are no other thē a pure nothing, and it causeth vs to hould this esteeme of our selues: the better to vnderstand this, you must knowe, that there are in vs, two kinds or sortes of goods, some, which are in vs, and of vs, and others which are in vs, but not of vs. when I say we haue goods which are of vs, I doe not say, that they come not from God, and that we haue them of our selues, for in veritye of our selues, we haue no other thing then miserye and nothing, but this I meane, that they are goods which God hath so placed in vs, that they seeme to be of vs, these goods are health, riches,

riches, sciences, arts, and the like. Now Humilitye hindreth vs from glorifying, and esteeming our selues for theses goods, for so much as it maketh no more account of them, then of nothing, yea a meere nothing: and in effect reason doth make it cleare; these goods not being of any stabilitie, nor rēdring vs more acceptable to God but mutable, and subiect to fortune: and if it weare not so, there is nothing of lesse assurāce then riches which depend of time and seasons; thē beautie which fadeth in let thē nothings a little durt on the face is sufficient to take away all the luster thereof; and concerning sciences and arts, a little trouble of the braine, causeth vs to loose and forgett all that we haue knowne; Is it not thē great reason, that humilitie make no reckoning of all the foresayed goods? but how much the more it causeth vs, to abase our selues, by the knowledge of what we are of our selues, and by the little esteeme that it maketh of all that is in vs, and of vs: so much the more doth it cause vs, to esteeme our selues because of the goods which are in vs, and not of vs; which are fayth, hope, and the loue of God, how little soeuer, we haue of them in vs; as also a certayne capacitie which God hath giuē vs, to vnite our selues to him by meanes of his grace, and touching vs, our vocatiō which giueth vs as much assurance (as we can haue thereof in this life) of the possession of Glorie and eternall felicitie; and this great esteeme that humilitie maketh of these goods, to witt fayth, hope and charitie, is the foundation of Generositie of spiritt: Behould thē the first goods whereof we haue spokē appertayne to humility for her exercise: and these other to Generositie for hers. Humilitie maketh vs beleeue that we are able to doe nothing, in respect of the knowlegd of our pouertie, and weaknesse in so much as is of our selues: and on the cōtrarie Generositie maketh vs say with S. Paule; I can doe all things in him that cōforteth me. Humilitie maketh vs to distrust our selues, and Generositie causeth vs to cōfide in God. You see thē that these two vertues of Humilitie and Generositie are so ioyned and vnited the one with the other, that they neuer are nor cā be seperated. There are certayne persons, who relye vppō a false and childish Humilitie which hindreth thē frō regarding in thēselues, that good which god hath placed there: They are very much deceaued, for the gifts that God hath endowed vs with all, should be acknowledged, esteemed and greatly honoured, ād not held in the same rāke of base esteeme, which we ought to hould of those, that are with in vs and of vs. Not onely true christians haue acknowledged, that they ought to regard these two sortes of goods, which are in vs, the one kind to hūble vs, the other to glorifie the Diuine boūtie, which bestowed thē vppon vs: but also the Philosophers: for this worde so common amōg them, know thy selfe, ought not onely to be vnderstood of the knowledge of our vilitye and miserie; but likewise of the excellencye and dignitye of our soules, who are capable to be vnited to the Diuinitie, by his Diuiue bountye who hath setled a certayne instinct in vs the which causeth vs allwaies to tend to, and pretend this vnion. Wherein consisteth all our felicitye.

§. 2. The Humilitie which doth not produce Generositie, vndoubtedly is false for after that she hath sayed, I can doe nothing, I am no other then a pure nothing, she yealdeth immediatlye the place to Generositye of spiritt, the which sayeth, There is not any thing, neither can there be any thing to be had that is not in my power, for so much as I put all my confidence in God, who can doe all: and vppō this cōfidēce, she enterpriseth couragiously to performe all that they cōmaund her. But marke that I say all that is cōmaūded her, or coūselled, how difficult soeuer it be: for I cā assure you that Humilitie iudgeth

it not

it not to be a thing impossible for her to worke miracles, being commaunded so to doe: if she put her selfe to the execution of the commaundement in simplicitie of hart, God will rather worke a miracle, then be wanting to giue her abilitie to accōplish her enterprise: because she did not vndertake the action vppon any other ayde, then vppon the cōfidēce she hath in his streingth: yea she is grounded vppon the estimation that she hath of the gifts that God hath imparted vnto her and so she maketh this discourse within her selfe: if God doe call me to so high an estate of perfection, that there is not a more high estate in this life, what is that which shall hinder me to attayne there vnto, since that I am most assured that he, who hath begū the worke of my perfectiō, will perfect it? but take heed that this be done with out any presumptiō: for so much as this confidence hindereth not, but that we must allwaies keepe our selues vppon our gard, for feare of being deceaued; but rather it maketh vs more attentiue ouer our selues, more vigilant and carefull to doe that, which may serue vs for the aduancement of our perfection. Humilitie consisteth not onely in the distrust of our selues, but also that we confide in God: and the diffidēce of our selues and of our owune forces, produceth confidence in God and from this confidence springeth Generositie of spiritt of which we speake.

3. The most holie virgin Our Bl. Ladie did furnish vs with a most remarkable exāple for this subiect, when she pronūced these wordes, Behould the hand mayde of our Lord, be it done to mee according to thy worde: for in that she sayeth, the seruāt of our Lord, she maketh an act of the greatest humilitie that she could doe for so much as she opposed against the praises that the Angell gaue her, that she should be the mother of God, that the child

child which should be borne of her should be called the Sonne of the most High (the greatest dignitie, that euer had bene or could be imagined:) she opposed (I say) to all these praises and greatnesses, her basenes and vnworthines, saying she was the handmayd of our Lord. But consider that after she had rendred her due to humilitie, she practiced incontinently a most excellent act of Generositie, saying: Lett it be done to me according to thy word. It is true (as if she would haue sayed) that I am not in any sorte capable of this grace, if respect be had to what I am of my selfe; but since that which is good in me is of God, and that wich thou tellest mee is his most holy will, I beleeue that he is able, and that he will effect it; and therefore she sayed, Let it be done to me as thou hast sayed.

§. 4. Likewise for want of this Generositie, very few acts of true contrition are made; for so-much as after we be humbled and confounded, before the diuine maiestie in consideration of our great infidelitye, we approch not to make an act of confidence, in taking hart by the assurance we ought to haue, that the diuine bountie will giue vs his grace, from henceforth to be more faythfull to him, and to correspōd more perfectly to his diuine loue. After this act of confidence should immediatlye follow, that of Generositie, saying, since that I am most assured that the grace of God shall not be wanting to mee, I will further beleeue, that he will not permitt me to fayle in corresponding to his grace.

§. 5. But you will say to mee, If I be wanting to grace, it will also be wanting to me. It is true, if then it be so, who shall assure me from this time forth, that I shall not fayle to cooperate vvith grace since I haue so oftentimes heretofore lett it passe carelesslie? I aunsvvere that Generositie causeth the soule

soule boudly to say, with out any feare: no; I wilbe no more vnfaytfull to God; and because she feeleth in her hart this resolution of neuer being disloyall, she vndertaketh with out any feare, all that she knoweth is in her power to yeald acceptable seruice to God, with out exception: and enterprising all, she beleeueth she hath abilitye for all, not of her selfe; but in God, vppon whome she hath fixed her confidence: therefore she attempteth what soeuer is commaunded or councelled her.

§.5. But you will demaund of mee, if it be neuer permitted to doubt, whether we bee capable or not, to doe those things that are commaunded vs? I aunsweere, that Generositie of spiritt, doth neuer permitt vs to enter into any doubt. To this end you must distinguish, (as I haue bene accoustomed to tell you) the superiour part of your soules from, the inferiour: Now whē I say that Generositie doth not permitt vs to doubt, this is as touching the Superiour part: for it may very well bee that the inferiour will be top full of deubts, and will haue much difficultye to receaue the charge, or imployment that is appointed vs: But for all this, the soule that is Generous scorneth it, and maked no account ther-of; but simply putteth her selfe to the exercise of the charge not so much as speaking one worde, nor shewing any action to discouer the feeling she hath of her incapacitie. But we poore creatures, are so ioyfull, as of nothing more, to witnesse that we are very hūble, and that we haue a base esteeme of our selues; and the like things, which are nothing lesse then true humilitie, which doth neuer permitt vs to resist the iudgment of those whom God hath giuen vs to be our Guides. I haue put in the booke of the introduction an example which serueth to my purpose, and which is very remarkable: it is of king Achab who being reduced to extreeme affliction, by the

greuous

greeuous warre that two other kings did make against him,hauing beseeged Herusalem· God cōmaunded the prophet Isaye, that he should goe to comfort him in his name, and to promise him he should haue the victorie, and remayne triumphant ouer his enimyes.And moreouer the prophet sayed to him,that for proofe of the truth of what he spake he should demaund of God a signe in heauē aboue, or in the earth below,and God would grant it him: then Achaz distrusting the bountie of God, and his liberality, sayed, I will not doe it, for so much as I will not tempt God.But the miserable man,sayed not this for the honour he did beare to God: for contrariwise, he refused to honour him, because God would at that time be honored by miracles: and Achaz did refuse to demaūd one of him, which he had signified vnto him, he desired to doe: he offended God in refusing to obey the Prophet,that God sent to signify his will vnto him. VVee ought then neuer to be doubtfull that we cannot doe that which is commaunded, for so much as those, who commaund vs, knowe sufficiently our capacitye.

§. 6. But you tell me, that peraduenturē you haue many interiour miseries ad imperfections, that your superiours knowe not of, and this that they doe is vppon exteriour apparences, by the which it may be you haue deceaued their spiritts, I say,wee must not allwaies beleeue what you saye, pushed forwardes it may be with discouragment, that you are miserable,and wholy filled with imperfections,no more thē we must beleeue that you haue them not, whē you say nothing of them,they ordinarilie being such as your workes make them appeare. Your vertues are knowne by the fidelitie you haue in practicing of them,and euen so imperfections are knowne by their acts. VVe cannot, as long as we feele no malice in our hart deceaue the

 spiritt

ſpiritt of our ſuperiours.

§.7. But you tell mee that wee ſee many Sts. make great reſiſtance, that they might not receaue thoſe offices and charges others would haue giuen them. That which they haue done, hath not bene onely, becauſe of the baſe eſteeme they had of thẽſelues; but principally becauſe they did ſee, that thoſe that would haue them vndertake theſe charges grounded themſelues vppon apparent vertues, as are faſtings, Almces deeds, penãces and auſterities of bodye, and not vppon the true interiour vertues, which they kept cloſe, and couert vnder holye humilitie; and they weare ſought ont, and followed by the poeple, who did nott knowe them otherwiſe then by the fame they heard of their vertu: in this caſe, it should be (as it ſeeemeth) permitted to make ſome reſiſtãce: but doe you know to whome? I will tell you. To a Religious of Dijon, for example, to whome a Superiour of Aneſſy should ſend commaundement to be Superiour, hauing neuer ſeene nor knowen her. But a Religious of that place, to whom she should make the ſame commaundement, should neuer endeuour to bring any teſtimonie, that she is repugnant to the commaundement: but rather she should endeuour to put her ſelfe to the exercise of her charge, with as much peace and courage, as if she thought her ſelfe very capable for the performance thereof. But I ſee very well the craft of the diuell, we feare forſoothe the ſucceſſe thereof will not proue to our honour, we haue our reputation in ſo great recommendation, that we would not be held for learners in our charges, but for maiſters and Miſtriſſes, that neuer committ faultes.

§.8. You now by this vnderſtand inough, what the ſpiritt of ſtreingth and Generoſitie is, which we ſo much deſire should be eſtablished amongſt you,

to

to the end it may banish all childishnes, & effeminacie which serue for nothing else, then to stop vs in our way, and to hinder vs from making any progresse in perfection. These tendernesses are nourisht by the vaine reflectiōs wee make vppō our selues, principallie when we haue stūbled in our way by any faulte; for in this place by the grace of God we haue neuer yet seene any directlye to fall; but if they stumble now and then, and in steed of hūbling themselues mildly, and redressing themselues couragiously (as we haue sayed) they enter into consideration of their pouertie, and there vppon they begin to compassionate themselues saying, Alas my God! how miserable am I. I am fitt for nothing: and afterward we passe into discouragment which causeth vs to saye: O no, there is nothing more for to be hoped for of me, I shall neuer doe any thing of worth, it is time lost to speake to mee: and cōsequentlie we would almost that they should leaue vs there, as if they weere very well assured neuer to be able to gayne any thing with vs. Good God how farre are all these things from the soule that is generous, and who maketh a great esteeme, as we haue sayed, of the talentes God hath endowed her with all? for she is not astonished eyther at the difficultyes of the way, she hath to goe, or at the greatnesse of the worke, or the leanght of time that must be imployed therein, or in fine at the delaying of the worke which she hath vndertaken. The Religious of the Visitation are all called to most great perfection, and their enterprise is the most high and excellent that can be thought of: for so much as they haue not onely the pretense in vniting themselues to the will of God, as all creatures ought to doe; but moreouer their pretensiō is to vnite themselues to his desires, yea euen vnto his intentions, I say, euen in a manner before they be scarse signified vnto them, and if they could cōceaue vvhat vveere more perfect, and one degree of perfection more thē to conforme thēselues to the will of God, his desires, and intentions, they would with out doubt vndertake to mount thereunto, since they haue a vocation, which obligeth thē thereunto: and therefore their deuotion ought to be a strong and generous deuotion, as we haue sayed many times.

§. 7. But besides this that we haue sayed of this Generositie, this must furthermore be declared heere to witt, that the soule which possesseth it, receaueth equallie drinesse of spiritt, and sweetnesse of consolations; interiour anguishes, vexations, and oppressions of spiritt. as the fauoures and prosperitie of a spiritt, filled with peace and tranquillitie; and this because she cōsidereth, that he which giueth her the consolations, is the very same that sendeth her afflictions, vvho sendeth the one and the other with the same loue, which she her selfe acknowledgeth to be exceedinglie great: because that by the interiour affliction of the spiritt, he pretendeth to drawe her to most high perfectiō, which is the abnegation of all sortes of cōsolatiōs in this life: remayning most assured that he who hath depriued her of them in this world, will not eternallie depriue her of thē in the height of heauē. You will say to mee, that we cānot in the thickett of these great darknesses make these considerations: seeing as it seemeth, we cānot speake so much as one onely word vnto our Lord: truly you haue reason to say, as it seemeth to you, for so much as in veritie it is not so. The sacred councell of Trent hath determined thus, and wee are obliged to beleaue it, that God and his grace doe neuer abādon vs in such sort, that we cannot haue recourse to his bountie, and protest that against all the trouble and wrestling of our soule, we wilbe wholie his, and that we will not willinglie offend him. But marke well, all this is in the superiour part of our soule, and because the inferiour perceaueth not any thing at all of this, but that she remayneth allvvaies in her payne, that is it, that troubleth vs, and maketh vs to esteeme our selues very miserable: and further more we begin to bemoane our selues excessiuelye as if it weare a thing very worthy of compassion, to see our selues vvith out consolation. Alas, Alas, for Gods sake let vs cōsider, how our Lord and maister hath very willinglie bene exercised by these interiour anguishes, and that beyōd all imaginatiō. Lett vs harkē vnto those wordes that he spake vppō the crosse: My God, my God, why hast thou forsakē mee? he was reduced to so great extremitye that he had no other thing left thē the point of the spiritt, which was not ouer whelmed with dolours: but yet cōsider that he betaketh himselfe to speake to God, for to shewe vs, that it should not be impossible for vs to doe the same

§. 8. VVhich is better say you, at this time, to speake to God of our greife, and miserie, or else to speake to him of some other matter? I tell you that in this case, as in all sortes of temptations, it is better to diuert our spiritt frō the vexation and trouble ther-of discoursing with God of some other thing, then to speake to him of our vexation: for vndoubtedly if we doe it, it will not be with out a kinde of bemoaning and tendernesse ouer our hart, augmenting a nevv our grife, our nature being such, as it cannot see or thinke of her dolours with out hauing great compassion of them. But you say to me except you be attentiue to your greifes, you shall not remember then hovv to declare them, & what matter is it; truely we are as children, vvho are very glad to goe to their mother, if a Bee haue stung them, to tell it her, to the end she may bemoane them, and blow vppon the place, which is alreadie whole: for we willinglie goe to our mother to tell her we haue bene very much afflicted, and we aggrauate our affliction, recounting the very least things, not omitting any little circumstance which may cause vs to be bemoaned a little: Now doe you not see this extreeme childishnes? if wee haue committed any infidelitie, it is good to declare it, if we haue bene faythfull it must be also tould, yet breiflie, with out exaggerating either the one or the other, for all ought to be declared to those that haue charge of our soules.

§. 9. You will say now, that when you haue had a great motion of choller, or of any other tentation there allwaies commeth some scruple into your minde vnlesse you confesse it: I say it ought to be spoken in the reuewe of our selues, but not by way of confession: but for instruction how to cōport our selues in the like occasions, I say, when we doe not clearelie see, that we haue giuen some kind of consent; for if you saie: I accuse my selfe that two dayes together I haue had great motions of choler, but I consented not there vnto, you declare your vertues, in place of telling your faultes, but if I be in doubt whether I haue committed some fault therein or no: I must consider maturelie if this doubt haue any ground: it may be, that about a quarter of an hower, in the space of these two dayes you haue bene somewhat negligent in diuerting your thoughts from that motion; if it be so tell simply, that you haue bene negligent in diuerting your selfe from a motion of choller that you haue had, during the space of a quarter of an hower, with out adding the tentation hath continued two dayes: except you would say it either to receaue some instruction from your Confessour, or otherwise because it is of your ordinarie reuewe; for then it is very good to declare it. But for ordinarie confessions, it wilbe better not to speake of it,

since

since you doe it to no other end then to satisfie your selues, and if it put you to some little payne in not doing it, it ought to be suffered, as some other accident, in which we are not able to procure redresse. God be Blessed.

LIVE JESUS.

THE SIXT ENTERTAIN-MENT OF HOPE.

VPPON THE DEPARTVRE OF THE Visitation, that went to found a new house of their Institute.

1. AMong the praises the Holy Sainctes haue giuen to Abraham S. Paul extolleth this aboue all the rest, that he increased in Hope against hope, it selfe; God Almightie had promised him, that his seede should be multiplied as the stars of heauen, & as the sandes of the sea: yet notwithstanding he receaued a commaundement to sacrifice his sonne Isaac: poore Abraham did not loose his Hope for this, but hee expected beyond hope it selfe, that being obedient to the commaundement giuen him of sacrificing his sonne, God vvould not therefore fayle to performe his promise made to him: great truely vvas his hope: for in no sort did he see where-on it might depend, but onely vppon the worde which God had giuen him. O; that word of God is a most true and solide ground and foundation, for it is infallible; Abraham then proceeded to accōplish the will of God with an incōparable simplicitie; for he made no more conside-

 ration,

ratiō, nor reply, then he did vvhē God had cōmaunded him, saying: goe forth out of thy country, and from thy kindred, and goe to the place that I will shewe thee, not specifying it vnto him, to the end he should imbarke himselfe, most simply in the ship of his Diuine prouidence: walking then forwards three dayes and three nights, with his sonne Isaac, carrying the wood for the sacrifice, this Innocent soule demaunded of his Father vvhere was the Holocaust? to vvhome good Abraham aunswered; My sonne, our Lord will prouide it O good God! hovv happie should wee bee, if vve could accustome our selues to make this aunswere to our hartes, vvhen they are in care for any thing; our Lord vvill prouide therefore, and that after this vve had not any more anxietie, trouble, or impression, then Isaac had: for he held himselfe silent and quiett, beleuing our Lord vvould prouide, euen as his father had sayed; Certainelye God requireth that the confidence vvee haue in his fatherlie care and Diuine Prouidence should be great: But wherefore should we not haue it? seeing there hath neuer bene any personne deceaued therein, nor any one confided in God that hath not receaued the fruit of his confidence. I speake this amongst our selues; for touching these of the vvorld, their confidence is accompagnied vvith apprehension; and therefore is of no vvorth before God. Lett vs consider I beseech you, vvhat Our Lord & Maister sayed to his Apostles, to establish in them this holy and louing Confidence. I haue sent you into the world vvith out scrip, mony, or other prouisions, either for your nourishment or clothing, hath there bene any thing vvanting to you? and they sayed no: goe, sayed he, to them, and meditate not in your mind, whereof you shall eate, or vvhat you shall drinke, or vvhere vvith you shalbe clothed, nor likewise likevvise vvhat you shall speake, being in the presence of the great Lords and magistrats of the prouinces through vvhich you shall passe: for in euery occasion your heauenlie Father vvill prouide for you, all that is necessarie; neither doe you premeditate vvhat you shall speake, for he vvill speake in you, and put into your mouth the wordes that you shall haue to say. But I am so dull, and ill-spoke (some one of our sisters will say) I knovve not hovv to conuerse with great ones, and Noble people, I haue no learning: that is all one, goe, and confide in God: for he hath sayed. Although a vvomā should happen to forgett her child yet vvill I neuer forgett you: for I beare you ingrauen in my hart, and on my hands; Thinke you that he vvho hath care to prouide foode for the foules of the ayre, and the beastes of the earth, which neither sovv nor gather into barnes, can euer forgett to prouide all that shalbe necessarie for the man that vvil confide totallie in his Prouidence, since that man is capable to be vnited to God our Souueraigne good?

§. 2. This my most deare Sisters hath seemed good to me to speake to you vppon this subiect of your departure; for although you are not capable of Apostolicall dignitie because of your sex, neuer thelesse you are in some sort capable of the Apostolicall office: and you may render many seruices to God, procuring in some sorte the aduancement of his glorie as the Apostles did. Certaynelie, my Deare Daughters, this ought to be a motiue of great consolation vnto you, that God will serue him selfe of you for so excellent a worke as this to which you are called, and you ought to hould your selues greatlie honored before the Diuine maiestie. For what is that, that God desireth of you, but that which he did ordayne to his Apostles?

 and

and that for which he sent them into the World, which was that for which our Lord himselfe came to worke in this world, to witt, to giue life to men, and not onely this, sayed hee, but to the end they should liue more abundantlie, that they may haue life and better life, which he hath wrought by giuing the his grace: The Apostles were sent of our Lord throughout the world for the same subiect: for our Lord sayed vnto them, euen as my Father sent mee I send you: goe and giue life to men; but you must not content your selues with this, but endeuour that they liue, and that a most perfect life; by the meanes of the doctrine that you shall teach them, they shall haue life in beleeuing my worde that you expose to them: but they shall haue more abundant life by the good example that you shall giue them: and therefore take no care whether your labours fructifie according to your pretended desire, for it is not of you the fruits shalbe demaunded, but onely whether you haue imploied your selues faythfully to cultiuate the sterill and dry ground: it will not be demaunded whether you haue had a good haruest: but onely if you haue had care to sowe vvel. In like manner my deare daughters you are now comaunded to goe hether and thether, into diuers places to the end that soules hauing life, by your meanes may liue a better life, for what is that vvhich you goe to doe, but to giue knowledg of your Institute, and by meanes of this knowledg to dravve many soules, to imbrace all the obseruances, which are comprised and contained therein! but with out preaching and conferring the Sacraments, and remitting sinnes as the Appostles did. Goe you not to giue life to men? but to speake more properly, goe you not to giue life to vvomen, since it may be a hundred and a hūdred virgins which would haue bene lost in the vvorld, shall by your example, retyring them selues

selues vvith in your Religion, goe to enioy in heauen for all eternitie, incomprebēsible felicitye: and is not this by your meanes, that their life shalbe giuen them, and that they shall liue a more abundant life, that is to say, a life more perfect and pleasing to God, a life that shall make them capable to vnite themselues more perfectly to the diuine Bountie: for they shall receaue from you necessarie instructions, for to attayne the true and pure loue of God, with is that more abundant life, which our Lord IESVS is come to giue to men? I haue brought, sayed he, fire into the earth, what is that I demaund, or what doe I prretend, but that it burne? And in another place he cōmaundeth that fire burne continually vppon his Altar, and therefore that it should neuer be put out, to shewe with what ardour he desireth that the fire of his loue be allwaies kindled vppō the Altar of our harts. O God, what a grace is this, that God doeth bestowe on you? he maketh you Apostles, not in dignity, but in office and meritt, you preach not; for your sex is not permitted it, although S. Marie Magdalene, and S. Martha her Sister hath done it, but you omitt not therefore to exercise the Apostolicall office, in the communicatiō of your manner of life, euen so as I say. Goe then with courage to accomplish that to which you are called, but goe in simplicitye; if you haue apprehensions, saye to your soules, Our Lord will prouide for vs: if the consideration of your weaknes disharten you; cast your selues into the armes of God; and confide in him. The Apostles for the most part weere sinners and ignorant, God made them learned, according as was necessarie for the charge that he would giue them: doe you therefore confide in him, depend vppon his prouidence and feare nothing: doe not say, I haue not the talēt to discourse well, it impor-
teth

teth not, goe with out making discourse: for god will giue you that which you shall haue to saye, and to doe when it shalbe time, if you haue indeed no vertue, or at least perceaue none in you, lett it not trouble you; for if you enterprise for the Glorie of God: and the fulfilling of obedience, the gouerment of soules, or any other exercise whatsoeuer it bee, God vvill haue care of you, and shalbe obliged to prouide for you all that shalbe necessarie, as well for you, as for those God hath giuen you in charge: it is true that this which you vndertake is a matter of great consequence and importance; but hovv soeuer you should doe amisse, if you would not expect good successe, since you doe not interprise it, by your owne choise, but for your obligation to Obedience. VVithout doubt we haue great cause to feare when vve seeke after offices and charges, be it in Religion, or other where, and that they be granted vs through our importune suite; but vvhen it is not so: Lett vs bovve humbly our necke vnder the yoke of holy Obedience, and Lett vs accept of the burthen with a good hart humbling our selues, for this ought allwaies to be practiced: but lett vs allvvaies remember to establish Generositie vppon the acts of humilitye, for vvith out it, these acts of humilitie are vvorth nothing.

§. 3. I haue an extreeme desire to graue in your harts one maxime, vvhich is of incomparable profitt: not to aske any thing, nor to refuse any thing: no my Deare Children demaund nothing, nor refuse nothing: receaue that which they vvill giue you, and doe not demaund vvhat they shall not present, or that they vvill not giue you: in this practice you shall find great peace to your soules: yea, my Deare Sisters, hould your harts to

this

this holy indifferencie, to receaue all they vvill giue you, and not to desire that vvhich they vvill not giue you: I say in a vvorde desire nothing, but leaue your selues, and all your affayres totally and perfectlie to the care of the Diuine Prouidence: permitt him to doe with you; euen as Children leaue themselues to be gouerned by their Nourses, if it carrye you on the right arme or on the left, lett it all be as it shall please him, for a child vvould not bee discontented thereat. vvhether it bring you to bed, or raise you from bed, lett it alone for it is a good mother, that knovveth better vvhat you vvant, then you your selues. I advise you, if the Diuine prouidence permitt, that affliction or mortifications happen to you, not to refuse them: rather accept them with a louing and peacefull hart: and if they be not sent you by it, or that it be not permitted that they happen vnto you: desire them not, nor aske for them: likevvise if consolations or comfortes be giuen you, receaue them vvith the spiritt of gratitude, and thankesgiuing to the Diuine bountie: and if you haue them not; doe not desire them, but endeauour to haue your hart prepared to receaue the diuersitye of euents from the Diuine Prouidence vvith an equall hart as much as may bee. If in Religion they appoint obediences to you, vvhich seeme dangerous for you, as are those of superioritye, refuse them not, if they are not appointed you, desire them not, and euen so of all thinges, I meane of things of this vvorld: for so farr as concerneth vertues, We may and ought to aske thē of God: and the loue of God comprehendeth them all. You cannot beleeue vntill you haue experienced it, hovv much profitt the practice of this will bring to your soules, for in place of musing to desire now these meanes, and after

others

others to perfect your selues, you will apply your selues more simply, and faythfullie, to those that will encounter you in your way.

§. 4. Casting my eyes vppon the subiect of your departure, and vppon the ineuitable feelings that euerie one of you shall haue, in being separated one from an other, I thought my selfe bound to make some little speache to you, to lessen your greife, although I will not say, that it is not lawefull to weepe a little, for it must be done, for so much as ye shall not be able to restraine it, hauing remayned so sweetly and louinglie together, a long time in the practice of one and the same exercises; the which hath so vnited your hartes that with out doubt they cannot suffer any diuision or separatiō: My Deare Sisters, you shall not be deuided nor separated, for all goe, and all remayne; those that goe remayne; and those that remayne goe; not in their person: but in the person of those that goe: and likewise those that shall goe, shall remayne in the person of those that remayne, this is one of the principall fruites of Religion (to witt) this holye vniō that is made by charitie, which is such an vniō that of many harts there is but one hart, and of many members there is made but one bodye: all are so made one in Religion; that all the Religious of one order (as it seemeth) are but one onely Religious. The laye Sisters sing the Diuine Office in the person of those that are dedicated to the Quire, and the quire Nūnes serue in domesticall offices in the person of those who doe them: and euen so the reason is most euident. For so much as if those that are in the quire, to sing the office, weare not there, the others should be there in their place, and and if they had not domesticall Sisters to dresse their dinner, the Sisters of the Quire should be imployed therin: and if such a Sister weare not superiour, thē

there

there should be another: euen so those who doe goe, doe remayne, & those who remayne goe: for if those that be named to goe, could not performe it, those that remayne should goe in their place: but that which ought cause you either to goe or remayne willingly, my deare daughters, is, the almost infallible assurance which wee ought to haue, that this separation is made no otherwise then touching the bodye, for touching the spiritt you remayne most perfectly vnited; this corporall separation is but a small matter, the which wilbe done, will wee, or will wee not: but the separation of harts and disvnion of spiritts, this is it alone that is to be feared. Now touching vs, we will not onelie remayne vnited together: but further more this our vnion shall euerie day increase to more perfection, and that most sweete and amiable bond or corde of charitie shall be allwayes more twisted and tied together, according to the measure that we shall aduance our selues, in the way of our owne perfection: for as much as becomming more capable to vnite our selues to God, the more we shall vnite our selues one to and other, so that by euery communion that we make, our vnion shalbe made more perfect: for vniting our selues with our Lord we shall allwaies remayne more vnited together: also the receauing of this sacred and celestiall Bread and of this most odoriferous Sacrament is called Communion, that is as much to say, as, common vnion. O good God, what an vnion is that, which is betweene, each Religious of one and the same order; such an vnion that their spirituall riches are so intermixed together, and reduced into common, as their exteriour prouisions are. A Religious persō hath nothing in particular to himselfe, because of the sacred vowe that he hath made, of voluntarie Pouertie, and by the holy profession that Religious make

make of most holy charitie. all their vertues are cōmon, and all participat of the good workes of
one an other, and shall enioy the fruite of the
same: prouided that they keepe themselues allwaies
in charitie, and in obseruance of those Rules of
Religion vvherevnto God hath called them; so
that that person which is in any domesticall office, or in any other exercise vvhatsoeuer it be, con-
templateth in the person of her that is in prayer
in the quier: she that reposeth, participateth of the
labour another hath, vvho is in exercise by the
commaundement of the Superiour. Behould then
my deare Children, hovv those that goe, doe remayne, and those vvho remayne doe goe, and
therefore you ought all equallie, louinglie and couragiously to imbrace Obedience as vvell in this occasiō as in all others, since those vvho doe remayne
shall haue part of the labour and fruite of the voyage of those vvho depart: euen as they shall haue part
of the tranquillitie and quiet of those who remayne. Doubtlesse all of you, my Deare children, haue
neede of much vertue, and of great care to practice
it, aswell to depart, as to stay. For euen as they vvho
depart, haue need of much courage & confidence
in God, louinglye and with the spiritt of humilitie
to enterprise that vvhich God requireth of them,
vanquishing all the feelings which may laye hould
or come vppon them to leaue the house, in vvhich
God hath first placed them, the Sisters they haue
so dearely loued, and vvhose conuersation brought
so much consolation to their soule; the tranquillitye of their retired life, which is so deare, their
parents and acquaintance, and I knovv not vvhat
many other things, to which nature is tyed whiles that vve liue in this life; They likewise vvho
remayne haue the same neede and necessitye of
courage, asvvell to perseuere in the practice of
holy

holy submission, humilitie, and tranquillitye, as also to prepare themselues, to goe forth, vvhen they shalbe commaunded: since, that euen, as, you see, your Institute, My Deare sisters, beginnegth, to extend it selfe, into all parts, in so many diuers places: in like manner you ought to endeauour, to increase and multiply the acts of your vertue, and to stringhten your conrage, for to make your selues capable to bee imployed, according to the vvill of God.

§.5. Truely it seemeth to mee, vvhen I regard and consider the beginning of your Institute, that it verye vvel representeth the historie of Abraham: for vvhen God had giuen his vvord to him, that his seede should be multiplied as the stars of the firmament, and as the sandes of the sea: he commaunded him neuerthelesse to sacrifice his sonne: by vvhome the promise of God vvas to be accomplished. Abraham did hope and strenghten himselfe in his hope, agaynst hope it selfe, and his hope vvas not in vaine, but fruitfull: in like manner vvhen the first three Sisters did ranke themselues together, and embrace this kind of life, God had designed from all eternitie to blesse their generation, in giuing them one vvho should be greatlie multyplied: but vvho could haue beleeued this? since vvhen they enclosed themselues vvith in their little house, vve thought no other thing then to make them dye to the world? they vveare not sacrificed, but they did voluntarilie sacrifice themselues, and God contented himselfe so must vvith their sacrifice, that he hath not onely giuen them a nevv life for them selues: but a life so abundant, that they may by his grace communicate it to many soules, euen as vve allreadie see. And truelie it

seemeth

seemeth to mee that these three first Sisters, are verye well represented by the three graines of wheat that weare found among the strawe, which was put on the chariott of Triptolemus, the which graines did serue to conserue his armye. For being brought into a countrye, where there was not any wheate, these three graines weare takē, and cast into the ground, which did produce others in such quantitie, that with in a fewe yeares all the groundes of that country weare sowed there with. The Prouidence of our good God casting with his blessed hand these three Religious into the ground of the Visitation: and hauing remayned there somtime hidden from the eyes of the world, they haue produced the fruite that we see at this present: in such sort that within a short time, all this country shalbe made participant of your Institute. O how happie are those soules who dedicate themselues truely and absolutely to the seruice of God? for God neuer leaueth them barren nor vnfruitefull; for, for a very nothing that they haue leaft for God: God giueth them incomparable recompences, aswell in this life as in the other. VVhat a grace is this I praye you, to be imployed in the seruice of soules, whom God hath so dearelye loued, and for whose saluation our Lord IESVS hath suffered so much? truely it is an inestimable honour, and you ought) my deare children) to make a very great esteeme thereof, and to employ your selues faythfully therein, not cōplayning neither of payne nor care, nor labour: for you shalbe most dearely recompensed for all, allthough this ought not to serue as a motiue to encourage you but rather, because by the same you become more pleasing to God, and thereby augment his Glorie so much the more; Goe then, and remayne couragiouslie in this exercise, and doe not studie to cōsider, that you see not in your selues what is necessarie, I meane meanes talentes proper for the offices you shalbe imployed in: it is better that you doe not see them in your selues, for this will keepe you in humilitye, and giue you more ample subiect to distrust your selues, & your owne forces, and cause you more absolutelie to put your vvhole confidence in God, in so much that as long as we haue not necessitie to practice a vertue, it is better we haue it not: when vve shall haue vse thereof (prouided that we bee faythfull in those that vve haue present practice of) lett vs hould our selues assured that God will giue vs euery vertue in his time; lett vs not studie to desire, nor to pretend any thing, lett vs indeed leaue our selues vvholie in the handes of the diuine prouidence that he doe vvith vs vvhat shall please him: for to vvhat purpose is it, to desire one thing rather then another? ought not all things to be indifferent vnto vs? prouided that vve pleale God, and that vve loue his diuine vvill, this ought to suffice vs. For my part, I admire hovv it can bee, that vve should haue more inclinatiō to bee imployed in one thing then in another; principallie being in Religion, vvhere one charge, and one busines is as pleasing to God as another: since it is Obedience that giueth the prise to all the exercises of Religiō: if the choice vveare giuen vs the most abiect should bee the most desirable, and these vve should imbrace most louingly; but this not being in our choice, lett vs imbrace the one & the other with the same harty good vvill: vvhen the charge that is giuē vs is honorable before men: lett vs hould our selues humble before God: vvhen it is more abiect before men, lett vs esteeme our selues more honored before the diuine Bountie.

§. 6. In fine, my deare daughters, retayne cherefully and faythfully, that which I haue sayed to you, vvhether it respect the interiour, or the exteriour,

vvill

vvill nothing but what God vvould haue you to vvill: imbrace louinglie the euents ad diuers effects of his diuine will, not troubling your heades about any other thing, and now what can I say more, my deare Sisters, since it seemeth that all our happinesse is comprised in this most amiable practice ? onelie I will represent to you the example of the Isralites: with the which I vvill ende: they hauing bene a long time vvith out a king, had a desire to haue one (great certaynelie is the spiritt of humayne estimation,) as if God had left them vvith out a guide, or that he had not had care to Rule, gouerne, and defend them, for this cause they did addresse themselues to the Prophett, vvho promised in theire name to demaund one for them of God, the vvhich he did, and God being irritated vvith their demaũd, made them this aunsvvere, that he vvould grant their request: but that he should aduertise thẽ, that the king that they should haue, should take such dominion ouer them, that he should take their children from them, & as for their sonnes, he should make some of them, vnder officers, others souldiers, and captaynes, and for their daughters, he should make some of them cookes, others Bakers, and others perfumers: Our Lord doth the same, Most deare daughters, to those vvho dedicate themselues vnto his seruice, for (as you see in Religion) their are diuers charges, and diuers offices: but vvhat is it that I will say ? no other thing, but that it seemeth to mee, that the diuine Maiestie hath chosen you, vvho are to goe, as perfumers, yea truelie, for you are deputed by him, to goe and povvre forth the most svveete sauour of the vertues of your Institute; and as young damsells are louers of svveete smelles, (as the sacred spouse sayeth in the Cãticles) that the name of her beloued is an oyle or balme, vvhich spredeth all ouer its Odoriferous and fra-

grant

grant fauour: for this cause she addeth, the young damisells, haue followved him (being dravven by his Diuine perfumes) My deare sisters, as perfumers of the diuine bountie, goe your way to povvre forth through all partes the incomparable odour of Most sincere humilitie, svveetnesse, ād Charitie, that many young maydens may be dravvne, to follovv after your perfumes, and to imbrace your manner of life, by which they may bee able, as yourselues, to inioy in this life a holy and amorouse peace and trāquillie of soule, and by this meanes, in the other life, to possess eternall felicitye. Your congregation is as a hiue of Bees, the vvhich hath allreadie cast diuers svvarmes: but neuerthelesse vvith this difference, that the Bees come forth to retyre themselues vvith in another hiue, and there to begin a nevv houshould; euery svvarme choising their particuler king vnder vvhome they fight, and make their retraite: but touching you, my deare soules, although you goe vvithin a nevv hiue (that is to saye, begin a nevv house of your order) neuerthelesse you haue allvvaies the selfe same king, that is our Lord IESVS Crucified: vnder vvhose authoritie you shall liue in securitie vvheresoeuer you shall bee: feare not the vvant of any thing, for he vvill be allvvaies vvith you, so long as you doe not make choise of another: onely haue a great care to increase your loue and fideliue to his diuine Goodnes; hould your selues as neere to him as you can possibly, and all vvill succeede to your good: learne of him to doe all that you shall haue to doe, and doe nothing vvithout his councell. for he is the most faythfull freind, vvho vvil conduct, gouerne, and haue care of you, as vvith my vvhole hart, I humbly beeseech him. God bee Blessed.

LIVE JESUS.

THE

THE SEAVENTH ENTERTAYNMENT.

VVHEREIN THE PROPERTIES of Doues are applyed to the Religious soule by vvay of Lavves.

1. YOu haue demaunded of mee some nevv Lavves, in the beginning of the yeare, and considering vvhat might bee most profitable and conuenient for you, I haue cast the eyes of my cōsiration vppon the Gospell of this day, vvherin is made mention of the Baptisme of our Lord IESVS and of the Glorious apparition of the holie Ghost in the forme of a Doue, vppon the vvhich apparitiō I haue layed hould: and considering that the Holy Ghost is the loue of the Father, and of the Sonne; I haue thought that I ought to giue lavves all of loue the vvhich I haue taken from the Doues, in consideration of this, that the Holie Ghost hath vouchsafed to take the forme of a Doue: and also so much the more vvilinglie, because that all the soules vvho are dedicated to the seruice of the Diuine Maiestie are obliged to bee as chast and louing Doues. Euen as vve see the spouse in the Canticles is often named by this name, and vvith very good reason: for there is a great correspondence betvvene the quallities of the Doue, and those of the beautifull louing Doue of our Lord, the lavves of Doues are all exceedinglie agreable: & it is a most svvete meditation to consider them. VVhat is a more goodly lavve, I pray you, then that of cleanlines? for their is not any thing more neate then Doues: they are vvōderfull

full handsome, although there is nothing more foule then a doue-cote, and the place vvhere they make their nests: notvvithstanding vve neuer see a foule Doue; they haue allvvaies their feathers bright vvhich make a delightfull aspect in the sunne. Lett vs consider I pray you, hovv gratious the Lavve of their simplicitie is? Our Lord IESVS himselfe hath praised it, saying to his Apostles; bee as simple as Doues, and as prudent as the serpent. But in the third place, good God hovv delightfull is their Lavv of svveetnesse. For they are vvith out galle, and vvith out bitternesse: and a hundred other lavves they haue, vvhich are exceeding amiable and profitable for soules to obserue vvho are dedicated in Religion, to the more peculier seruice of the diuine Bountie. But I haue considered, that if I giue you some lavves, that you haue allreadie had, you vvould make small esteeme of them, I haue therefore chose onely three, vvhich are of an incomparable profitt, being vvell obserued, and vvhich doe bring a very great svvetnesse to the soule vvho cōsidereth them, because they are all vvholie of loue, and extreemely delicious for the perfection of spirituall life, & are so much the more excellent for attayning perfection, as they are lesse knowne vnto those that make profession to gett it, at least for the most part: but vvhat then are these Lavves?

§. 2. The first that I haue designed to giue you is that of the shee-doues, vvho doe all for their mate and maistre Doue, and nothing for themselues, it seemeth they say no other thing but; My deare doue is all for mee, and I all his, he is allvvaies inclining tovvardes mee, and I attend, and assure my selfe of him, and rely on him, lett this vvelbeloued doue then flie, to seeke vvhere it pleaseth him, I vvill not enter into diffidēce, or Ielousie of his loue, but vvill confide fully in his care. It

may

may bee you haue seene but not marked, that the shee-doues, vvhiles that they hache, or sitt on their egges, stirre not of them, vntill such time as their little young ones be hasthed, and vvhen they bee hacthed, they continue to couer and keepe them vvarme so long as they haue neede, and all this time the hēn goeth not to gather for to nourish her selfe, but she leaueth all the care to her deare companiō; who is so faythfull to her, that he not oncly goeth to search out the graines to nourish her, but hee also bringeth vvater in his bill to quench her thirst: he hath an exceding care that nothing be vvanting vnto her that is necessarie, yea so great, that it vvas neuer seene that any doue did dye in this time for vvant of foode; the Doue then doeth all for her beloued one, she couereth and keepeth her little ones vvarme, for the desire she hath to please him, in giuing him generation: and the cocke-Doue taketh care to nourish his deare hen, vvho hath left the care of her selfe to him; she hath no other thought then to please him; and he in counterchāge thinketh onely hovv to sustayne her. O vvhat a delightfull and profitable lavve is this? to doe nothing but for God: and to leaue all the care of our selues to him: I speake not onely for that which regardeth the temporallitye (for I vvill not speake thereof, for there is none of you heere, but vnderstand this vvithout speaking,) but I speake for that which concerneth the spiritualitye, and the aduancement of our soules in perfection. Ah: doe you not see that the Doue thinketh nothing but of her beloued, and to please him, she moueth not of her eggs, and in the meane time nothing is vvantting to her: he recompensing her confidence, vvith his care. O hovv happie, shoulde vve bee, if all vve did vveere for our most amiable Doue the Holy Ghost! for he vvould take the care of vs, and according to the
measure

measure that our confidence, wherely we should repose in his prouidence, should become more great, so much more also should his care extende it selfe ouer all our necessities, and we should neuer doubt that God would leaue vs: for his loue is infinitt for the soule that putteth her trust in him. O how happie is the Doue to haue such confidence in her deare one! this is that which causeth her to liue in peace and tranquillitie: A thousand times more happie is the soule that leaueth the totall care of her selfe, and all that is necessarie for her, to her most deare and welbeloued beautiful Doue, hauing no other thought, then to couer and cherish her little ones to please him and produce him issue: for she enioyeth in this life such tranquillitye and so great peace, that there is nothing to bee compared therevnto, nor any repose equall to hers in this world; but onely in the height of heauen, where she shall fully for euer enioy the chast imbracemēts of her celestiall Spouse.

§. But what are our egges that we must sitt on vntill that they bee hatched, for to haue little young Doues? our eggs are our desires, the which being well couered and cherished, the little young doues come forth out of them, which are the effects of our desires: but among our desires there is one which is supereminent aboue all the other, and deserueth much to be very well cherished and couered for to please our Diuine louer the Holy Ghost, who will allwaies be called the sacred Spouse of our soules: So great is his bountye and loue towards vs. This desyre is the same which we haue brought with vs comming into Religion, which is to imbrace Religious vertues, it is one of the branches of the loue of God, and one of the most high that are in this diuine tree. But this desire must not extend it selfe further, then the meanes which are sett downe in our Rules and constitutions, for to attayne to this perfection which wee haue pretended to gayne, in obliging our selues to the persuite thereof: But it must be cherished, and keept in the first vigor all the dayes of our life, to the end that this desire may become a beautifull young doue, which may resemble her Father, which is perfection it selfe: And yet wee must haue no other intention then to keepe our selues vppon our egges, that is to say, enclosed within the meanes that are prescribed vs for our perfection, leauing all the care of our selues to our onelye and most amiable Doue, who will not permitt that any thing shalbe wantting to vs of that which shalbe necessarie to please him.

§. Trulie it is a verye great pittie to see soules, whereof the number is too great, who pretending perfection imagin within themselues, that all consisteth in making a multitude of desires, and constraine themselues very much to search out now this meanes, and immediatlye another to attayne there vnto, & are neuer content nor quiett in thẽselues. for from one desire that they haue, they endeauour quickly to cõceaue another, and it seemeth they are as hennes, who hauing layed an egge, presentlie charge themselues with another, leauing the same which they made without brooding it, in such sort that they haue no issue of chickens: the Doue doth not so, for she couereth, hatcheth, and cherisheth her little ones, vntill such time as they are capable to flye, and gather wherewith to nourish themselues: The henne if she haue little ones, is extreemlye sollicitous, and ceaseth not clocking, & making a noise: But the Doue retayneth her selfe quiett, and patient, she clocketh not, nor troubleth not her selfe: euen so there are some soules, who cease not to clocke, and to enforce themselues after their little ones, that is to say, after the desires they

haue

haue to perfect themselues, and neuer find persons sufficient to speake vnto, and to demaund of them proper and new meanes therefore: in breife they studie so much to speake of the perfection they pretend to gett, that they forgett the principall meanes for the practice thereof; which is that same of keeping themselues quiett, and putting all their confidence in him, who onely can giue the increase to that they haue sowne and planted.

§. All our good dependeth of the grace of God in whome we ought to place all our confidence: and neuerthelesse it seemeth, by the egernesse that they haue to doe much, they place their confidence in their labours, and in the multiplicitye of exercises that they imbrace, and in seemeth to them they are neuer able to doe enough. This is good, prouided that it weere accompaned with peace, and with a louing care of doeing well all that they doe, notwithstanding allwaies depending vppon the grace of God, and not on their exercises: I would say, not to expect any fruit of their labour, without the grace of God: it appeareth that these soules forcing themselues in the inquirie of their perfection, haue forgotten, or else they knowe not, that vvhich S. Hierom sayeth: O poore man what doest thou confiding in thy labour, and in thy industrye? knowest thou not, that it appertaineth to thee to cultiuate the earth, to plovve and to sovve it: but it is the part of God to giue the grovvth to the plãtes, and to cause thee to haue a good haruest, and to rayne fauorably vpon thy sowed grounds? thou mayest water them, and it is well done; but yet for all that, it vvould serue thee for nothing, if God did not blesse thy labour, and giue thee of his pure grace and goodnes, a good haruest, and not by thy sweates: Depend then intirelie of his diuine Bountie. It is true, it is our dutye to cultiuate well,

 but

but it is God that causeth our trauaill to be follo-wed with good successe: the Holy Church singeth in euerie feast of the holy Confessours, God hath honored your labours, in causing you to drawe fruite of them, to shew that we of our selues are not able to doe any thing, with out thee grace of God, in which we ought to place all our confidēce, not expecting any thing of our selues. I pray you lett vs not bee too sollicitous in our busines, for, for to doe it well, wee must apply our selues care-fully: but quietly and peaceably, not putting confi-dence in our indeuours, but in God and in his grace. These anxieties of spiritt, that wee haue to aduance our perfection, and to see if wee be aduanced, are nothing pleasing to God, and serue for no other thing then to satisfie selfe loue; who is a great hurrier vp and downe, trotting hither and thither, and neuer ceaseth to vndertake very much, although it doe but little: one good worke well done with tranquillitie of spirit, is worth much more, then many better workes perfomed with ouer much egernesse.

§. The Doue museth simply of the worke she hath in hand to doe it well, leauing all other care to her deare companion: the soule truely colombine, that is to say, which loueth God dearely, applyeth her selfe simply to all, and with out impetuositye taketh the meanes, which are prescribed to perfect her selfe, not searching after others how perfect soeuer they may bee: my welbeloued, sayeth she, thinketh of mee, and I confide in him, he loueth mee, and in testimonie of my loue I am wholie his. A while since there weere some holie Religious women that sayed to me, My Lord, what shall we doe this yeare, the yeare past we did fast three dayes in the weeke, and tooke as many disciplines; what shall we now doe this yeare? it is necessarie we should

should doe some thing more, aswell to giue thākes to God for the yeare past, as to proceede allvvaies forward in the way of God: It is very vvell sayed, that vve ought to aduance our selues daylie, aunswered I: but our aduancement is not effected as you cōceaue, by the multitude of exercises of pietie, but by the perfection wherevvith vvee doe them, confiding allvvaies more in our Deare beloued Doue, & more distrusting our selues: The passed yeare you fasted three dayes in the vveeke, and tooke discipline three times, if you vvill allvvaies double your exercises, this yeare you must fast and discipline the vveke entire: but the yeare that is to come vvhat vvill you doe? you must make nine dayes in the weeke, or else fast twise in the day: what a great follye is it of those that busie their heades in desiring to bee martyred in the Indies, and neuer apply thēselues to that which they haue to doe, according to their cōdition: it is also a great deceat in them that will eate more then they can digest, we haue not spirituall heate sufficient to digest vvell all that vvee imbrace for our perfection, and yet we will not cutt of these anxieties of spiritt, that wee haue of desiring to doe much more, to read many spirituall bookes, espetiallie when they are new, to speake well of God, and of all the most spirituall things, to incite vs, say vvee, to deuotion, to heare sermons, to make conferences vpon euerie occasion, to communicate very often, and confesse oftē, to serue the sicke, to speake vvel of all that passeth in vs for to manifest the pretension that vvee haue to perfect our selues, and the soonest that possible may bee, and such like; are not these things very proper to make vs perfect, and to attayne to the end of our designes? yeas doubtles, prouided that all this be done according as it is ordayned, and that it bee allvvaies vvith dependance of the grace of God
 that

that is to say, that we put not our confidence in all this, hovv good soeuer it bee : but in one onely God, vvho onely can make vs to gather fruite of all our exercises.

§. But, my deare daughters, I beseech you consider a little the liues of the great Religious saint S. Antonye vvho hath bene honoured of God and men, because of his extraordinarie sanctitie; tell mee hovv did he attayne to so great sanctitye and perfection? vvas it by the force of reading, or by conferences, and frequent communions, or by the multitude of sermons, that he heard? not so: but he attayned there vnto, in seruing himselfe with the example of the holy hermitts, learning of one abstinence, of another prayer, euen so he went as a carefull Bee, picking and gathering the vertues of the seruantes of God, to compose of them the hony of holie edification. Hovv did S. Paul the first hermitt attayne vnto perfection, did he gayne it by good bookes? he had none: was it confessions or communions that he vsed? he neuer made but two in his life: was it conferences or preaching? he had them not; for he did neuer see any man with in the deserte but S. Antonye, vvho came to visitt him in the end of his life. doe you knovv vvhat made him a Saint? it vvas the fidelitye vvherewith he had imployed himselfe to that which he enterprised in the begining, to the vvhich he had bene called, and intertayned not any other cogitations. Those Holy Religious vvho did liue vnder the charge of S. Pachomius, had they bookes or preachings? none: conferences they had, but rarelie: did they confesse often? Somtimes vppon good feasts: did they heare many Masses? the sundayes and the feasts, on other dayes none; but vvhat wilbe sayed thẽ? that eatting so seldome of the spirituall foodes, that nourish our soules to immortallitye they weere allwaies in so good

good state, that is to say, so strong and couragious, for to vndertake the gayning of vertues, and to attayne to perfection, and to the end of their pretention: and wee vvho eate much more, are allwaies so leane, that is to saye so remisse and languishing in the poursuite of our enterprises: and it seemeth that we haue not, longer then spirituall consolations march before vs, any courage, or vigour in the seruice of our Lord? wee must then imitate these holy Religious, applying our selues to our affayres, that is to say, to that which God requireth of vs, according to our vocation, feruently, and humbly, not to thinke of any other thing then this: nor expecting to find any meanes fitter to perfect vs then it.

§. But it may bee you vvill reply, Sir, you say feruentlye, Good God! and hovv shall I doe this? for I haue not any feruour: no, not of that, which you vnderstaud, to vvitt not the feeling of feruour which God giueth to vvhom he thinketh good, and it is not in our power to gaine it when we please: I add also humbly, to the end none haue any subiect of excuse: for doe not say, I haue not humilitie, it is not in my povver to haue it; for the Holy Ghost that is bountie it selfe, doth giue it him that demaũdeth it of him: not that humilitie (that is to saye) that feeling of our littlenesse, which maketh vs so much to humble our selues so graciouslie: But I meane the humilitie that maketh vs knovve our owne abiection, and which causeth vs to loue it, hauing acknowledged it to bee in vs; for that is true humilitie. Mẽ did neuer studye so much as novv they doe. Those great Saints S. Augustine, S. Gregorie, S. Hilarie, whose solemnitie vve keepe this day, and many others, haue not studied so much, they had not time to doe it, composing so many bookes as they haue done, preaching, and performing all other things appertayning, to their charges. But they had so great confidence in God, and in his grace and so great distrust in themselues, that they attẽded not to thẽselues, nor cõfided any thing at all in their owne industry, nor in their labour, so that all the great workes that they haue done, weere done purelie by the confidence which they had in the grace of God and in his Allmighty povver: It is thou, O Lord sayed they, which makeest vs to labour, and for thee we labour; it shalbee thou alone vvich must blesse our sweats and paynes, and giue vs a good haruest: ãd so their bookes and their preachings did bring forth meruelous fruites; and wee who cõfide in our fayre wordes, in our exquisite fine speaches, and in our doctrine; all our paynes vanish as smoake, and yeald no other fruite thẽ vanitie. You must thẽ for cõclusion of this first lawe that I giue you fully cõ fide in God, ãd doe all for him, entirely quitting the care of your selues to your deare master Doue; who will exercise an exceeding care and foresight ouer you: and how much more true and perfect your confidence shalbe, so more peculier shall his prouidence bee ouer you.

§.3. I thought good to giue you for the secõd lawe the worde which the doues speake in their lãguage, The more they take, the more I make, say they; what meaneth that? the meaning is this vvhen their little pigeons are grovvne a little great, the maister of the doue-cote cõmeth and taketh them from them, and presently they put thẽselues to sitt for others; but if they did not take them, they would prouide for thẽ longer, and consequently, they would breed lesse: they say; The more they take from mee, the more I make: And to make you vnderstand the better what I would saye, I vvil presẽt an exãple vnto you: Iob that great seruant of God, praised by the mouth of God himselfe: did not permitt himselfe to be ouercome by any affliction, vvhich did come vppõ him: the more that God did take frõ him his young pi-

geons: the more did he begett: what is that which he did not doe, whiles he was in his first prosperitie? what good whorkes did he omitt? he speaketh of himselfe in this manner: I was a foote to the lame, that is to say, I caused him to be carryed, or I sett him on my asse, or camell; I was an eye to the blind, in causing him to be guided; I was in fine the prouider for the hungrye, and the refuge of all the afflicted; Now consider him in extreme pouertye: Hee complayneth not that God had takē frō him the meanes that hee had to doe so many good workes: but he sayeth with the doue, The more is takē frō mee, the more I doe: not Almes deeds; for hee had not wherewithall; but in this onely act of submission, and patiēce that he made, seeing himselfe depriued of all his goods, and of all his children, hee did more then euer hee had done by all the great workes of charitie that hee had wrought, during the time of his prosperitie, & yealded himselfe more pleasing to God, in this onely act of patience, then euer hee had done in so very many good workes, that hee had performed in his whole life: for of necessitie he must haue a loue more noble ād generous for this onely act, thē euer vvas needfull for all the others put together. VVe must then likewise doe the same to obserue this amiable lawe of Doues; giuing our selues ouer to bee depriued by our soueraygne maister of our little young pigeōs: that is to say, of the meanes to execute our desires, whē it pleaseth him to depriue vs of thē, how good soeuer they bee, neuer complayning of him nor lamenting as if he did vs great wronge: but rather we ought to double not our desires, nor our exercises, but the perfection with the which wee doe thē, endeuoring by this meanes to gayne more, by one onelie act (as vndoubtedly we shall doe) then we should haue done with a hundred other acts done according to our pro-
 pension

pension and affection: our Lord vvill not haue vs carrye his crosse, but onely by one ende, and he vvil be honoured therein, as great ladies vvho cause their traynes to be carried after them, his vvill is notwithstanding that vve should carrye the crosse, that he layeth vpon our shoulders, which indeed is our ovvne. But alas! vve doe nothing, for vvhen his Goodnes depriueth vs of the consolation which he vvas vvont to giue vs in our exercises, it seemeth that all is lost, and the meanes to performe our begun enterprise is taken from vs. Cōsider this soule hovv vvell she sitteth on her eggs in the time of consolation, and leaueth the care of her selfe to her onely vvelbeloued one. If she bee in prayer, what holy desires doth she not make to please him? hovv tenderly affected is she in his presēce? vvholye melting into her vvelbeloued, she putteth her selfe intirely into the armes of his Diuine Prouidence: O these are most amiable eggs, and all this is verye good, besides, the little pigions are not vvanting, which are the effects: for vvhat is it that she doth not? the vvorkes of her charitie are in so great nū-ber, her modestie appeareth before all the sisters, she giueth exceeding edification, she causeth admi-ration in all those that behould her, or vvho knovv her; mortifications, sayeth she, lost mee nothing at that time; they vveere rather consolations to mee: and for Obediences they vveere my ioyes: I no sooner heard the first sound of the Bell, but I vvas risen: I did not permitt one point of vertue to passe without practice, and I did doe all this vvith most great peace and tranquillitie. But novv that I am in disgust, and in driesse in prayer, I haue not any courage as it seemeth to mee, for my amendment; I haue not the feruour I vsed to haue in my exer-cises, in fine, the cold and frost hath wholy benum-med mee; I beleeue it vvell, Consider I pray you

her

this poore soule, hovv she lamenteth her disgrace, her discontent doth appeare euen in her face, she hath her countenance on the ground, deiected and melencholye, she vvalketh all pensiue & so cõfused as nothing more. Good God! vvhat haue you sister, (are vvee constrained to say to her.) O! vvhat haue I: I am so decayed in vigour nothing can content mee, all is disgustfull to mee, I am novv so confused: But vvhat confusion is it? For there are two sorts, one which cõducteth to humilitie, and to life, and the other to dispayre, and consequentlye to death, I assure you (quoth she) I am so neere it, that I haue allmost lost the courage to passe further in my vndertaken course of perfection. O Good God! what a vveaknes is this? consolation is vvanting, and by that occation, courage is lost. O vvee must not doe so; but rather the more God depriueth vs of consolation the more wee ought to labour, and confide in him, to giue him testimonie of our fidelitye: one onely act made with drinesse of spiritt, is more worth then many made with great tendernesse. Because, that, as I haue allreadye sayed, speaking of Iob: it is vvrought with a more strõg loue, allthough not so tender, nor so pleasing: so that the more they take frõ mee the more I make, is the secõd lavve, that I desire very much that you obserue.

§.4. The third lavve that I present to you of the Doues, is this, that they vveepe as if they did reioyce, they sing allwaies one selfe same tune, asvvell for their songs of reioysing, as for those of lamenting, that is to say, to bemoane themselues, and manifest their griefe. Behould them pearched on their branches, vvhere they bewaile the losse that they haue had of their little ones, which the vveasill or ovvle hath robbed them of (for vvhen any other taketh them, then the maister of the Douehouse, they are very much afflicted) consider them

also

also vvhen their companion commeth and approcheth to thē foe that they are wholie cōforted, they chang not their tune, but make the same mournfull grumling sound, to expresse their contentment, as they did to manifest their greife. This is that most holie Equallitie of spiritt, my Deare soules, that I vvish vnto you, I doe not saye, equallitie of humours, nor of inclinations, I saye equallitie of spiritt: for I make none, neither doe I desire that you should make any acount of the turmoyle, that the inferiour part of your soule causeth to trouble you, which is that which causeth vnquietnesse (whē the Superiour part doth not her duty, in making her selfe maister, nor doeth keepe good watch, to discouer her enimies, as the Spirituall Cōflict sayeth wee ought to doe; to the end she bee prōptly aduertised of the turbulent motions, and assaults, that the inferiour part raiseth, which proceed from our sences, and from our inclinations and passions, for to make warre against it and to subiect it to hir lawes) but, I say vve must retayne our selues allvvaies constant, and resolute in the Superiour part of our soule, to prosecute the vertue vvhereof vvee make profession, and to keepe our selues in a continuall equallitie, asvvell in aduerse things as in prosperous, in desolation, as in consolation, and in fine aswell in the thickest of ariditues, as in the midst of cherishings. Iob, of vvhome vve spake in the secōd lawe, furnisheth vs moreouer vvith an exāple of this subiect: for he did euer sing the selfe same ayre in all the songes that he hath cōposed, which are no other thē the historie of his life. what is that which he did saye, vvhē as God did make his goods to be multiplyed, giuing him children, and in fine he did send him, whatsoeuer his desire could wish in this life? vvhat sayed hee, but, the name of God be blessed? this was his song of loue, that he did sing in all occasiōs: for
consider

consider him reduced to the extremitye of afflictiõ, what doth hee doe, hee singeth his canticle of lamẽtatiõ vppõ the same ayre that hee did sing the other for reioyceing; we haue receaued sayeth hee good things of our Lord, wherefore should not wee receaue the euill? Our Lord hath giuen mee children, and goods, and our Lord hath taken them frõ mee, his holy name be blessed: allwaies the name of God be blessed. O this holy soule vvas a chast and louing young doue, exceedinglye cherished of her deare and onely one; euen so should wee doe My deare children, that is, in all occasions vve should take the good and the euill, our comforts and afflictions frõ the hand of our Lord, neuer ceasing to sing other then that most excellent canticle: The name of God be blessed, allwaies on the ayre of cõtinuall equalitye: for if this good happ arriue vnto vs we shall liue in great peace in all occurrences. But doe not you doe, as those that weepe when consolation fayleth, and doe no other thing but sing vvhen it is returned or cometh agayne: vvherin they are like to the Apes and Baboones, who are allvvaies sadd and furious, vvhen the ayre becometh raynie and cloudie; and neuer cease to leape & skipp, and turne heeles ouer head, vvhen it is fayre vveather.

§. 5. Consider then the three lawes that I giue you, the which neuerthelesse are lavves totallye of loue, obliging no othervvise then for loue. Lett loue then carrye vs vnto our Lord, that vve bee sollicitous to obserue and keepe them, to the end vvee may truely say, in imitation of the beautifull Doue of the Soueraigne spiritt, vvhich is the sacred spouse: My welbeloued is all mine, and I am all for him, doing no other thing then for to please him: hee hath his hart allvvaies tovvards mee by prouidence, as I haue mine tovvards him by by confidence: and hauing all this time of our life exhibited our selues for our vvelbeloued, he vvill haue care to prouide for vs his eternall Glorie, for recompence of our confiden e: & there vve shall see the happie estate of those, who quitting all superfluous & vnquiett care that vvee haue ordinarilye ouer our selues, and of our perfection, giuing them selues simply and intirel to their duty. abādoning themselues vvith out reseruation into the hands of the diuine goodnes, for vvhom onely they haue laboured; hovv their labours shallbe in the end followved with such peace and repose, as cannot be explicated: for they shall rest for euer within the breast of their vvellbeloued; The happie lott also of those vvho shall haue obserued the second lavve vvilbe very great; for permitting and giuing themselues ouer to bee depriued of their young pigeons by their maister which is our Lord, vvith out trouble or discontent, hauing had the courage to say, The more they take from mee, the more I make, remayning submisse vnto him vvho hath spoyled them, these shall sing, so much the more couragiously in the height of heauen, this Most mellifluous canticle, God be Blessed, in the midest of eternall consolations, as they haue song with a better courage in the thickest of the desolations, anguishes, and disgusts of this mortall and transitorie life, during the which wee ought to endeuour carefully to conserue this most amiable indifferencye of spiritt. Amen.

THE

THE EIGHT ENTERTAYNMENT.

OF DISAPPROPRIATION, AND depriuation of all things.

1. These little affections of, myne and thine, are the reliques of the world, where there is nothing so pretious as they: for it is the soueraigne felicitye of the world, to haue great store of things proper, and of which one may saye, This is mine: now that which maketh vs become affectionat to that which is ours, is the great esteeme wee haue of our selues: for wee hould our selues for such excellent creatures, that wee esteeme any one thing that appertayneth to vs aboue measure: and the little esteeme that wee haue of others, causeth that wee haue a dislike of that which hath serued them: but if wee weere truelie humble, and vnclothed of our selues, so that wee held our selues for nothing beefore God: we would make no reckoning of that should be proper for vs, and wee should esteeme our selues exceedingly honoured to be serued with that which hath bene for the vse of another. But we ought as well in this, as in euery other thing, to make a difference, betweene inclinations, and affections, for when these things are no other then inclinations, and not affections, vvee must not trouble our selues, because, it doth not depend of vs, to bee free from hauing euill inclinations, as it doth, from bad affections. So then, if it happen that in changing the garment of any sister, to giue her another of lesse worth, the inferiour part be moued

a little, it is not sinne, if that with reason she accept it willinglye for the loue of God, and so likevvise of all other motions that arriue vnto vs.

§. 2. Now these motions doe happen, because wee haue not put all our will in cōmō, which is a thing that oug t to bee done entring into Religion: for euery Sister should leaue her proper will without the gate, to the end, she haue no other vvill then the Will of God: happie is she that shall haue no other Will then that of the communitie, and vvho shall euerie day take out of the cōmon purse that which shall bee necessarie for her, euen so ought this sacred vvord of our Lord to bee vnderstood: Bee not carefull for to morrow: it regardeth not so much that which appertayneth to corporall foode or clothing as spirituall exercises: for if one should demaund of you, vvhat will you doe to morrow? you would aunsvver I knovve not, this day I vvil doe such a thing that is commanded mee, to morrow I doe not know what I shall doe, because I knowe not what they will cōmaund mee. whosoeuer vvill doe this, she shall neuer be vexed nor vnquiet, for where true indifferēcye is, there cannot be displeasure or sadnes. If there bee any that will haue Mine aud Thine, let her goe seeke it out of the house; for within it is not to be spoken of.

§. 3. Now wee must not onely vvill in generall disappropriatiō, but in particular: for there is nothing more easye thē to say in grosse, wee must renounce our selues, and quitt our ovvne will: but when it must come to practice, there lieth the difficulty; For this cause wee must make considerations vpon our condition, and vpon all things that depend thereof in particular, then in particuler, to renounce forthwith one of our proper wills, and incōtinently another, vntill such time as wee bee intirely vnclothed of them all, This true nakednes of all things is

wrought

wrought by three degrees. The first in the affection thereof, the which is begotten in vs, by the consideration of the beautie of this nakednes. The secōd degree is, the resolution that followeth the affectiō, for wee easilye resolue of a good that wee affect. The third is the practice, which is the most difficult. The goods vvhereof vvee must vncloth our selues, are of three sortes. Exteriour goods, the goods of the bodye, & the goods of the soule. Exteriour goods are all those things, that wee haue left out of Religiō: as housses, possessions, parents, freinds and the like. For to vncloth vs of them, vvee must renounce them into the hands of our Lord, and then demaund those affectiōs that hee would wee should haue for them: for vvee must not remayne with out affections, nor haue them all equall and indifferent, wee must loue euerie one in his degree. Charitie giueeth place and order to the affections. The second goods are those of the bodie, beautye, health and the the like things which wee must renounce, and then we must not goe to a looking glasse, to behould if we be fayre, nor care more for health thē for sicknes, at least touching the superiour parte; for nature will allwaies haue a sensible apprehension, and exclame somtimes, espetiallie vvhen the person is not verye perfect. VVee ought therefore to remayne equallie content, in sicknes and in health, and to take the remedies, and such sustenance as vvee find, I meane with reason allwaies; for touching inclinations, I lett them passe. The goods of the hart are the consolations, and svvetnesses that are found in a spirituall lif: and thes goods are very good, and wherefore (vvill you say to mee) must vvee then vncloth our selues of them? it must be done notvvithstanding, and they are to bee remitted into the hāds of our Lord, for to dispose thereof as it shall please him, and wee are to serue him, asvvell vvithout them

them as with them. There is another ſorte of goods which are neither interiour nor exteriour, that are neither goods of the body, nor goods of the hart, theſe are imaginarye goods, that depend vppon the opiniō of another, they are called honour, eſteeme, reputation: Now wee muſt vnclothe our ſelues of them wholye in an inſtant, and not vvill any other honour, then the honour of the congregatiō, which is in all things to ſeeke the Glorie of God; nor other eſteeme or reputation, then that of the communitye, vvhich is to giue good edification in all occaſions.

§. 4. The ſtripping of our ſelues of all theſe afore ſayed things, ought not to bee done out of contempt, but by abnegation, for the onely and pure loue of God. VVee muſt note heere, that the contentment that wee find, in meeting with perſons that wee loue, and the teſtimonies of affection that wee render them, in behoulding them, are not contrarie to this vertue of depriuation, ſo that it bee not inordinate, and the perſons being abſent our hart runne not after them: for how shall wee bee able (the obiect being preſent) to cauſe the powers not to bee moued? it is as if one should ſay to a perſon at the incounter of a lion or a beare, bee not affeard; this is not in our power. Likewiſe at the encounter of thoſe vvee loue, it cannot bee but that wee shalbe moued with Ioy and contentment: wherefore this is not contrarie to vertue. I ſay yet more, that if I haue a deſire to ſee any one for ſome profitable thing, and that vvould redound to the Glorie of God, if his deſigne to come happen to bee croſſed, and that I feele ſome ſorrovve, yea alſo that I ſomewhat force my ſelfe, to diuert the occaſions that retayne him, I doe nothing in this contrarie to the vertue of diſappropriation, ſo that I paſſe not into vnquietneſſe. Heere you ſee, that

vertue

vertue ,is not so terrible a thinge as some imagin it to bee;this is a fault that many make., they frame foolish imaginations in their spiritts, & thinke that the way to heauen is strãgly difficult,vvherein they greatly abuse and deceaue themselues, for Dauid sayeth to our Lord,that his lavve vvas verye sweet, and according, as the vvicked did diuulge it to be harde,, & difficult, this good king sayed it vvas more sweete then hony. VVe ought to say the same of our vocation, esteeming it not onely good and fayre, but also sweete and amiable.. If vvee doe so, we shall haue a great loue to obserue all that which dependeth there-on.

§.5. It is true,my deare Sisters, that vvee shall neuer knowe hovv to attayne to perfection, vvhiles that vvee haue affection to any imperfection, hovv little soeuer it bee;yea also vvhen it shalbe no more then to haue an vnprofitable thought, and you vvould not beleeue hovv much euill this bringeth to the soule; for after you haue giuen your spiritt libertye,to settle it selfe to thinke of an vnprofitable thing, it vvill aftervvards thinke of pernicious things:wee must then cutt of the euill, so soone as wee perceaue it,hovv little soeuer it bee:wee must also examine in good earnest,if it bee true,as somtimes it seemeth to vs, that wee haue not our affections ingaged:for example,if vvhen you are praysed, you begin to speake fome wordes which may increase the praise,that they giue you, or otherwise vvhen you seeke it by artificiall wordes,saying that you haue not so good a memorie, or so good a spiritt as you weere wonte to haue to discourse vvell. Alas! vvho perceaueth not that you pretend, they should tell you,that allwaies you speake exceedingly vvell? search then vvell into the depth of your conscience,if you find therein the affection to vanitie. You may easilie also knowe, if you bee tyed

tyed to any thing, vvhen you haue not commoditie to performe vvhat you haue purposed : for if you haue no affection therevnto, you will receaue as much contentment not to haue done it, as if you had effected it: and contrary-wise if you bee troubled, it is a signe, that you haue setled your affection there-on. Now our affections are so pretious (since they ought all to bee imployed in the loue of God) that vvee must take very great heede not to lodge them in vnprofitable things, and a fault, hovv little soeuer it may bee, cōmitted vvith affection, is more contrarie to perfection then a hundred others done by surprise and vvithout affection.

§.6. You demaund hovv you ought to loue creatures; I tell you breiflie, that there are certayne loues, that exteriourly seeme great and perfect in the eyes of creatures, vvhich before God vvill be found little and of no vvorth: because that these freindships are not grounded in true charitie, vvhich is God, but in certayne alliances, and inclinatiōs, and vppon some consideratiōs humaynlie worthy of praise and acceptation: in the contrarie there are others that exteriourlye seeme little, empty and nothing in the eyes of the World, which before God are found to be full fraught and very excellent, because they are made onely in God, and for God without mixture of our proper interest. Novv the acts of charitie that are done about those vvhom wee loue in this sorte, are a thousand times more perfect, for so much as they all tend purely to God: But the seruices and other assistance that vve giue to those vvhom vvee loue by inclination, are farr lesse vvorth in meritt, because of the great contentment and sattisfactiō that vve receaue in doing them, and that (ordinarilie) vvee doe them more for that motiue then for the loue of God. There is furthermore another reason, vvhich maketh these first freindships vvhereof vvee speake

speake, lesse then the second, to vvitt that they are not of continuance, because the ground-vvorke being fraile, assoone as there happens any crosse they vvax could, or chang themselues; the vvhich arriueth not to those vvho are settled and grounded in God, for that the cause is solide and permanent.

§.7. To this purpose S. Catherine of Sienne made a good comparison: If you take, sayed she, a glasse, and fill it vvithin a fountayne, and drinke in that glasse not taking it out of the fountayne, although you drinke as much as you vvill, the glasse will not be emptie; but if you take it forth of the fountayne, when you haue drõke, the glasse vvilbe emptie: eue so it is in freind ships, vvhen they are dravvne from their spring or fountayne they neuer vvither nor perish. The kindnesses and signes of frindship thẽselues which wee shevv contrarie to our ovvne inclinatiõ to the person to vvhom vvee haue an auersion, are better, and more pleasing to God, thẽ those that wee doe dravve with sẽsitiue affectiõ: and this ought not to bee called doublenesse or dissimulatiõ, for although I haue a cõtrarie feeling, it is but in the inferiour part, and the acts I doe, is vvith the force of reason, which is the principall part of my soule. In such manner, that whẽ those to vvhõ I doe these courtesyes, should knowe, that I doe them, bẽcause I haue an auersiõ from them, they ought not to bee offended at it: but rather to esteeme of them more then if they vveare imparted of sensible affection: for auersions are naturall, and of themselues they are not vvicked, vvhen as vvee doe not follovv them: contrarievvise, it is a meanes to practice a thousand sortes of vertues: and our Lord himselfe hath more liking to vs, whẽ with extreme repugnãce wee goe to kisse his feete, thẽ if vve went to doe it vvith much more sweetnes and cõtent. Also those

that

that haue nothing that is comelye and gratious, are very happie: For they are assured the loue vve beare them is excellent, since it is all for God, and in God. VVee thinke often that wee loue some persons for God, and wee loue them for our selues, seruing our selues of this pretext, saying: that it is for this cause that vvee loue them, but in veritie vvee loue them for the comfort vvee find in them: for is it not a thing more svveete, to see a soule come to you full of good affection, that follovveth exceedingly vvell your councells, and who goeth faythfully and peaceably on the way which you haue directed her? yes vvithout all doubt, thē to see another allvvaies vnquiett, perplexed, and weake to follovv good, and to vvhome one thing must bee tould a thousād times, which you therefore neglect, perchaunce it is not for God then that you loue the former; For this last person is also as deare to God as the first, and moreouer you should loue her more; because there is much more to be laboured for God. It is true that there vvhere there is more of God, that is to say more vertue, which is a participation of the diuine quallities, wee ovve more affection; as for example, if there bee found more perfect soules then that of your Superiour, wee ought to loue them more for that reason: notvvithstanding wee owe much more loue to our superiours, because they are our fathers and directours.

§. 8. Touching that which you demaund of mee, If vvee must be glad that a sister practice vertue to the cost of another; I say that wee ought to loue the good in our neighbour as in our selues, and principallie in Religion, vvhere all ought to be perfectly in common, neither ought vve to bee sorrie, that a sister practice some vertue to my losse: as for exāple, I find my selfe with one more young thē I at the gate, and I vvithdravve my selfe to giue

her

her waye: according to the measure that I practice this act of humilitie, she ought with sweetnesse to practice simplicitie, and to proue at another encoũter, to preuent it. Likevvise if I giue her a stoole, or retire from any place to giue it her, she should bee content that I make this little gayne, and by that meanes she shalbe partaker of it: as if she did say, since I could not doe this act of vertue, I am very glad that this sister hath done it, and vve must not onely not bee sorrie, but also ought to contribute all that vvee are able for this, euen vnto our skin, if it vveere needfull: for so as God be Glorified vvee should not care by vvhom: in such sort, that if an occasion should bee presented to performe some vvorke of vertue, and our Lord did demaund of vs vvho vvee should like best, to performe it, vvee must aunsvvere him, Lord she vvho shalbe able to doe it most to thy Glorie. Now not hauing this choise, vve ought to desire to doe itt; for charity begins first vvith it selfe: but if I cannot, I ought to reioyce, delight, and bee exceeding glade that another hath done it, and so vve shall perfectly put all things in common. Further I must say the same for that which concerneth the temporall: so that the house be accommodated, vve ought not to care, whether it bee by our meanes, or by another. If there bee found these little contrarie affections, it is a signe that there is yet, thine and mine amongst vs.

§. 9. In fine, you demaund, if vvee may knovve if vvee doe aduãce in perfection, or no. I aunsvvere, vvee shall neuer bee able to knowe our ovvne perfection: for it hapneth to vs, as to those that saile vppon sea, they doe not knovve vvhether they goe forvvard or no: But the maister Pilot, who knoweth the ayre where they saile, knovveth it; euen so we cannot iudg of our aduancement, but easilye of anothers;

anothers; for vvhen vvee doe a good action, vvee dare not assure our selues that wee haue performed it vvith perfection, for so much as humility doth forbid vs. Novv allthoug vvee may iudg of the vertues of another, yet must vvee not therefore at any time determine, that one person is better then another: because apparences are very deceaitfull; and such as exteriourlye seeme to bee very vertuous to the eyes of creatures, before the eyes of God maybe lesse then another vvho appeareth much more imperfect aboue all perfection. I vvish you humilitie, vvhich is not onely charitable, but svveet and tractable. For Charitie is Humilitie ascēding, and Humilitye is Charitie discending; I loue you better vvith more humilitye, and fevver other perfections, then vvith many other perfections and lesse humilitie.

THE NINTH ENTERTAINEMENT.

VVHEREIN IS TREATED OF MODESTIE; of the manner to receaue corrections; and of the meanes for a soule, so to establish her estate in God, that nothinge may be able to vvithdravve her from him.

§. 1. YOu demaund vvhat true Modesty is: I vvill tell you, There are fovvre vertues, that beare the name of modestie, the first is that vvhich beareth it by eminencye aboue the others; this is the comelinesse of our beauiour and exteriour gesture; There are tvvo vices opposite to this vertue, to witt dissolutnes in our countenāces and gestures: that is to say, lightnes; the other vice vvhich is no lesse con-

contrarie is an affected countenance. The second that beareth the name of modestie, is the interiour comlinesse of our vnderstanding, and will: this likewise hath two vices opposite, vvhich are curiositye in the vnderstanding, multiplicitye of desires to knovve and vnderstand all things; and instabilitie in our enterprises passing frō one exercise to another, not setling our selues vpon any one: The other vice is a certayne stupiditye & carelesnes of spiritt, that vvill not knovve nor learne things necessarie for our perfectiō: an imperfection which is no lesse dangerous thē ther other. The third kind of Modestie, consisteth in our conuersation, and in our wordes, that is to say, in our manner of speaking, and conuersing vvith our neighbour, auoyding the two imperfections that are opposite vnto it, to witt clownishnes, and ouer much babbling. vvhere of the one hinders vs from contributing any thing, to the intertaynment of honest conuersation; the other maketh vs so to speake that vvee take the time from others, that they cannot speake in their turne. The fourth is honestie and decencie in garments, and the contrarie vices are vncleanesse, and superfluitie.

Behould heere fowr sortes of Modestie, the first is exceeding much to bee commended, for many reasons: and first because it doth subiect vs very much: neither is there any vertue, in the vvhich so particular attention is requisite, and in that it subiecteth vs, consisteth the great valour thereof; for all that subiecteth vs for God; is of great meritt, and merueilouslye pleasing to God. The second reason is, that it doth not onely subiect vs for a time: but allvvaies, and in euerie place, asvvell being alone, as in cōpanie, and at all times, yea sleeping. A great Saint vvrote to a disciple of his, saying, that in the presence of God, hee ought to lay himselfe downe

F modestly

modestlye in his bed, euen as hee vvould doe if our Lord IESVS being yet aliue should command him to sleepe and lye dovvne in his presence, and although (sayeth hee) thou seest him not, nor vnderstandest not the commaundement hee giueth thee, hee omitteth not to doe it, euen as if thou didst see him: because that in effect hee is present vvith thee, and keepeth thee vvhilst thou sleepest.

O good God, hovv modestly and deuoutlye should vvee lay our selues to rest if vvee did see thee? vvithout doubt vvee should crosse our armes vvith great deuotion vpon our breasts. Modestie then doth allwaies subiect vs, and in all occasions of our life, because the Angells are allvvaies presēt, yea God himselfe; before vvhose eyes vvee ought to gouerne our selues modestlye. This vertue is also verye recommendable, because of the edificatiō of our neighbour, and I assure you that simple modestye in the exteriour hath conuerted many, as it hapned to S. Francis, vvho passed one time through a tovvne, vvith so great modestie in his behauiour, that vvithout giuing one vvord, a great number of young poeple follovved him (dravvne onely by this example) to be instructed of him. Modestie is a dumme exhortation, it is a vertue that S. Paul recommendeth very particularlie to the Philippians the 4. th Chap. saying: Lett your modestie appeare before all men: and this is that hee sayeth to his disciple S. Timothy a Bishope should bee adorned vvith, tovvit vvith Modestie, and not vvith rich garments: to the end that by his modest and milde demeanour hee giue confidence to euerie one to approch to him, equallie auoyding inciuility, and lightnesse, to the end that giuing freedome to the vvorldly poeple to resorte to him, they may not conceaue that he is vvordly as they bee.

2, The vertue of modestie, obserueth three things,

things, to vvitt, time, place, and person; for tell mee, should not she bee troublesome, that vvould frovvne and pout in the time of recreation, and not bee merrie vvith the companye? there are gestures and countenances, that vvould bee immodest out of that time vvhich are not so then: likevvise she that should laugh vvhen they are in the midst of serious affayres; and should giue freedome to her spiritt, as vvee reasonably doe in recreation, should she not bee esteemed light and immodest? vvee ought also to obserue the place, the persons, the cōuersations, vvith vvhom vvee are; but very particularly the quallitie of the person. The modestie of a vvoman in the vvorld is othervvise then that of a Religious vvoman; a virgin in the vvorld should not bee esteemed, if she vvould looke dovvnevvarde, as our sisters doe, no more then our sisters should be if they held not there sight more lovve then the maydens of the vvorld doe: that vvhich is modesty in one man, vvill bee immodestie in another man, because of his quallitie: grauitie becommeth an aged person exceedingly vvell, vvhich vvould bee affected in a young person, to vvhom is conueniēt a more respectiue and humble modestie. I must not omitt to tell you a thing that I read a fevv dayes past, because it regardeth the discourse that vvee make of modestye. The great Saint Arsenius (vvho vvas chosen by the Pope, S. Damasus to instruct and bring vp the sonne of the Emperour Theodosius Arcadius, vvho vvas to succeede him in the Empire) after that he had bene honoured many yeares in the court, and fauoured of the Emperour, as much as any man in the vvorld, in the end being vvearie of all these vanities (although he had liued no lesse christianly then honourably in the court) resolued vvith himselfe to retire into the deserte, vvith the holy Fathers the Hermitts, vvho did liue there; the which designe he did very couragiously execute. The Fathers, who had heard the renounc of the vertues of this great Saint, vvere very glad, and much comforted to haue him in their companie. Hee grevve particulerly familiar vvith two Religious, the name of one of them was Pastor, and hee had great freindshipe with them: on a day vvhen all the Fathers weere assembled, to make spirituall cōference (for it hath bene the custome in all former times, so to doe amongst pious persons) one of the Fathers aduertised the superiour, that Arsenius did ordinarilie vse an immodest manner in that he did crosse one legg ouer the other: it is true, sayed the Father, I haue very often noted it. But hee is a good mā who hath liued a lōg time in the world, ād hath brought this gesture from the court, how could hee doe otherwise? excusing him, for hee was troubled to reprehēd him for so small a matter, wherein there was not any sinne: yet hee had a desire to haue him corrected therfore, for hee had no other thing then that, wherein they might find vvhat to say against him. Thē the Religious Pastor sayed: Father doe not trouble your selfe, it vvilbe no great matter to tell it him, hee vvilbe very gladd, therefore, if you please to morrovv at the hour of the assēbly, I will sett my selfe in the same posture that hee doth, and lett mee receaue correction before all for it, and so he will vnderstād that hee must not doe it. The Father then correcting Pastor, the good Arsenius cast himselfe, at the feete of the Father, humbly demaunding pardon, saying, that although they had not marked it, hee had neuerthelesse allvvaies committed this fault, vvhich was his ordinarie behauiour in the court; then hee asked pennance for it, but it vvas not giuen him, and neuer after did they see him in this posture. In this historie I find many things very vvorthy of consideration; first the prudence

of

of the Superiour, not to trouble the good Arsenius by correction, for a matter of so small importance; neuerthelesse seeking the meanes to correct it, vvherein hee shewed very vvell, that they vvere all most exact in the least thing that appertayned to Modestie. More-ouer I note the noble vprightnesse of Arsenius, to yeald himselfe faultie, and his fidelitye in correcting himselfe, although this vvas so light a thing, that in it selfe vvas not inmodest being in the court, although being among the Fathers it vvas so. I marke also, that vvee ought not to bee astonished at our selues, if vvee haue as yet some ould habitt of the vvorld, since Arsenius had this hauing remayned a long time, in the companie of the Fathers in the desert: vvee cannot bee so soone ridd of all our imperfections, and vvee must neuer bee astonished to see many in our selues, so that vvee haue the vvill to vvithstand them. Furthermore I note, that it is not to bee thought an euill iudgment, that the superiour imposeth correction to another, for some fault that you commit asvvell as he, to the end, that vvithout reprehending of you, you of your selfe amend it: but you must humble your selfe profoundly, seeing that the superiour taketh notice of your vveaknesse, and knovveth very vvell, you vvould haue much feeling of the correction, if it vvere done to you. VVee must also dearely loue this abiection, and humble our selues as Arsenius did, confessing that vvee bee culpable of the same fault, prouided that vvee humble our selues allvvaies in the spiritt of svveetnes and tranquillitie.

§. 3. I perceaue very vvel, that you desire I should furthermore speake of the other vertues of Modestye: I tell you then, that the second, vvhich is the interiour, vvorketh the same effects in the soule, that this vvhich vvee haue spoken of doth in the body; this composeth the motions, gestures, and countenances of the body, auoyding the two extremities, vvhich are these tvvo contrarie vices, lightnes or dissolution, and a countenance too much affected. Likewise interiour modestie mayntaineth the povvers of the soule in tranquillity, and Modesty, auoyding as I haue sayed curiosity of the vnderstanding, ouer the vvhich she principally exerciseth her care, also cutting of from the vvill her multitude of desires, making it to apply it selfe piously to that onely one, that Marie hath chosen vvhich shall not be taken from her, that is, a vvill to please God. Martha doeth verye vvell represent the immodestye of the vvill, she is forvvard and eager, and setteth all the seruants of the house a vvorke, she goeth hither and thither, vvithout stay, so desirous is she to intreat our Lord vvell, and it seemeth to her there vvill neuer be sufficient seruices of meat to make him good cheare. Euen so the vvill vvhich is not restrayned by Modesty, passeth from one subiect to another, to prouoke it selfe to loue God, and to desire many meanes and vvayes to serue him, and yet notvvithstanding there is no necessitie of so many things, it vvould be better to vnite her selfe to God as Magdalene did; keeping her selfe at his feete, demaunding of him that hee giue vs his loue, then to thinke hovv, and by vvhat meanes vvee may gett it. This Modesty bridleth the vvill, cōtinually setling and closing it in the exercise of the meanes of her aduancement in the loue of God, according to the vocation in vvhich vvee remayne. I haue sayed that this vertue doth principally imploy it selfe to subiect the vnderstanding, because the naturall curiositie that vvee haue is very dangerouse, and causeth that vvee neuer perfectly knovve any one thing: for so much as vvee take not

time

time sufficient to learne it vvell. It flieth also the other extremitie of vice, vvhich is opposite to it, that is dulnes and negligence of spiritt, vvhich vvill not knovve that vvhich is necessarie. Novv this subiection of the vnderstanding is of verye great importance, for our perfection: for look how much the vvill vveddeth it selfe to any thing, so much the more earnest it is in the pursuite of it: and if the vnderstanding shevve vnto the vvill the beautie of another, it deuerteth it from the first. The Bees haue no setled place, vvhiles they haue not a king, neuer ceasing to fly through the ayre, dispersing & scattering themselues hauing allmost no repose in their hiue: but so soone as their king is borne, they gather themselues all together round about him, and goe not forth but by the permission of their king to gather their honnye. In like manner our vnderstanding and vvill, our passions, and the faculties of our soule, as spirituall Bees, vntill such time as they haue a king, that is to saye, vntill such time as they haue made choise of our Lord IESVS for their king, haue no repose, our senses neuer ceasing to vvander curiously, and to dravve our interiour faculties after them, to disperse them, somtimes after one subiect, then after another, and by this meanes there is no other then a continuall labour, and vnquietnesse of spiritt, vvhich maketh vs to loose the peace and tranquillitie of spiritt vvhich is so necessarie for vs, & this is that vvhich the immodestie of the vnderstanding, and will, causeth vs. But from the time that our soules haue chosen Our Lord IESVS for their onely souueraigne king, her povvers like chast mysticall Bees, put themselues in order neere to him, and neuer goe forth from their Hiue but for to gather the exercises of charitie, that this holy king commaundeth them to practice, towards their neighbour, and presently after, they returne modestly

 into

into this holy and amiable presence of their Lord, for to gather and mannage discreetlye the honny of holy and amorous conceits and affections, vvhich they dravve from his sacred presence : and so they shall auoyd the tvvo extremities aforesayed : cutting of on the one side curiositie of the vnderstanding, by a simple attention to God All, mighty and on the other side stupiditie, and lazines of spiritt, by the exercises of Charitie that they shall practize tovvards their neighbour, vvhen it shalbe requisite and necessary. But behould another example touching this subiect. On a day a certayne Religious man came to the great Sainct Thomas, and demaũded of him vvhat hee should doe, to become verye learned; In reading one onely booke, sayed hee. I read these dayes past, The Rule that Sainct Augustine made for Religious vvomen, vvhere hee sayeth expressly, that the sisters may neuer read any other bookes, then those that shalbe giuen them by their Superiour: and after hee gaue the same commaundement to his Religious mẽ. So much knowledg had hee of the euill, that the curiositie of willing to knovve other things, then that vvhich is necessarie for the better seruice of God (vvhich are very fevv things) bringeth to the soule: for if you vvalke in simplicitye, by the obseruance of your Rules, vvithout povvring out your selues, or searching to knovve other things, you shall perfectly serue God. Science or knowledg is not necessarie to loue God; (as sayeth Sainct Bonauenture) for a simple vvoman is as capable to loue God, as the most learned men in the vvorld. There must bee little knovvledg, and very much practice, in that vvhich concerneth perfection. I remember vpõ this discourse, the danger there is in the curiositie of the vvill to knovve so many meanes for the perfiting of it selfe, I spake vvith tvvo Religious vvomen of tvvo orders vvell reformed, one of them by the frequent reading of the bookes of the Bl. S. Teresa, learned to speake so like her, that she seemed to bee a little Mother Teresa, and she beleeued it, so imagining in her selfe, all that the holy Mother Teresa had done vvhilest she liued, that she thought to doe the very same, so farr as to haue had the bindings of the spiritt, and suspensions of the povvers of the soule, euen so as she did read the Sainte had, so that she spake very vvell thereof. There are others, who haue so effectually thought on the life of S. Katherin of Sienna, and of the life of S. Katherin of Genes, that they also thought thēselues to bee S. Katherins. Such soules as these, at the least haue contentment in themselues, by the imagination they haue of being Saints, although their contentment be vaine. But the other Religious vvoman, I spake of, vvas of a verie different humour: for so much as she neuer had contentment, because of the auiditie she had to seeke, and desire the vvay, and method to perfect her selfe; and although she laboured for it, neuerthelesse it allvvaies seemed to her, that there vvas some other manner to perfect her, then that vvhich others did teach her. The one of these Religious womē did liue content in her imaginary sanctitie, and did not seeke nor desire any other thing: and the other did liue discontent, because her perfectiō vvas hidden, and therefore she did allwaies desire some other thing. Interiour modestie retayneth the soule betweene these tvvo estates in mediocritye to desire and knovv that vvhich is necessarie, and no more. In fine it must be noted, that the exteriour modestie vvhereof vvee haue spoken, serueth verye much to the interiour, and to the peace ād trāquillitie of the soule. The proofe that all the holy fathers haue made thereof, who haue made great professiō of prayer, doeth witnesse it. For they haue all

 judged,

iudged, that the most modest posture ayde th most therein; as to sett themselues on their knees their hands ioyned together, or their armes a crosse, or the like.

§. 4. The third kind of Modestie regardeth our wordes, and manner of conuersing. There are speeches vvhich should bee immodest out of the time of recreation, vvhere iustly and vvith good reason, vvee ought to vnbind the spiritt a little; and vvhosoeuer vvould not speake, nor permitt others to speake; but of high eleuated matters in this time, shonld doe immodestlie: For haue vvee not sayed that Modestye regardeth the time, the place, and the persons? To this purpose I did read the other day, that S. Pachome vppon his entry into the desert, to lead a monasticall life, had verye great tentations, and the vvicked spiritts did appeare to him often in diuerse formes. He that wrote his life sayeth, that one day going to the vvoode to hevv, there came a great troupe of infernall spiritts to fright him, vvho ranked themselues as soldiers, that sett the gard, all verye vvell armed, calling one to the other: Make place for the holy man; S. Pachome that knevve very well, these vveere the soundes of the wicked spirit t, began to laugh saying, you mocke mee, but I wilbe one, if it please God. Novv the diuell seeing that hee could not intrap him, nor make him enter into melancholie, thought that he vvould ouertake him with ioy, since he had laughed at their first enterprise, so he went about to tye a great number of huge cordes to a leafe of a tree and many diuells did sett themselues about these cordes, to dravve them with great violence, crying and swëating, as if they had had great difficultie, the good Sainte lifting vp his eyes, and seeing this folly, did represẽt to himselfe our Lord IESVS Crucified on the crosse, they seeing that the S. did apply himselfe to the fruite of the tree

and

and not to the leafe, went their waies all cōfounded and ashamed. There is a time for laughing, and a time not to laugh: as also a time to speake, and a time to keepe silence, as this glorious S. sheweth vs in his tentations. This Modestie cōposeth our manner of speaking that it may bee acceptable, speaking neither too high nor too lowe, neither too slowly nor too fast, retayning our selues within the tearmes of holy mediocritie, permitting others to speake without interrupting them, (for that sauoureth of babling) yet speaking in our turne to auoyde rusticallnesse, which hindreth vs from being of good conuersation. Also oftentimes a person meeteth with occasiōs, vvhere it is necessarie to speake with modestie, equallitie, patience, and tranquillitye.

§. 5. The fourth vertue named Modestie appertayneth to apparell, and manner of dressing: where-of it is not needfull to speake any other thing, then that sluttishnes, and vnseemelinesse, in the manner of apparelling of our selues, must be auoyded, as also the other extremitie, that is ouer much great care of dressing our selues vvell, with affected curiositie to bee verye fine, which is vanitye. But ciuilitye ād cleanlines hath bene very much commended by S. Bernard, as being a great signe of the puritie and sanctity of the soule. There is an example in the life of S. Hilarion, vvhich seemeth contrarie to this, for one day speaking to a gentleman that vvas come to see him, hee sayed to him, that there was no apparence to looke after cleanlines in a haire shirte, as if hee had sayed, that vvee must not seeke neatnes in our bodies, vvhich are no other then stincking carrion, and top full of infection. But this was more admirable in this great S. then imi-table.

Truely wee must not haue too much delicatnesse, yet notwithstanding vvee must not bee sluttish, that

that which made this Saint speake in this sort, was (if I be not deceaued) because he spake before courtiers, that hee did see so giuen ouer to delicatnesse, that it was needfull for him to speake a little more sharplye, as those that will make straight a yoũg tree, they doe not onelie sett it straighte; but they bend it euen to the other side, to the end it retourne not to its former crookednes. Behould there what I had to say of modestie.

§.6. You desire in the second place, to know, what wee must doe to receaue correction well, that the feeling thereof remayne not in vs, or drinesse of hart: To hinder the motions of choller to be felt in vs, and the bloud not to rise in the face, will neuer bee. Happie shall vvee bee, if wee may bee able to haue this perfectiõ, a quarter of an hower before our death. But to keepe drinesse of spiritt, in such manner, that after the feeling is past, wee cannot speake, with so much confidence, sweetnesse and tranquillitie as before, ô this, vvee must haue a great care not to doe; You dismisse the feeling farr of, saye you, but it ceaseth not to retourne. I assure you, my deare daughters, that you send it from you, it may bee, as doe the Cytizens of a tovvne, vvherein is made a sedition in the night, vvhen they chase a vvay the seditious persons and enimies; but they put them not out of the tovvne, so that they hide themselues going from street to street, vntill the day come, and then they cast themselues vppon the inhabitants, and in fine remayne Masters: you reiect the feeling you haue of the correction, that is giuen you, but not so couragiously and carefully, that it hideth not it selfe in some little corner of your hart, at least some part of the feeling. You vvill not haue the feeling: neither vvill you submitt your iudgment, vvhich maketh you beleeue, that

that the correction hath bene giuen you vvrongfully, or else that it hath bene done by passion, or the like: vvho seeth not, that these makebates vvill sett vppon you, and ouervvhelme you quickly, vvhith a thousand sorts of confusions? beleeue mee, you chase them not farre of. But vvhat must bee done in this time? vvee must dravve neere vnto our Lord IESV, and speake to him of some other thing. But your feeling is not quieted, but it suggesteth to you to regard the vvrong hath bene done you. O God, this is not the time; submitt your iudgment, to make it beleeue and confesse, that the correction is good, and that it vvas giuen verye iustlie; O no, this is to bee done after your soule shalbe quiet agayne and pacified; for in the time of trouble wee must not speake, nor doe any thing, vppon any ter mes or reasons, but remayne constant and resolute, not to consent to our passion; for vvee shall neuer vvant reasons at that time, they will come thicke and threefold: But not one must bee hearkned vnto, hovv good soeuer they seeme to bee; But vvee must keepe neere to God as I haue sayed; diuerting our selues, after vvee bee humbled and prostrate before his Maiestie; speaking to him of some other thing.

But marke this vvorde, that pleaseth mee verie much to speake, because of the profitt thereof, humble your selues vvith a svvete and a peacefull humilitye, and not vvith a melancholy and troubled humility: for this is our vnhappinesse, that vvee bring before God acts of troubled & spitefull humilitye, and by this meanes our spiritts are not pacified, and these acts are vnfruitfull. But if on the contrarie vvee make these acts before the diuine bountie, vvith a svveet confidence,

dence, wee should come away all cherefull and trãquille, and after wee should verie easilye disauowe all the reasons, (very often and ordinarilye unreasonable) that our iudgement and proper loue doth suggeit vnto vs, and wee should goe with the same facilitye to speake to those, who haue giuen vs this correction, or contradiction as before. You ouercome your selfe indeed (say you) to speake to them, but if they doe not aunsvvere to you as you desire, this doth redouble the tentation, all this proceedeth of the same euill that wee haue sayed: what imports it you, whether they speake after one fashion or another, so that you doe your dutie? Therefore all being well counted and deducted, there is not any person that hath not auersion to bee corrected. S. Pachome after that he had liued forty or fiftye yeares in the desert in great perfection, had a reuelation from God, that hee should gayne a great number of soules, and that many should come into the deserts, to place themselues vnder his conduct: hee had allreadie some Religious with him, and the first hee receaued was his Brother named Iohn, vvho was his elder Brother: S. Pachome then began to inlarge his monasterie, and to make a great number of cells, his Brother Iohn, either because hee did not knovve his designe, or otherwise for the zeale hee had to pouertie, one day reprehended him verye sharplye, saying vnto him, is it so, that you ought, and meane to imitate our Lord Iesv, who had not where-on to rest his head, vvhilest hee was in this world, to make so great a conuent? and other the like wordes to that purpose. S. Pachome although he weare a great S. had such a feeling of this reprehension, that hee tourned himselfe on the other side, to the end (if I bee not deceaued) that the feeling hee had there-of might not appeare in his face: Then hee wet, and cast himselfe on his knees

before

before God, demaunding pardon for his fault, and complayning, for that, after he had remayned so long within the desert, he was not yet mortifyed, making so humble and feruent prayer, that he obteyned grace, neuer more to bee subiect to impatience. Likewise S. Francis, towards the end of his life, after hee had had so many rapts, and amorous vnions with God: after hee had done so much for his glorie; and surmounted himselfe in so many sortes; one day when hee planted colworts in the garden, it hapned that a Brother seeing that hee did not plant them well, reprehended him, and the S. was moued with so povverfull a motion of cholere at his reprehension, that hee had almost vttered iniurious words against that Brother, that had reprehended him. Hee opened his mouth to pronounce it: but hee restrayned himselfe, and taking of the dung, that hee did burie with the collworts: O wicked toung sayed hee, I will teach the to iniurye thy Brother, and presently prostrating himselfe on both his knees, hee besought the Brother to pardon him. Now what reason is there I praye you that wee should bee astonished to see our selues apt to cholere, and if wee haue a feeling vvhen wee are reptehended, or when some contradiction happneth vnto vs? vvee must therefore take example from these Saints who did surmount themselues incontinentlye, the one hauing recourse to prayer, and the other humbly demauuding pardon of his Brother; and neither the one nor the other did any thing in fauour of their motion, but amended thẽselues and made their profitt of it. You tell mee that you accept of the correction with all your hart, that you approue it, and find it iust & reasonable, but this giueth you a certayne coufusion, in respect of the superiour, because you haue displeased her, or giuen her occasion to bee angrye, and that this taketh from you the confidence to approch vnto her; notvvistanding you loue the abiection that commeth on you for the fault. My daughter, this is done by the commaundement of selfeloue; knowe you not (it may bee you doe not) that there is in our selues, a certayne Monasterie, whereof the Superiour is selfeloue, and therefore it imposeth penances, and this payne is the penance it imposeth vppon you, for the fault you haue committed in displeasing the superiour; because it may bee she will not esteeme you so much as she hath done, if you had not fayled in your duty; This is enough for those vvho receaue correction; I must speake a word for those that giue it. They ought to vse verye great discretion, to take a proper time for it, and to doe it with all due circumstances; besides, they must not bee astonished or meruaill; nor bee offended to see those to whome they giue it, to haue a feeling or trouble thereof; for it is a thing verye greeuous to a person to see himselfe corrected.

§. 7. Thirdly you demaund, how you may bee able to carrye your spiritt vp rightly before God, not svvaruing on the righr hand, or on the left. My Deare daughter, your proposition is very pleasing to mee, for so much as it bringeth his aunswere with it. You must doe that you speake, goe to God, looking neithor on the right hand, nor on the left. But it is not this that you demaund, I see well; but vvhat you may bee able to doe, to fix your spiritt in God in such sorte, that nothing may vntye nor dravve it backe. Tvvo things are necessarie for this, to die, and to bee saued. For after this there shall neuer bee any separation, and your spiritt shalbe indissolubly fastned and vnited to God. You say yet, this is not that which you demaund; but it is, what you may doe to hinder, that the least fly doe not withdrawe your spiritt from God, as it doth, you

would

would say the least distraction. Pardō mee, my daughter, the least fly of distraction doth not withdrawe your spiritt frō God, so as you say: For nothing withdraweth vs from god but sinne; and the resolution we haue made in the morning, to keepe our selues vnited to God, and attentiue to his presence, causeth that wee remayne allwaies there, yea also vvhen vvee sleepe, since wee doe it in the name of God, and according to his most holy vvill: it seemeth that his diuine bountye hath sayed to vs, sleepe and rest, and in the meane time, I vvill watch ouer you, for to keepe and defend you from the roreing lion, vvho goeth allwaies round about you to defeat you: Consider then if you haue not reason to take your rest modestly, as I haue sayed: for the meanes to doe all things vvell that vvee doe, is to bee attentiue to the presence of God; for seeing that hee doth behould vs, vvho of vs will offend him? veniall sinnes of themselues are not capable to diuert vs out of the way, that conducteth vs to God: they stay vs vvithout doubt a little in our way, but they doe not therefore turne vs backe, and much lesse simple distractions, and this I haue declared in the Introduction; As for prayer, it is no lesse profitable to vs, nor lesse pleasing to God, for hauing manye distractions: but it may bee, it shall proue more profitable, then if we had had many consolations; because there is more labour therein, prouided notwithstādiug that wee must haue fidelitie to withdrawe our selues from these distractions, and not willinglie permitt our spiritt to rest, or pause on them. The same is to be sayd of the paine that wee haue all the day long to settle our spirits in god, and celestiall things: so that we haue care to retayne our spiritt, from running after these flyes & butter flyes, as a mother doth with her child, seeing her little one affected to runne after the butterflyes, thinking to catch them, she withdraweth him, withhoulding him presentlye by the armes, saying to him, My child, thou wilt take cold to runne after those butter flyes in the sunne, it is better that thou stay with mee: this poore child remayneth vntill such time as hee seeth another, after the which hee should be as readie to runne, if his mother did not withhould him as before; but what must wee doe then, wee must haue patience, and not bee wearie of our labour, since it is vndertaken for the loue of God? But if I bee not deceaued, when wee say that wee cannot find God, and that it seemeth to vs that hee is farr from vs: wee would say that wee cannot haue the feeling of his presence; I haue obserued that manye make no difference betweene God and the feeling of God: betvveene fayth & the feeling of fayth, which is a very great defect: it seemeth to them, that whē they feele not God, that they are not in his presence, and this is ignorance: For a person vvho goeth to suffer martyrdome for God notwithstanding should not thinke on God at the present, but on the payne: although he haue not the feeling of fayth: he is not excluded from meritt in respect of his first resolution, but executeth an act of great loue. There is a great difference, to haue the presence of God (I vnderstand to bee in his presence) and to haue the feeling of his presence. There is not any but God him selfe, that may grant vs this grace: For to giue you the meanes to obteyne this feelieg is not possible for mee. Doe you demaund what must bee done to hould ones selfe allwaies with great respect before God, as being most vnworthye of his grace? There is no other meanes to doe it, then as you saye: consider that hee is our God, and that we are his weake creatures, vnworthy of this honour, as S. Francis did, who passed a whole night, interrogating with

God in these termes, who art thou? and who am I? In fine if you demaund of mee what I shall doe to obteyne the loue of God? I will tell you, in desiring to loue him, and in place of applying your selues to thinke and aske, what you may doe to vnite your spiritt to God, sett your selues to practice it, by a continuall application of your spiritt to God, and I assure you, you shall sooner arriue to your pretence by this meanes, then by any other waye: for according to the measure that we disperse our selues, so much lesse are wee recollected, and therefore lesse capable of vniting our selues with the diuine maiestie who will haue vs all without any reseruation. Truely there are soules who busye themselues so much to thinke, what they shall doe, that they haue not time to doe it; and notwitstanding in that which regardeth our perfection, which consisteth in the vnion of our soule with the diuinitie, to knovve little, and to doe much, is our way without doubt: it seemeth to me, that those of vvhom you aske the way to heauen, haue great reason to aunswer, as they who say, that to goe to such a place, you must allwaies goe, setting one foote before another, and by this meanes, you shall come where you desire, walke allwaies, say they, to these soules desirous of their perfections, walke in the way of your vocation in simplicitie, and lett your studie be to effect, more then to desire, this is the shortest vvay.

§. 8. But behould a subtilitie, that I must, if it please you to permitt mee, discouer vnto you, without offending you; to vvit, you would I should teach you a way of perfection allreadie perfected, in such sort as there weere no other thing to be done, then to put it ouer your head, as you doe your habitt, and then, by this meanes you should find your selues perfect without payne, that is to say

I should

I should giue you in an instant perfection allreadie made; For that, I say, wee must doe, is not agreable to nature; is not this that vvee vvould haue? O truely if this were in my povver, I should bee the most perfect man of the vvorld; For if I could giue perfection vnto others vvithout doing any thing, I assure you I vvould first learne it my selfe. It seemeth to you that perfection is an art, that if one could find the secreat there-of, hee should haue it vvithout labour. Truely you deceaue your selues, for there is no greatter secreet then to vvorke and labour faythfully in the exercise of diuine loue, if you pretend to vnite your selues to the vvelbeloued. But I vvould vvillinglie that you did marke: that vvhen I saye you must vvorke, I allvvaies intend to speake of the superiour part of our soule: For notvvitstanding all the repugnances of the inferiour, vvee must bee no more astonished, then passengers are at doggs that barke a farre of. They vvho at a feast, take a tast of euerie dish, eatting somvvhat of each kind of meat, vvith this varietie ouerturne their stomacke, and cause so great indisgestion that it hindreth them from sleeping all the night, neither can they doe any other thing then spitte: euen so the soules that desire to tast of all methodes, and meanes that leade, or may conduce to perfection, doe the very same; for the stomacke of their vvill not hauing sufficiēt heat to disgest, and put in practice so many meanes, there is made there a certayne cruditie, and indisgestiō, vvhich taketh avvay their peace and trāquillitie of spirit to dravve neere vnto our Lord, vvhich is the onely thing necessarie that Mary hath chosen and shall neuer bee taken from her.

Lett vs passe novv to that other demaund, that you proposed to mee, that is, vvhat you may doe to strengthen your resolutions so vvell, that they

may

may spring forth and come to good effect. There is no better meanes (my child) then to put them in practice: but you say you are allvvaies fraile, and that although you doe often make strong resolutions, not to fall into the imperfections that you desire to amend, if the occasiō present it selfe, you faile not to stumble, and lay your nose on the ground. would you haue mee tell you, vvhy vvee remayne so vveake? it is because vvee vvill not abstayne from vnwholsome meates: it is euen as if a parson that vvould not haue the payne of the stomacke, did aske of a phisition vvhat she should doe: hee vvould aunsvvere her, that she must not eate of such and such meates, because they engender crudities, vvhich doe cause payne aftervvardes: but she vvill not abstayne from them. VVee doe euen the very same, wee would (for example) loue correctiō vvell: but we vvill neuerthelesse bee obstinate: O what a folly is this? this cannot bee, you vvill neuer bee able and strong to support correctiō couragiously, whiles you eate of the fruit of proper estimation. I vvould verye vvillingly keepe my soule, recollect, & neuerthelesse I vvill not abridge so many sortes of vnprofitable reflections. This may not be. Good God! I vvould bee inuariable, and very feruent in my exercises; but also I would not willinglye haue so muche payne; in a worde I would find the busines allreadie dispatched: this may not bee grāted during this life, wherein we shall allwaies haue difficultie and labour. The feast of the Purification (as I haue sayed to you once before) hath not an Octaue. Of necessitie wee must haue two equall resolutions, the one to see vveedes grovve in our garden; and the other to haue the courage to see them pluckte vp by the rootes, and to plucke them vp our selues: for our selfe loue will neuer dye vvhiles wee liue: it being selfe-loue, that causeth

causeth these impertinent productions. Moreouer it is not to bee fraile, to fall sometimes into veniall sinnes, so that wee raise our selues immediatlye by the retourne of our soule to God, meeklie and gentlye humbling our selues: wee must not thinke to liue vvith out committing some: for there hath not bene any, (Our Bl. Ladie excepted) that hath had this priuiledge: truely although they staye vs a little (as I haue sayed) they doe not diuert vs so much out of the vvay, but that one onely regard of God abolisheth thẽ, in fine wee must knowe, that we ought neuer to cease from making good resolutions, although wee see very well, that according to our ordinarie wee practice them not; yea when wee perceaue verye vvell, it is impossible to practice them when occasion shall present it selfe; and this must bee done with more stabilitie, then if we felt in our selues, sufficient courage for to bring our enterprise to good effect, saying to our Lord, it is true, O Lord, that I shall not haue the strenght to doe, or support such a thing of my selfe, but I reioyce for so much as it shalbe thy streinght which will worke it in mee; and vppon this foundation wee must goe to battaill couragiously, and doe not doubt, but you shall haue the victorie. Our Lord doeth tovvards vs, euen the very same that a good Father or Mother, who permitt their child to goe alone, when hee is in a softe medovve vvhere the grasse is vvell grovvne, or vppon moss: because if hee happen to fall it vvil be no great harme: but in the ill and dangerous vvaies they carrye him carefully in their armes. VVe haue often seene soules to support couragiouslye diuers great assaultes, not hauing bene ouercome of their enimies, who within a while haue bene ouercome in slight encounters; & why so? because our Lord seeing it could doe them no great harme to fall, left them to goe alone by them-

themselues, the vvhich hee did not doe vvhen they vveere in the desperate termes of great temptatiõs, out of vvhich hee drewe them by his Allmighty povver. Paula vvho vvas so generous to forsake the world, quitting the citty of Rome, and so great abundance of all things, and vvho could not be shaken by the Motherly affection she bare to her children, so resolute vvas she to forsake all for God, after she had effected all these great meruailes, she permitted herselfe to bee surmounted, by the tentation of her proper iudgment, vvhich made her beleeue, that she ought not to submitt her selfe to the aduise of many holie persons, vvho did desire her to vvithdravve somevvhat of her ordinarie austerities, vvherein S. Hierome auovveth that she vvas reprehensible. Lett vs marke vvell for conclusion, that all vvhatsoeuer vvee haue declared in this discourse, are things verie delicate concerning perfectiõ, and therefore lett none of you that haue heard them bee affrighted or afflicted, if she find not her selfe to haue arriued to this perfection, since by the grace of God, you haue so good courage to desire, and pretend, the attayning therevnto.

LIVE IESVS AMEN.

THE TENTH ENTERTAINEMENT.

OF OBEDIENCE.

§. 1. OBediẽce is a morall vertue, vvhich dependeth of Iustice: novv there are certayne morall vertues vvhich haue so great affinitye with the vertues Theologicall (which are Fayth, hope, and

and charitie) that they seeme as it weere Theologicall, although they bee in a degree verie inferiour, as Penance, Religion, Iustice, and Obedience: Novv Obedience consisteth in tvvo points, the first is to obey Superiours, the second to obey our equalles, and inferiours: But this second appertayneth rather to humilitie, gentlenesse and charitie, then to Obedience; For the person that is humble, thinketh that all others surpasse her, and are better then she, in such sort that she esteemeth them her Superiours, and beleeueth that she ought to obey them. But touching the Obedience that regardeth the Superiours, that God hath established ouer vs to gouerne vs, it is of Iustice and necessity, and wee ought to render it vnto them with entire submission of our vnderstanding & vvill. Novv this Obedience of the vnderstanding is practized, when being cōmaunded, vvee accept and approue the commaundment, not onely vvith our will; but also vvith our vnderstanding, approuing and esteeming the thing that is commaunded, and iudging it better, then any other thing that they might haue commaunded vs vppon this occasion. VVhen one is come to this, then they loue so to Obey, that they desire insatiably to bee commaunded, to the end that all they doe, bee done by Obedience: This is the Obediēce of the perfect, and that which I desire for you which proceedeth from the pure gift of God, or othervvise is gotten vvith long time and labour, and by a great number of reiterated acts, and produced with a liuely force, by the meanes vvhereof vvee gayne the habitt and facillitye therof. Our naturall inclination allwaies carrieth vs to desire to commaund, and giueth vs an auersion to Obey: and notvvithstanding it is certayne that wee haue much capacitie to Obey, and it may be wee haue none at all to commaund.

§.2. Obe

§. 2. Obedience most ordinarilye hath three conditions, the first is to accept vvith a good vvill the thing that they commaund vs, and to apply our vvill svveetly thereuntolouing to bee commaunded; for it is not the way or meanes to yeald our selues truelye obedient, to haue no person to commaund vs: as likewise it is not a meanes to bee milde to remayne alone in a desert. Cassian reporteth that being in the desert, he was somtimes in choler, and taking his pē to write, if it did not write well, hee should cast it from him; vvhere-fore sayed hee, it serueth for nothing to bee alone, since that wee carrye cholere with vs. Vertue is a good of it selfe, that dependeth not of the priuation of his contrarie. The second condition of obedience is promptitude, to the which sloth, or spirituall sadnes is opposite; For it rarelye hapneth, that a sorovvfull soule doth any thing promptly, and diligentlye, (in Theologicall termes, sloth is called spirituall sorrowe) and this is it vvhich hindereth from executing obedience couragiouslie, and promptlye. The third is perseuerance: for it sufficeth not, that vvee consent to the commaundement, and that wee execute it for some space of time, if wee doe not perseuere therein, since it is this perseuerance that obteyneth the crovvne. There are euerie where to be found admirable examples of perseuerance: but particularlye in the life of Saint Pachome; there is mention of diuers monkes, that perseuered vvith an incredible patience, all their life imploying thē-selues, in one and the selfe same exercise, as the good Father Ionas, vvho neuer in his life did any other thing (besides gardening) then make matts, and hee vvas so habituated, that hee made them, his windowe being shut close, meditating and making his prayer, and the one did not hinder the other in him, in such sorte that they found him dead vvith his knees acrosse, and his matts fastned vpon them: hee did dye doing of that which hee had done all his life. This vvas an act of great humilitie, for obe-bedience to imploye himselfe in this selfe same exercise being so abiect all his life: For strong temptations might arriue vnto him, that he should be capable of some office of more vvorth. Now this third condition is most difficult of all, because of the lightnes ad inconstancie of humayne spiritts; for at this present vvee loue to doe one thing, and by and by wee will not regarde it. if vvee would follow all the motions of our spiritt, or that it weere possible for vs so to doe, without giuing scandall ther-in, or dishonoring our selues, wee should see no other thing then chang and instabilitye. Now wee would bee in one condition, and a while after wee would seeke for another, so extrauagant and inconstant, is the spiritt of man: Therefore it must be stopped by the force of our first resolutions, to the end wee may liue equallie, in the throng of the inequallities of our feelings, successes, and euents. Now to giue our selues affectionatly to Obedience, when wee shall find our selues tempted, vve ought to make considerations of the excellencie, beautie, and meritt, yea also the profitt thereof: for to encourage vs to passe onvvarde; This is to bee vnderstood for those soules, that are not yet well established in Obedience: but vvhen there is no question but of a simple auersion, or disgust of the thing cõmaunded, wee must make on act of loue, and put our selues to the vvorke. Our Lord Iesvs himselfe in his passion, did feele a very great distaste, and a mortall auerfion to suffer death: hee sayeth it himselfe: but vvith the subtile point of his spiritt hee was resigned to the will of his Father; all the rest was but a motion of nature. Perseuerance is most difficult in interiour things; for the exteriour and materiall

materiall are easie enough, which proceedeth from this, that wee are troubled to subiect our vnderstanding, for this is the last peece that vvee submitt, and notwithstanding it is intirelie necessarie, that wee subiect our thoughs to certayne obiects; in such sort, that vvhen our superiour doth giue vs sett exercises, or practice of vertue, wee remayne in those exercises, and submitt our spiritt. I doe not call it want of perseuerance when wee make some small interruptions, so that vvee quit it not alltogether: as it is not vvant of Obedience, to bee defectiue in one of her conditions, prouided that vvee are not obliged but to the substance of the vertues, and not to the conditions: For allthough that vvee doe obey vvith repugnance, and allmost as it weere by force, by the obligation of our condition, our Obedience notwistanding omitteth not therefote to bee good, in vertue of our first resolutiō: But it is of an infinitt worth and meritt, when it is performed vvith the conditions that wee haue nominated, for any one thing hovv little soeuer it bee, being effectuated vvith such Obedience, is of excellent vvorth.

§.3. Obedience is a vertue so excellent, that our Lord IESVS vvould guide all the course of his life by Obedience, euē so as hee sayed manye times, that hee vvas not come to doe his vvill, but that of his Father: and the Apostle sayeth, that hee vvas made Obedient euen vnto death, and the death of the crosse: and he would ioyne to the infinite meritt of his perfect Charitie, the infinitt meritt of perfect Obedience, Charitie giueth way to Obedience, because Obedience dependeth of Iustice. also it is better to pay that vvee ovve, then to giue an almes, that is to say, it is better to Obey, then to doe acts of Charitie by our ovvne proper motion.

The second point v[illegible]-in Obedience consisteth

is rather humilitie then Obedience, for this kinde of Obedience is a certayne flexiblenes of our will, to follovv the will of another, and this is a vertue that is exceedinglye pleasing, which causeth our spirit to winde it selfe in all occasiōs, and allwaies disposeth vs to doe the vvill of God: For example, if in passing to one place I meete a sister that desireth mee to goe to another: the will of God in mee is, that I doe as she desireth, rather thē that I vvill. But if I oppose my opiniō to hers, the will of God in her is, that she giue mee way, and the like in all things that are indifferent: But if it happen vppon this first opiniō both will yeald and giue way, they must not staye there contesting: but they shall haue regard to that vvhich is best and most reasonable, and simply doe it, but in this wee must bee guided by discretiō, for it should bee farre from the purpose, to quitt a thing that vvere of necessitie, to condescend to a thing indifferent. If I would execute an action of great mortificatiō, and another sister should come to mee, and bidd mee not to doe it, or that I doe some other. I would remitt my first designe if it vvere possible vntill another time, for to doe her will, and then after wardes, I vvould dispatch my vndertaken mortification; But if I could not omitt or remitt it, and that this that she vvould haue of mee, were not necessarie, I ought to doe that, which I had first vndertaken: and then if I could, I would regaine the cōmoditie to doe that vvhich the sister did desire of mee. But if it happē that a sister request vs to doe something for her, and that through sodaynesse, or surprise, wee shewe our selues disgusted therevvhith, the sister must not bee ielous, or mistrust, nor make semblance of knowing or marking it, neither must she desire that it be not done, for it is in our power to hinder our eyes and our countenance from demonstrating the cōbat that wee haue

vvith

within vs, allthoug reason would gladlie performe what is desired: For these are messengers that come vvithout sending for, and although wee bidd them retourne, ordinarilie they doe not stirre. To vvhat purpose then, would not this sister haue mee to doe that she desired, onely because she knovveth, I haue had repugnãce thereunto? she ought to desire that I make profitt of this for my soule. You vvill say, it is because she feareth that she hath displeased you. No, it is selfe loue that would not that I should haue the least thought, that she is importune; I shall haue it notwitstãding, although I stay not my selfe therein. Moreouer, if to the signes of my repugnance, I add words, that plainly witnesse, I haue no desire to doe that which this sister desired of mee, she may and ought sweetly to praye mee, that I doe it not, when the persons are equall: for those that haue authoritie must hould thẽselues resolute, and they must cause their inferiours to bee pliable to them. Now al-thoug a sister should absolutelye refuse mee some-thing, or manifest the disgust she hath, I ought not to loose cõfidence to imploy her another time, neither ought I to bee disedified with her imperfectiõ; For at the present I support her, and within a vvhile she will support mee; Now she hath auersion frõ doing of this thing, and another time she will willinglie doe it: Notwitstãding if I haue had experiẽce, that this was such a spiritt, as were not as yet capable to bee intreated in this mãner, I would expect a while vntill such time as she were better disposed. we are all of vs capable of the defectes one of another, and wee must in no sorte whatsoeuer bee astonished to incounter thẽ, for if wee remayne sometime with-out falling into a fault, with in a while it will happẽ that wee shall doe no other thing then fayle, and committ manye great imperfections, vvhereof it followeth, that wee must profitt our selues, by the
abiection

abiection that hapneth to vs there-vppon. VVee ought also to suffer the delay of our perfection with patience, allvvaies doing that which wee are able for our aduancement, and that hartelye, and vvillinglie.

§.4. O hovv happie are those, vvho liuing in expectation, are not vvearied out vvith expecting! this I say for many, who hauing a desire to perfect themselues, by the acquisition of vertues, vvould haue them all in an instant, as if perfection consisted in no other thing then to desire it. It vvould be an exttaordinarie great benefitt, if wee could be humble, euen so soone as wee haue a desire to bee so, vvithout further payne. we ought to accustome our selues, to examine diligently the successe of our perfection, according to the ordinarie vvaies, in trãquillitie of hart, doing all that is in our power to gayne vertues by the fidelitie that wee shall haue to practice them, each one according to her condition and vocation, and expecting vvith patience the attayning, soone, or late, the end that vvee pretend, committing this to the diuine prouidence, who will haue care to comfort vs, in the time hee hath appointed for it: and if this should not bee vntill the houre of our death, vvee ought to suffer it, prouided that we doe our dutye, in performing allwaies that which is in our power, wee shall haue soone enough that vvee desire, when that wee shall obteyne it, & that it shall please almighty God to giue it vs. This attending and resignation is most necessarie: for the want there-of hindreth and troubleth a soule very much. wee must bee content to knovve that we doe vvell by him vvho gouerneth vs, and not to seeke after feelings, or particuler knovvledg: but vvalke as blind, within this prouidence and confidence in God: yea euen in the thickest of desolations, feares, darknes, and all other

Kind of crosses, if it please our Lord that wee shall haue them: : remayning perfectly abandoned to his gouerment, with out any exception or reseruation whatsoeuer, permitting him to doe all, casting vppō his bounty the vvhole care of bodye and soule, resting also vvholie resigned and immoueable in God, vnder the gouerment of Superiours, hauing no other care then to obey. Now the meanes to obteyne this flexiblenesse to the will of another is in prayer to make acts of indifferencye verie often and seriouslie, and then to put them in practice when occasion shall present it selfe: For it is not enough to cast our selues before God, for so much as this being done onely vvith the Imagination, there is no great matter in it; but when it is to bee performed in effect, and that comming to giue our selues vvholie to God wee shall find a creature that will commaund vs, wee shall find a difference, and heere it is where wee must shewe our courage. This gentlenesse and condescendance to the vvill of our neigbour is a verie pretious vertue, and resembleth much the prayer of vnion: for as this prayer is no other thing, then a renouncing of our selues in God; when the soule sayeth vvith veritie, I haue no other vvill but thine O Lord, then is she wholie vnited vnto God; likevvise allwaies renouncing our vvill to doe that our neighbour desireth, is true vnion with our neighbour, and all this must bee done for the loue of God. It happneth often that such persons as are little and vveake, both in bodie and spiritt, vvho vvill exercise themselues but in small matters, will doe them vvith such Charitie, that they shall farre surpasse the meritt of great and eleuated actions; for ordinarilie these high and great acts are made with lesse charitie, because of the attention, and of diuers considerations that are made about them. Yet neuerthelesse if a great vvorke bee done vvith as much Charitie, as a little one, vvithout doubt hee shall haue much more meritt and revvarde that doeth it. In fine, Charitie giueth the prize and vvorth to all our vvorkes, in such manner that all the good that vvee doe, vvee must doe it for the loue of God; and the euill that vve auoyd, must bee avoyded for the loue of God. The good actions that vvee doe, vvhich are not particularlie commaunded vs, and vvhich cannot dravve their meritt from Obedience, it must bee giuen them by Charitie, allthough vvee may doe all by Obedience; In breife vvee must haue a good courage, and depend of God onely, For the Character of the Religious of the Visitation is, to regarde the vvill of God in all things and to follovve itt.

§.5. You haue asked of mee heretofore, if you may saye particular prayers. I aunsvvere, that touching those short prayers, that you haue deuotion vnto sometimes, it is not amisse, so that you doe not tye your selues vnto them, in such sorte, that if they bee not sayed you haue a scruple there-of: or that you determine to say euerie day, or during a yeare, or a certayne time, some prayer according to your fantasye, for this must not beedone, but sometimes in the time of silence, if vve haue deuotion to say an *Aue Maris stella*, or a *Veni Creator*, there is not any difficultie, but that vvee may say it, and it is good, but vvee must bee verie warye, that this bee done vvithout preiudice of a greater good, as for example, if you haue deuotion before the Bl. Sacrament, to say three *Pater nosters* in honour of the Blessed Trinitie, and that you bee called to doe some other thing, you should rise presentlie, and readilie goe to performe that action to the honour of the Blessed Trinitie, in stead of the three *Pater nosters*: therefore vvee must not prescribe to our selues the making of a certayne number of genu-

flections

flectiōs, and Iaculatorie prayers, and the like daylie practices, or during any time, vvithout declaring it to the Superiour, although we must bee very faythfull in the practice of eleuations, and aspirations to God. Novv if you thinke that it is the Holy spiritt, vvho inspireth you to make those kind of exercises you wilbe willing to demaund leaue, yea likevvise not to performe them, if they vvill not permitt you, for so much as there is nothing so acceptable as Religious Obediēce. You must not promise a person to say any number of prayers for them: if they praye you to doe it, you must aunsvvere you vvill aske leaue: but if they recommend themselues simply to your prayers, you may aunsvvere that you vvill doe it vvillingly, and euen in the same time raise vp your spiritt to God for that person: euen so likevvise in the Blessed Sacrament, for you may not communicate vvithout leaue for any person, this is not to bee vnderstoode vvhen being readie to receaue our Lord Iesv, in the Sacramēt; if there came into your mind the necessitie of any one of your freinds, or the common necessitie of the poeple, that you may not recommend them to God, in supplicating him to haue compassion of them. But if you vvould communicate particularlye for any thing, you must aske leaue, if it bee not for your ovvne necessities, as to obteyne streinght against some tentation, or else to obteyne some vertues of our Lord, vvho bee euer Blessed. Amen.

THE ELEAVENTH DIS-COVRSE.

VPPON THE SAME SVBIECT OF Obedience; Of the vertue of Obedience.

§. 1. THere are three sortes of pious Obedience, vvhere-of the first is generall to all Christians, vvhich is the Obedience due to God, and to the Holye Church, in the obseruance of their commandementes. The second is Religious Obedience, which is of farre greatter price then the other, because it is not onely tyed to the commaundemētes of God: but subiecteth it selfe to his coūcells. There is a thurd Obedience, vvhich is this where-of I intēd to speake, as being the most perfect, vvhich is called amorous Obedience: and this is that same, which our Lord hath shevveed vs example of, all the time of his life. The holy Fathers haue giuen to this kind of Obedience many properties and conditions: but among them I vvill choose onely three, vvhere-of the first is, that it is (as they name it) blind: The second, that it is prompt, the third that it is perseuerant. Blind Obedience hath three properties or conditions: The first that it looketh not on the face of the Superiours, but onely on their authoritie; The second that it informeth not it selfe of reasons, nor of the motiues the Superiours haue to commaund such or such a thing, it suffiseth, to knowe, they haue commaunded it; and the third, that it enquireth not the meanes, vvhich it must haue to doe that vvhich is commaunded, being assured that God, by vvhose inspirations the commaundment is made, will also giue abilitie to accomplish it: but in stead of enqui-

ring

ring how she shall doe it, she putteth her selfe to it. Religiouse Obedience, the which should bee blind submitteth her selfe Louingly to doe all that is cōmaunded her simply, vvithout euer regarding whether the commaundement be well or ill made, so that they who commande haue power to commaunde, and that the commaundement serue to the coniunction of our spiritt with God: for out of it true Obedience neuer doth any thing. Many are greatly deceaued about this condition of Obediēce, who haue beleeued, that it consisteth in doing all that should bee commaunded vs, bee it right or wrong, weere it euen against the commaundements of God and Holy church: vvherein they haue greatlye erred, imagining follye in this blindnes, where there is none: for in all that vvhich concerneth the commaundements of God, as the Superiours haue neuer any povver to make any commaundement contrarie, so likevvise the inferiours neuer haue any obligation to obey in such case. For if they should Obey therin, they should sinne. Now I know verye well, that many haue done things cōtrarie to the cōmaundements of God by the instinct of this Obedience (which will not onelie Obey the commaundements of God and Superiours, but also their councells and inclinations) Many haue precipitated themselues to death, by a particuler inspiration from God, vvhich vvas so strong that they could in no sorte gaynsaye it: for otherwise it had beene in them a greuous sinne. It is related in the third booke of the Machabees, that one named Razias vvho being thrust forvvard with an ardēt zeale of the Glorie of God, vvent and exposed himselfe to blovves vvherof hee knewe hee could not auoyde vvoundes and death: and feeling himselfe to bee vvoūded in the breast, hee drewe out all his entrails by this vvound, then hee cast them in the ayre, in the

the presence of his enimies. Saint Apolonia cast her selfe into the fire which the enimyes of God, and of Christian fayth had prepared to put her into, to kill her Sainct Ambrose reporteth the historie of three virgines, vvho to auoyde the losse of their chastitie cast themselues into a riuer, and vvere drowned in the vvaters, but these had other manner of reasons to doe thus, vvhich vvould bee too long to declare in this place. There are diuers others, that haue precipitated themselues to death, as hee that cast himselfe into a burning fornace: all these examples ought to bee admired not imitated: for you knovv sufficiently, that vvee must neuer bee so blind, as to thinke to please God by transgressing his commaundements.

§. 2. Amorous Obedience presupposeth that vvee bee obedient to the commaundement of God, they say that this Obedience is blind, because it obeyeth equally to all Superiours. All the antient Fathers haue blamed those verye much, vvho vvould not submitt themselues to the Obedience of those, vvho vvere of lesse qualitie then themselues: Of vvhom they did demaund, vvhen you did obey your Superiours; vvherefore did you doe it? vvas it for the loue of God? nothing so; For hath not this person the same place amōgst vs, as the other had? vvithout doubt hee is the vicar of God, and God by his mouth commaundeth vs, and causeth vs to vnderstand his vvill by his ordinances, euen as hee did by the mouth of the other. You therefore obey the Superiours, because you haue an inclination to them, as for respect of their persons. Alas, Alas! you doe no more then vvorldlings; for they doe the verie same, and not onely obey they the commaundements of those vvhom they loue, but they vvould not esteeme their loue vvell satisfied, if they did not followe as neere as they could their inclinations and affections, euen as the true Obedient doth towardes his superiours as to god himselfe. The Panimes, as wicked as they were, haue shewed vs example of this; for the diuell spake to them in diuers sortes of Idoles, some of them were statues of men, others of Rats, doggs, liones, serpents, and the like things, and these poore poeple did equallie adioyne fayth to all, being as obedient to the statue of a dog, as to that of a man, and to that of a ratt, as to that of a lion, without any difference: why did they this? because they did respect their Gods in these statues. Sainct Paul comaundeth vs to obey our Superiours allthough they should be wicked. Our Lord, Our Ladie, and Sainct Ioseph haue taught vs very well this manner of Obedience, in the voyage they made from Nazareth to Bethleem: for Cesar hauing made an edict, that all his subiects should assemble to the places where they were borne for to bee enrolled, they went louingly thither to satisfie this Obedience, although Cesar was a Panyme and Idolater. Our Lord would shew by this, that wee neuer ought to regard the face of those who commaund, prouided they haue power to commaud.

§.3. Lett vs now passe to the second property of blind Obedience. After this point is gayned, not to consider those who commaund, but to submitt our selues equally to all sorts of superiours, she may passe further, and come to the second, which is to obey without consideration of the intion, or the end wherefore the commaundement is made, contenting her selfe to knowe that it is made, without consideration, whether it bee well, or ill, or whether they haue reason, or not, to make

such

such or such a commaundement. Abraham became verye recommendable in this Obedience. God called him, and sayed to him, Abraham goe forth of thy country, and from thy kindred, that is to say, out of thy citty, and goe vnto the place, which I will shevve thee. Abraham went without reply. Alas, might not hee very vvell haue sayed; Lord thou bidst mee goe out of the citty, tell mee then if thou please by which side I shall goe forth? hee sayed not a vvorde, but vvent his vvay whither the spirit carryed him, not regarding in any sorte, whether hee went well or ill, wherefore, or for what intention. God had giuen him this commaundement so sodaynely, that he had not so much as appointed him the way which hee should take. O! certaynlie true Obedience maketh no discourse, but setteth it selfe simply to the worke, not inquiring any other thing then to obey. It seemeth that our Lord himselfe vvould shevv vnto vs, hovv much this kind of Obedience vvas acceptable vnto him, when hee appeared to Sainct Paul to conuert him; for hauing called him by his name, hee made him fall to the ground, and strooke him blind: doe you not note how to make him his disciple, hee cast him dovvne to humble him, and subiect him to himselfe? then in an instāt hee made him blinde, and cōmaunded him to goe into the citty to seeke out Ananias, and that hee must doe all that, which hee should commaund him. But vvherefore did not our Lord himselfe tell him what hee shoulde doe, without referring him to another, since hee had vouchsafed to speake to him for his conuersion? S. Paule did all that vvas commannded. It had cast our Lord nothing to haue tould him himselfe, that which hee caused Ananias to doe: but hee vvould that vvee should knovv by this example, how much hee loueth blind Obedience, since that it seemeth, hee had not made Sainct

Paul

blind,but to become trulie Obedient. VVhen our Lord gaue sight to the man borne blind, hee made clay, and put it vpon his eis, commaunding him to goe wash in the fountayne of Silo. Might not this poore blind man haue bene amazed at the meanes, where-of our Lord made vse to heale him, & say vnto him; Alas, what will you haue mee to doe, if I weere not blind, this weere enough to make mee loose my sight? Hee made none of all these considerations, but obeyed simply: euē so the true Obedient, beleeue simply they can doo all that any can commaund them, because they hould that all the cōmaundements come from God, or are made by his inspiration, the which cannot bee impossible by reason of the power of him who commaundeth. Naiman the Syrian, did not the like, vvhereby hee exposed himselfe to danger: for being a leaper, hee vvent to finde out Eliseus to heale him, because that all the remedies, that hee had made vse of to recouer his former health, did serue him to no purpose. Hearing that Eliseus did worke great meruailes, hee went vnto him, and being arriued, hee sent vnto him, one of his seruantes, to beseech him to bee pleased to cure him. VVherevppon Eliseus not comming forth of his chamber, sent him a message by his seruant, that hee should vvash himselfe seauen times in Iordayne, and bee healed. At this aunswer Naiman begā to bee displeased, and sayed: Are there not as good vvaters in our country as those are of the River of Iordan? and he vvould not goe thether: But his followers did shewe vnto him that hee should doe well to doe as the Prophett enioyned him, since it was so easie a thing. Hee being perswaded by their wordes, vvashed seauen times and was healed. You see hee put himselfe in danger not to recouer his health, by making so many considerations vppon that vvhich vvas commaunded.

§. 4. The

§.4. The third propertie of blind Obedience is, that she cōsidereth not, nor enquireth not so much by what meanes she shalbe able to doe that which is cōmaūded her. She knoweth that the way wherby she ought to goe is the Rule of Religion, and the cōmaundements of superiours; she taketh this way in simplicitye of hart, without exception, whether it were better to doe so, or so, prouided that she obey all equallye: for she knoweth verye well, that this sufficeth to bee acceptable to God, for whose loue she obeyth purely & simply. The second condition of louing Obedience is, that it is prompt: Now promptitude of Obediēce hath allwaies bene recomended to the Religious, as a most necessarie peece to obey well, & perfectly to obserue that which they haue vowed to God. This was the tokē that Eliezer tooke to knowe the virgin, that God had ordayned to bee the spouse of his Maisters sōne. Hee sayed to himselfe, the virgin of whome I shall demaund drinke, and she shall aunswere mee, I will not onely giue you, but furthermore I will drawe water for your camells, by this I shall knowe her to bee a worthy spouse for the sōne of my Maister, and as he thought vppon this, hee sawe a farre of the fayre Rebecca: Eliezer seing her so fayre and so gratious, drewe neere the well, where she should drawe water for her sheepe, hee made his demaūd, and the damsell aunswered, according to his designe yeas, sayed she, not onely to you, but to your camells also. Marke I pray you how readie and gratious she was, she did not spare her labour but was verye liberall thereof: for she did not faile to drawe water for so many camells as Eliezer brought with him, which would require much water. O! Truly the Obediences that are performed in an ill māner are not acceptable. There are some who obey, but it is with so much lazines and so frowarde a countenance

tenance, that they diminish very much the meritt of this vertue. Charitie and Obedience haue such vnion together, that they cãnot bee separated. Loue maketh vs to obey readilie; For hovv difficult soeuer the thing bee that is cõmaũded, hee who hath amorous obedience, vndertaketh it louingly: for Obedience being a principall part of humilitye, vvhich exceedingly loueth submission, consequentlie a sister truelie Obedient loueth the commaundement: and perceauing it a farre of, vvhatsoeuer it may bee, whether it may bee according to her gust or not, she imbraceth it, houldeth it deare, and cherisheth it tẽderlie. There is in the life of Sainct Pachome, an example of this promptitude of Obedience, that I will tell you: Amongst the Religious of Saint Pachome, there was one called Ionas, a man of great vertue, and sãctitie, who had the charge of the gardẽ, wherein hee had a figg Tree, that did beare verye fayre figgs. Now this figg Tree did serue for a tẽptatiõ to the young Religious, for euerie time they passed neere vnto it, they allvvaies cast their eyes on the figges. Saint Pachome hauing noted it, walking one day through the garden, looking towardes the figg Tree, savve the diuell on the topp, vvho vevved the figgs from the topp to the bottome, as the Religious did from the bottome to the topp. This great Saint vvho did no lesse desire to direct his Religious to a totall morfitification of their sences, then to the interiour mortification of their passions & inclinations, called Ionas, and commaunded him, that the next morning hee should not faile to cutt dovvne the figg Tree, vvhereto the good man replyed, Ah; My Father, these young poeple must bee a little supported, they must bee recreated in some thing, it is not for mee that I desire to keepe it. VVhereto the Father aunsvvered verie svveetlie; My Brother, you

vvill

vvil not obey simply and readilye, vvhat vvill you saye, that the tree shalbe more obedient then you? else vvhich hapned: for the next morning they foud the Tree dry and without sap, & neuer bare more fruite. The Good Ionas did say verie truelie, that it was not for himselfe that hee vvould keepe the Tree, for they noted, that from 75. yeares that hee had liued in Religion, and was gardiner, hee neuer had tasted any fruit of his garden, but hee was verye liberall to his Brethrē, but heerby hee learned hovv commendable prompt obedience vvas. Our Lord hath giuen vs continuall examples all the time of his life, of this promptitude in Obedience, for there could not bee any thing found so pliable and prōpt as hee was to the vvill of euerie one, and according to his example wee must learne to bee verie prōpt in Obedience, For it sufficeth not the amorous hart to doe that is commaunded, or that vvhich other make shewe to desire of him: if hee doe it not prōptlie, hee cannot see the houre come soone enough for to accomplish what is ordayned, to the end they may of nevv commaunde him some other thing. Dauid did but onely desire to drinke of the Cesterne of Bethleem, and instantly three valiant warriours departed inclining themselues, and crossed through the armie of the enimies to gett it for him. They weare exceeding readie to follovv the desire of the king: euē so vvee see that innumerable saints haue done to follovve, as it appeared to them, the inclinations and desires that the king of kings our Lord Iesvs had. VVat commaundement I beseech you did our Lord make, that might oblige Saincte Katherin of Siēna, to drinke or licke vvith her toūg the filth vvhich came forth of the wound, of that poore woman whom she did serue? and Lewis king of France to eate vvith the leapers, to encourage them to eate? certaynelie they weere not any waies

waies obliged to this, but knowing our Lord did loue it, and had demonstrated his inclination to the loue of our proper abiectiō, they thought in doing of such things to gratifie him, by following his inclination, with verye great loue, (allthough it weere verie repugnant to their sence). VVe are obliged to helpe our neighbour whē hee is in extreeme necessitie: neuerthelesse because almes is a counsell of our Lord, many willingly giue almes, as much as their meanes vvill permitt them. Novv vppon this Obedience to the councells amorouse Obedience is grafted, vvich maketh vs enterprise to follovv precisely euerie point of the desires, and intentions of God, and our superiours.

§.5. But I must aduertise you heere, of one deceate, into vvhich vvee may fall: For if those that vvould vndertake the practice of this vertue verie exactlie, vvould allvvaies keepe themselues attentiue, thereby to knovve the desires and inclinations of their Superiours, or God, they should loose their time infallibly; as for example, vvhilest I should enquire vvhat is the desire of God: I should not busie my selfe in keeping my repose & tranquillitie in being neere him, which is the desire hee hath now, since hee hath not giuen mee any other thing to doe: euen as hee who to followe the inclination, that our Lord hath manifested of succouring the poore, vvould goe from towne to towne to seeke them, vvho knovveth not that whiles he is in one, hee shall not serue those that are in another? I must goe to this busines in simplicitie of hart, giuing my almes vvhen I shall meete vvith the occasion, and not goe musing through the streats, from house to house, to enquire, if there bee any poore that I knowe not of: likevvise vvhen I perceaue the superiour desireth something of mee, I must yeald my selfe readie to doe it, not sifting vp and dovvne, if I if I may bee able to knovve that she hath some inclinatiō that I doe some other thing: for this would take away the peace and tranquillitie of hart, vvhich is the principall fruite of Louing Obedience.

§.6. The third condition of Obedience is perseuerance. Now our Lord hath taught vs this verye particularlye; as sainct Paul declareth in these termes, Hee hath beene made Obedient vntill death and magnifying this Obedience vnto death, the death of the crosse sayeth hee: In these wordes, vntill death, is presupposed, that hee had bene Obedient all the dayes of his life: during the vvhich there vvas no other thing seene then the traces of Obedience yealded by him, asvvell to his parents, as to many others, yea likevvise to the vvicked and impious; and as hee did begin by this vertue hee did likevvise end therevvith the course of this mortall life. The good Religious man Ionas hath furnished vs vvith tvvo examples about this subiect of perseuerance, and allthough hee did not so promptlye obey the commaundement that Saint Pachome gaue him, hee vvas notvvitstanding a Religious of great perfection; for from the time that hee entred into Religion vntill his death, hee continued in the Office of gardener vvithout euer changing it, during Sixtie fiue yeares that hee liued in that Monasterie, and the other exercise, vvherein hee did perseuere all his life time (as I haue before sayed) vvas to make matts of bulrushes, interlaced vvith leaues of Palmes; so that hee dyed making of them. This is verie great vertue to perseuere so long in such an exercise: for to doe a thing ioyfully that is commaunded for one time, as often as they vvill, this costs nothing; But vvhen one shall say to you, you shall allwaies allvvaies doe this, all the time of your life; heere it is vvhere vertue shineth or vvherin the difficultie lieth. Consider then vvhat I haue sayed to you touching Obedience, but yett one worde more. Obedience is of so great vvorth, that she is companion to Charitie, and these tvvo vertues are those that giue the prize & vvorth to all the others; in such sort that vvithout them, all the others are nothing: if you haue not these tvvo vertues, you haue no vertue at all: if you haue these, you haue vvith them all the other vertues.

§. 7. But lett vs passe further, and leauing apart the generall Obedience to the commaundments of God, lett vs speake of Religious Obedience. I say then if the Religious obey not: they shall neuer haue any vertue; For it is Obedience principallie that maketh vs Religious, as being the proper and peculier vertue of Religion: yea, euen to haue the desire of martirdome for the loue of God is nothing, if you haue not Obedience, VVe read in the life of Sainct Pachome, that one of his Religious, (vvho all the time of his Nouitiat had perseuered in exemplar submission and humilitie) came to Saint Pachome transported vvith great feruour, and sayed to him; that hee had a verye great desire of martyrdome, and that hee should neuer bee sattiffyed vntill hee did attayne it; and besought him very humbly, that hee vvould praye to God that it might bee accomplished. The Holy Father endeauored to moderate this feruour; but the more that hee did saye, the more hott the other vvas in the pursuite of his desire: The Saint sayed to him; My sonne, it is more vvorthe to liue in Obedience, and to dye euerie day liuing, by a continuall mortification of a mans selfe, then to martyr our selues in our imagination; Hee dieth a good Martyr vvho mortifieth himselfe well;

vvell: it is a greater martirdome to perseuere all a mãs life in Obediẽce, then to dye vvith one stroke of a svvorde. Liue in peace, My sonne, and quiet your spiritt, diuerting it from this desire. The Religious who assured himselfe that his desire proceeded from the Holy Ghost, abated nothing at all of his heat, continually soliciting the Father that hee would praye, that his desire might bee fullfilled. After some shorte time, they had nevves proper for his consolation; For a certayne Saracene a captayne of theeues, came to a Mountayne neere to the Monasterie: wherevppon Sainct Pachome called the Monke to him, and sayed to him, well my sonne, the houre is come that you haue so much desired, goe in good time to cut vvood in the mountayne. The Religious being wholie replenished vvith ioy went his vvay chanting and singing psalmes to the praise of God, and giuing thankes vnto him, that hee had vouchsafed to doe him the honour, as to giue him this occasion to die for his loue: in fine, hee thought of nothing lesse, then that the successe vvould fall out as it did. Novv behould so soone as those theeues had perceaued him, they came towardes him, and began to laye hould of him and to threaten him; for a while hee vvas verye valiant: Thou art dead, sayed they; I demaũd no other thing sayed hee then to dye for God, and the like aunswers. The Saracẽs led him to the place vvhere their Idoll was, to make him adore it; vvhen they savve that hee did constantlie refuse it, they began to sett themselues vppon him to kill him. Alas, this poore Religious man, so valiant in his owne imagination, seeing the blade at his throate; Ah, of pittie sayed hee, doe not kill mee, I vvill doe all that you desire of mee, I am yet yõg take pittie on mee, it would bee a great losse to shortẽ my dayes. In fine, hee adored their Idoll, and these miscreants mocking and beating

beating him soundlye, left him to retourne to his Monasterie. VVhere being arriued more dead then aliue, all pale and gastlie, Sainct Pachome, vvho was gone forth to meete him, sayed to him: well my sonne, hovv goeth it, and and vvho is hee that hath thus vsed you? Then the poore Religious ashamed and confused in himselfe, because hee had had so great Pride, vvas not able to support himselfe. seeing hee had commited so haynous a crime, but casting himselfe before the Father confessed it, vvhom the Father readilye did helpe, causing the brethren to pray for him, and making him aske pardon of God, putt him in good estate, and then gaue him good aduertisments, saying: My sonne, remember thy selfe, that it is more vvorth to haue good desires to liue according to the communitie, and to haue no other vvill, then fidelitie in obseruance of the Rules, not enterprising, nor desiring any other thing, then that which is contayned in them, then to haue great desires to put in execution imaginarie meruailes, vvhich are good for no other thing, then to make our hartes svvell with pride, and to cause vs to despise others, esteeming our selues better thē they. O hovv good it is to liue vnder the shelter of Holy Obedience, rather then to retire our selues out of her armes, to seeke for that which seemeth more perfect vnto vs: if thou vvouldest haue bene contēt to doe as I aduised thee, to mortifie thy selfe liuing, then thou vvouldest haue desired nothing lesse then death, & shouldest not haue fallen as now thou hast done: but bee of good courage, and remember henceforth to liue in submission, and assure thy selfe that God hath pardoned thee. Hee obeyed the councell of the saint, comporting himselfe vvith much more humilitie all the time of his life.

§. 8. I say yet furthermore, that Obedience is of

of no lesse meritt the Charitie, for to giue a cupp of water for Charitie is vvorth the kindome of heauē, our Lord himselfe hath sayed it; doing so much for Obedience you vvill gayne the same: The verye least thing done for Obedience is most acceptable to God: eate for Obedience, your eating is more pleasing to God, then the fasts of Anchoritts, if they bee done without Obedience; if you rest by Obedience, your repose is much more meritorious, and acceptable to God, then voluntarie labour: but you will say to mee, what profitt shall come to mee for practiceing this louing Obedience so exactly vvith the foresayed conditions, blindlie, promptlye, and perseuerantlie? O my deare Daughthers! the person that vvill performe it, shall enioy in his soule continuall tranquillitye, and the most holie peace of our Lord vvhich surpasseth all vnderstanding: Hee shril haue no account to render of his actions, since they haue all bene exercised by Obedience, as vvell touching the Rules, as the Superiours. what happines more profitable and desirable then this? Certaynely the true Obedient (speaking this by the way) loueth hir Rules, honoureth thē, and esteemeth them dearely, as the true vvay wherein hee ought to walke to the vnion of his spiritt vvith God: Therefore hee neuer departeth from this vvaye, nor frō the obseruance of those things that are appointed therein in forme of direction, no more then from those that are there commaunded.

The soule truelie Obedient shall liue as svvetlye and peaceably as a childe vvho is in the armes of his deare mother, vvho troubleth not himselfe vvith that vvhich may happen: whether the Mother carrie him on the right hand, or on the left, hee taketh no care; euen so the true Obedient, lett them commaund him this, or that, hee troubleth not himselfe: prouided that they commaund him, and hee bee

allvvaies

allwaies betwene the armes of Obedience (I would, say in the exercise of Obedience) his content. Now to such a one, I may very well assure on the part of God the Paradice of eternall life, as also dureing the course of this mortall life hee shall enioy true tranquillitie, for it cannot bee doubted.

§. 9. Now you demaund, if you bee obliged on payne of sinne to doe all that the Superiours tell you, you must doe as when you render account, if you must hould for a commaundement all that the Superiour hath sayed to you, which is proper for your aduancement, O no, my Daughter, Superiours no more then confessours haue not intention allwaies to oblige the inferiours by the commaundements they make, & when they will doe it, they vse that worde of commaundement, vppon payne of disobedièce, and then the inferiours are obliged to obey vnder payne of sinne, allthough the commaundement were verie light, and the thing but little: but otherwise not: for they giue aduise in three sortes, some by forme of commaundement, others by way of councell, and others by way of simple direction. In the Cōstitutions & Rules it is euen the verie same, for their are articles that say: The sisters may doe such a thing: and others that saye, they shall doe itt, or take heede they doe it not: some of these are councells, and others commaundements, those who would not subiect themselues to the councells and direction, they should transgresse against louing Obedience, and this should witnesse in them great remisnesse of hart, and of hauing verie little of the of God: to doe but onelie that which is commaunded, and no more: and allthough they doe not transgresse the Obedience that they haue vowed, which are those of cōmaundements, and councells which they are not subiect vnto direction, neuerthelesse they trangresse louing Obedience, vvhich all the Religious of the Visitation ought to pretend and practice.

§. 10. You aske me if a person might not verie vvell thinke, vvhen they change your Superiour, that she is not so capable, as the other you haue had, and that she hath not so much knovvledg of the vvay, whereby she ought to guid you. Certaynelie vvee are not able to hinder our thoughts; but to resolue or abide in thẽ, this is that which vvee ought not to doe; For if Balaam vvas so vvell instructed by an asse, vvith much more reason ought vvee to beleeue, that God, vvho hath giuẽ vs this Superiour vvill cause her to teach vs according to his vvill, although it may bee not according to our vvill. Our Lord hath promised that the true obedient person shall neuer erre. No truelie, the person vvho vvill follovv indistinctlye the vvill and direction of the Superiours vvhõ God shall establish ouer him; although the Superiours vvere neuer so ignorant, and did leade their inferiours according to their ignorãce, yea through rugged and dãgerous waies: the inferiours submitting thẽselues, to all that is not manifestlie sinne, nor against the cõmaundements of God, and the Holie church, I can assure you that they shall neuer erre. The true obedient person, sayeth the holye scripture, shall speake of victories, that is to saye, hee shall become victorious in all difficulties through vvhich hee shalbe carried by Obedience, and shall come forth of the vvaies through vvhich hee did enter by Obedience, vvith honour, hovv dangerous soeuer they may bee: it should be a pretty kind of Obedience, if vvee vvould not obey but those Superiours who should be pleaseing to vs: If this day you haue a Superiour of great esteeme, asvvell for her quallitie, as for her vertues, you vvillinglie obey vvith a good hart; to morrovv you shall haue another, vvho vvill not bee

so

so much esteemed, ād you doe not obey her With so good a hart as the other, yealding her the like Obedience: not esteeming so much, that vvhich she sayeth to you, nor performing your dutye vvith that satisfaction. Ah! vvho seeth not, that you did obey the other out of your inclinations and not purelie for God· if it vvere so, you should haue as much pleasure, and make as great esteeme, of that which this telleth you, as you did of that vvhich the other did saye. I haue often vsed to speake one thing, that is good allvvaies to bee spoken of: because it ought allvvaies to bee obserued, to vvitt: That all our actions ought to bee practiced according to the superiour part: for it is so that vvee must liue in this house, and not according to our sences, and inclinations. VVithout doubt I shall haue more satisfaction, touching the inferiour part of my soule to doe that vvhich one superiour to whome I haue an inclination, shall cōmaund mee, then to doe that another biddeth mee, to vvhome I haue it not: but if I doe obey equallie touching the superiour part, it sufficeth, and my Obedience is vvorth more, whē I haue lesse content in doeing it, for heerein vvee shevvé it is for God, and not for our pleasure that wee doe obey: There is nothing more common in the vvorld, then in this manner to obey those vvee loue: but for the other, it is exceeding rare, and not practiced but in Religion. But it may bee you vvill say, Is it not permitted to disapproue that vvhich this Superiour doeth, nor to speake, or consider vvherefore she maketh these ordinances, which the other did not? O! truly no, neuer my deare daughters, so that it bee not manifestlie against the commaundements of God: for then vvee must neither obey nor approue it: but in vvhatsoeuer else, the inferiours ought allvvaies to make their proper iudgmēt to beleeue and cōfesse, that the Superiours doe verie vvell, and that they haue good reason to doe it: she that should doe otherwise, should make her selfe Superiour, ād the Superiour her inferiour, since shee maketh her selfe examiner of her cause: No, vvee must bovve our shoulders vnder the burthen of holie obedience, beleeuing that both these Supeciours haue had good reason to make the cōmaundements they haue done, although different, and contrarie the one to the other.

§. 11. But shall it not bee lavvefull for one that hath allreadie liued long in Religiō, and vvho hath done great seruices therein, to vvithdravve herselfe a little from obedience, at least in some small matter? O good God! vvhat should this bee, but to doe as a Maister Pilot, vvho haueing brought his barke to the haeuē, after hee had lōg & painfullie laboured to saue it frō the rageing vvaues of the sea, would in the end, being arriued in the hauen, breake his shipp, and cast himselfe into the sea; should not one iudge rightlie that hee vvere a foole? For if he had intended this hee needed not to haue laboured so much to haue brought his barque within the hauē.

The Religious man vvho hath begun, hath not done all, if hee doe not perseuere vnto the ende, we must not say, that it appertayneth but to Nouices to bee so exact; although that vvee see ordinarilie in all Religions, the nouices verye exact & mortified. It is not that they bee more obliged then the Professed, O no; for they are not obliged as yet any thing at all; but they perseuere in obedience, for to obtayne the grace of Profession. But the Profest are obliged thereunto in vertue of the vowes they haue made, vvhich hauing done, it is not sufficient to bee Religious, if they obserue them not. The Religious vvho thinketh she may bee remisse in any thing after her Profession, yea after she hath liued a long time in Religion, deceaueth her selfe exceedingly.

Our

Our Lord shevved himselfe mu h more exact in his death, then in his infancye, permitting himselfe to bee handled, and vsed as I haue sayed, and this is enough of obedience, for to vvinne your affection thereynto.

§. 12. It resteth onely to speake a word touching the question was made to mee yesterday in the euẽing; to witt, if it bee lavvfull for the sisters to tell one an other, that they haue bene mortified by the Superiour, or Maistresse of Nouices vppõ any occasion? I aunsvvere, this may be spoken of, in three sortes; The first is, that a sister may say: good God! sister, our Motherknoweth verie well howto mortifie mee; being verie glad, because she hath bene worthy of this mortification, and because the Superiour by this meanes hath caused some little gayne to her soule; saying she had good reason so to doe, and not to spare mee. Therby imparting her content to her sister, to the ende that she assist her to thanke God: The second manner in vvhich one may speake, is to disburdẽ her selfe, finding the mortificatiõ or correctiõ to bee verie heauie, she goeth to discharge it vppõ her sisterto whome she imparteth it, who bemoaning her, litghtneth in some sort her trouble: ãd this mãner is not alltogether so supportable as the first, because they cõmitt an imperfectiõ to cõplayne: but the third should bee absolutely naught, to witt, to speake by way of murmuratiõ and dispite, and to make it knowẽ that the Superiour hath done wronge. Now, as for this kind, I knowe verie well they doe it not in this house by the grace of God: of the first kind although it bee not euill tospeake, it shouldbe notvvitstanding verye good not to speake, but rather to exercise them selues internallie and reioyce vvith God. In the second manner truelye it must not bee done, for by meanes of our complayning, wee loose the meritt of mortification. Doe you knowve what must bee done, when we are corrected and mortified? wee must take this mortification as an apple of loue, and hide it in our hart, kissing it and cherishing it the most tenderlye that is possible for vs. Furthermore, to saye, I come from speaking vvith our mother, and I am as dry as I vvas before; I see there is no other course but to adhere to God: For my part I receaue not any consolation from creatures, I haue bene lesse comforted then I vvas, this is not to the purpose. The sister to vvhome she speaketh this, should aunsvvere verie gently: my deare sister, if you were so vvell vnited to God, as you say you must be, before you goe to speake to our mother, then you vvould not haue any discontent, because she hath not comforted you. But in the sence you speake of, that one must endeauour to vnite herselfe to God, take heede that in seeking God when creatures faile, hee permitt not himselfe so to bee found: For hee vvil bee sought before all things, and in the contempt of all things; Because creatures doe not contēt mee, I vvill seeke the creator; O no, The Creator doth deserue that I forsake all for him, euen as his vvill is, that wee should doe. Therefore vvhen vvee depart from the Superiour, full of ariditye, not hauing receaued one onely dropp of consolation, of necessitie wee must beare our ariditie and drinesse as a pretious balme, made of the affections that weē haue receaued in holy prayer, as balme, I say, and lett vs bee very carefull not to spill any part of this pretious liquor, which hath bene sent vs from heauen as a noble gift, to the end wee may perfume our hart, vvith the depriuation of consolation, vvhich vvee thought to meete with, in the vvordes of the Superiour. But there is a thing to bee noted vppon this subiect, vvhich is this, diuers times you carrie a dry and hard hart,

vvhen

vvhen you goe to speake to your Superiour, which cannot bee capable to bee vvatered, or moistned vvith the vvater of consolation, for so much as it is not susceptible, nor able to receaue vvhat the Superiour sayeth: and although she speake verie well according to your necessitie: notvvitstanding it seemeth not so to you. At another time whē you shall haue a tender and well disposed hart, she shall not speake aboue three or four vvords, much lesse profitable for your perfection, then the other vvere, but shall comfort you: and vvherefore? because your hart vvas disposed for it. It seemeth to you that Superiours haue consolation vppon the top of their lipps, and that they can povvre it forth easilye into the harts of vvhom they please: which neuerthelesse is not so: for they cannot allvvaies bee of one humour, no more then others: happie is that person that can keepe equallitie of hart, in the thrōg of all this inequallity of successes: one vvhile vvee shalbe comforted, a little time after wee shall haue a dry hart, in such sort that it will cost vs extreme deare to produce a word of comfort.

§. 13. Further you demaunded of mee, vvhat I had to say to you touching some exercise proper to kill selfe iudgment; to vvhich I aunsvvere, that it is best, faythfully to abridge it from all sortes of discourse, wherein it will become maister, making it to knovve that it is but the seruant. For, my deare Daughters, it is by reiterared acts that wee gayne vertues; allthough there haue bene some soules, to vvhom God hath giuen them all in an instāt. Therefore vvhen you find in youre selfe a suggestión to iudge, vvhether a thing bee vvell or ill ordayned, cutt of the discourse of your ovvne iudgment: and a little after vvhen one shall say to you, that such a thing must be done in such a manner, doe not studye to discourse or discerne, if it vvould bee better othervvise: but make your proper iudgment to bee confident, that it could neuer bee done, then in the manner that they haue tould you. If they appoint you any exercise, permitt not your iudgment to discerne, whether it bee proper for you, or not, and bee warie, for although you doe the thing, euen as it is commaunded, proper iudgment verie often obeyeth not, I vvould say, submiteth not it selfe; For it approueth not of the commaundement, the vvhich is ordinarilie the cause of the repugnance, that wee haue, to submitt our selues to doe that vvhich is desired of vs, because the vnderstanding and the iudgment represent to the will, that this ought not to bee so, or, that other meanes must bee vsed, to doe that vvhich they ordayned, then those that are appointed vs, and she cannot submitt her selfe, for so much as she allvvaies maketh more account of the reasons, that proper iudgment shevveth her, then of any other; For euerie one beleeueth his ovvne iudgment is the best, I neuer mett vvith any vvho did not esteeme his iudgment, but tvvo, vvho did confesse to mee, that they had not any iudgment: and the one comming to mee at a time, sayed: Sir, I pray you speake some what to me of such a matter, for I haue not iudgment enough to comprehend it; This did astonish mee verie much. VVee haue in our age a verye remarkable example, of the mortification of proper iudgment in a great doctour, a man of great renovvne, vvho composed a booke that hee intituled Of Dispensations and commaundement, the which booke falling into the hands of the Pope, hee iudged that it cōtayned some erronious propositiōs, and did write to this Doctour, that hee should raze thē out of his booke. This Doctour receauing the cōmaundement, submitted his iudgmēt so absolutelie, that hee vvould not cleare, nor explaine his

vvoorke

vvorke, to iustifie himselfe, but contrarivvise beleeued hee had done amisse, and that hee was deceaued by his ovvne iudgment, and going vp into a pullpitt, hee read alovvde the letter that the Pope had written, tooke the booke and rent it in peeces, saying vvhith a lovvde voice, that the Pope in iudging this fact, had iudged very well, and that hee did approue with all his hart the Censure, and Fatherlie correction that he had vouchsafed to giue him, as being most iust and svveete to him, who did deserue to bee rigorouslie punished, and that hee vvas much astonished that hee had bene so blinded, as to bee deceaued by his ovvne iudgment, in a thing so manifestly wicked. Hee was in noe sort obliged to doe this, because the Pope did not commaund it, but onely that hee should raze out of his booke certayne things that did not seeme good: For (vvhich is verie remarkable) it vvas not hereticall, nor so manifestly erroneus, that it might not bee defẽded. Hee gaue testimonie of great vertue in this occasiõ, and an admirable mortification of proper iudgment. VVee mortifie verie often our sences, because selfe-will intrudeth it selfe to mortifie thẽ; and it would bee a shamefull thing to shewe ones selfe stubborne in obedience: what would they say of vs? but in proper iudgment, verye rarelie, are any foũd vvell mortified. For to approue that vvhich is commaunded, to bee good, to loue and esteeme it as a thing which is good and profitable for vs aboue all other things, O this is that wherein Iudgmẽt is foũd backward and stubborne. For there are many who say, I will willinglie doe that you desire; but I see well it would bee better otherwise. Alas! vvhat doe you, if you nourish your iudgment in this manner? without doubt it will make you drũke: for there is no differẽce betweene a drunkẽ person, and hee who is full of his owne iudgmẽt. Dauid one day being in the country vvhich his souldiers wearyed, & tyred out vvith famine, not hauing any thing left vvhere-of to eate, hee sent to the husband of Abigaill for victualls: by ill happ this poore man was drunke, and talking like a drunkard sayed, Dauid after hee hath eatten vp all his robberies, hath sent to my house to ruine it as hee hath done other places. And so would not giue him any thing. Liue God, sayed Dauid, I will repay the not acknovvledgment, of the good that I haue done to this man in sauing his flockes, and not permitting that any thing of his should perish, nor any harme befall him. Abigaill vnderstanding the designe of Dauid, the next morning went to meete him, vvith presents to appease him, vsing these tearmes: My Lord vvhat vvill you doe to a foole? yesterday my husband vvas drunke, hee spake wickeddlye, but hee spake in drinke and as a foole, Sir lett your anger bee appeased, and lay not your hands vppon him, For you vvilbe sory, to haue layed your hands vppon a foole. The same excuses may bee made of our iudgment, as of a drunkē person, for the one is no more capable of reason then the other. VVee must therfore haue a very great care to hinder the making of these considerations, to the end wee bee not drunke with the reasons of proper iudgment, principallie in that vvhich concerneth obedience.

In fine you desire to knovve, if you ought to haue a great confidence, and care to aduertise one an other in charitie, of your defects. Yea, without doubt, my Daughter, this must bee done; for to what purpose doe you see a defect in your sister if you endeuour not to take it away by the meanes of an aduertisment, Neuerthelesse you must bee discreete in this busines, for it will bee no time to aduertise a sister, vvhiles you see her indisposed, or troubled vvith melancholie: for if you make it then, thē, she willbee in danger to reiect the aduertisimēt, at the first onsett. You must expect a vvhile, and then aduertise her in confidence and Charitie. If a sister speake vvordes to you, that sauour of murmuration, and that othervvise she haue her hart quiet, vvithout doubt you may say vnto her confidentlye, verilie sister this is not vvell done; but if you perceaue she hath some passion moued in her hart, then the discourse must bee changed the most dexterousl that you can. You say you feare to aduertise a Sister so often of the faultes that she hath committed, because it vvill take from her assurance, and make her sooner faile, through force of feare: O God! vvee must not iudg thus of the Sisters heere inclosed; for this appertayneth not to any other then to the maydens of the vvorld; to loose assurance vvhen they are aduertised of their faults: Our Sisters doe loue their ovvne abiection too much to doe so, although they bee troubled: but on the contrarie they vvill take greater courage, and more care to amend themselues, not to avoyde the aduertisments (for I suppose they doe exceedinglye loue all that vvhich may make them become vile and abiect in their owne eyes) but to the end, they may better performe their dutie, and yeald themselues more conformable to their vocation.

THE

THE TVVELFTH ENTER-TAINEMENT.

OF SIMPLICITIE AND RELIGIOVS Prudence.

§. 1. THe vertue whereof we are novv to treat, is so neceſſarie, that allthough I haue oftentimes ſpoken there-of, notwithſtanding, you haue deſired, that I make an entire diſcourſe of the ſame. Novv in the firſt place muſt bee made knovvne, what this vertue of Simplicitie is. You knovve that, commonlie vvee call a thing ſimple, vvhen it is not imbrodered, pleated, or of many coullours: For example, wee ſaye, behould a perſon that is ſimply apparelled, becauſe he hath no lineing in his garmēt: I meane his habitt is but of one ſtuffe, and this is a ſimple garment. Simplicitie therefore is no other thing, then a pure and ſimple act of Charitie, which hath but one onely end, vvhich is, to attayne to the loue of God. And our ſoule is then ſimple, vvhen vvee haue no other pretenſion in all whatſoeuer wee doe. The famous hiſtorie of the hoſteſſes of our Lord, Martha, and Magdalene, is verie remarkable for this ſubiect: For doe you not ſee that Martha, although her end was laudable, to vvitt, to entertayne our Lord in the beſt manner: yet she vvas not free from being reprehended by this diuine Maiſter, for ſo much as beſides the verie good end, that she had in her ouer-buſie care, she did yet behould our Lord in as much as hee vvas man, and therefore she did beleeue hee vvas as others, vvhom not one onely meate, or one manner of dreſſing, vvould ſuffice, and this vvas that vvhich

caused

caused her to stirr vpp and dovvne so much, to prepare many dishes: and so she doubled this first end of the loue of God in her exercise, vvith diuers other petty-pretenses, for which she vvas reprehēded of our Lord: Martha, Martha, thou troublest thy selfe vvith many things, allthough one onely is necessarie, which is, this that Magdalene hath chosē, and vvhich shall not bee taken from her. Therefore this act of simple charitie, which causeth vs not to regard, nor haue any other eye in all our actions then the sole desire to please God, is the part of Marie, which is onely necessarie, and this is Simplicitie, a vertue vvhich is inseparable with Charitie; forsomuch as it looketh right towards God: neither cā it suffer any mixture of proper interest: for otherwise, it would not bee Simplicity; for she cannot suffer any doubling of creatures, nor any consideration of them, God alone findeth place in her. This vertue is purely Christiā. The Panymes, yea those who haue discoursed best of vertues had not any knovvledg thereof, no more then of Humilitie. For of Magnificēce, Liberallitie, and Constancye, they haue writtē verie well, but of Simplicitie, and Humilitie, nothing at all. Our Lord himselfe is descended from heauen to giue knovvledg to mē, asvvel of the one, as of the other vertue, othervvise this so necessarie doctrine had allvvaies bene vnknovvne. Bee prudēt as serpents, sayeth hee to his Apostles; but moreouer bee as simple as Doues. Learne of the Doue to loue God in simplicitye of hart, hauing but one onely pretence, and one onely end in all that you shall doe, but imitate not onely the simplicitie of the loue of Doues, in that they haue allvvaies but one mate, for vvhom they doe all, and vvhō onely they will please, but imitate them also in the simplicitye that they practice in the exercise and testimonie that they yeald of their loue; for they bucsie not them-thēselues vvith many things, nor many loue toyes, but they make simply their little gronings and mournings about their young ones, and content themselues with their companie, when they are present. Simplicitie banisheth from the soule, the vnprofitable care and solicitude that many haue to seeke out diuersitie of exercises and meanes for to bee able to loue God: so as they say, that if they doe not all vvhich the sisters haue done, in their opiniō they knovve not hovv to bee contēt. Poore people they torment themselues to find the art hovv to loue God, and knovve not, that it hath no other point then to loue him; they thinke there is a certayne subtilitie to attayne this loue, the vvhich notvvithstanding is not found but in simplicitye.

§. 2. Now vvhen vvee say, that there is not any art therein, it is not to dispise certayne bookes which are intituled: *The art hovv to loue God*: For these bookes teach that there is no other art then to sett themselues to loue: that is to say, to put themselues into the practice of those things, that are pleasing vnto him, vvhich is the onely meanes to find and attayne this sacred loue; prouided that this practice bee vndertaken in simplicitye, vvithout trouble and solicitude. Simplicitye embraceth truely the meanes, that are prescribed to each one according to their vocatiō, for to attayne to the loue of God, in such sort, that she vvill not haue any other motiue, to gayne or to be incited to the search of this loue but the end it selfe: otherwvise she should not bee perfectlie simple; For she cannot endure any other aspect, hovv perfect soeuer it may bee, thē the pure loue of God vvhich is her onely pretence. For example, if one goe to the office, and you aske her whether goe you? I goe to the office aunsvvereth she, but vvherefore goe you thither? [illegible] ...ise God; but wherfore at this hower rather [illegible] to p[illegible] ...then at another?

ther? it is because the clocke hath stroken, if I doe not goe I shalbe noted. To goe to the office to praise God is verie good; but the motiue is not simple: For simplicitye requireth, that vvee goe thereunto drawne vvith desire to please God vvithout any other respect, and the like is to bee sayed in all other occasions. Novv before wee passe further, a deceyt must bee discouered, vvhich is in the spiritt of diuers, touching this vertue; for they thinke that Simplicitye is contrarie to Prudence, and that they bee opposite the one to the other; it is not so, for vertues doe neuer contradict the one the other; but haue a verie great vnion together. The vertue of simplicitie is opposite, and contrarie to the vice of craft and deceaite; a vice vvhich is the source and spring from vvhence proceedeth policye, subtiltye and doublenesse: Crafte is a masse of subtilties, deceytes, and threacheries; it is by the meanes of crafte that vvee find out inuentions to deceaue the spiritt of our neighbour; and of those vvith vvhom wee haue to doe, for to leade to the point vve aime at, vvhich is to make them vnderstand, that wee haue no other meaning in our hart, then the same wee manifest by our wordes, nor any other knovvledg of the subiect vvhereof there is question; a thing which is infinitly contrarie to simplicitye, vvhich requireth that vvee haue the interiour entirely cōforme to the exteriour.

§. 3. I intend not therefore to say that wee must demonstrat our motions of passions by the exteriour, euen as vvee haue them in the interiour; for it is not against simplicitye to sett a good countenance on the matter, so as they may conceaue nothing amisse. There must be allwaies made a difference betweene the effects of the Superiour part of our soule, and the effectes of the inferiour part. It is true that by fitts vvee haue great cōmotions in the

interiour

interiour of our soule, vppon the encounter of a correction, or of some other contradiction: but this commotiō proceedeth not from our vvill: but all this sensible apprenhension passeth in the inferiour part, the superiour part consenteth not at all to this; but agreeth, accepteth, and findeth this encounter good. we haue sayed, that Simplicitye hath her continuall aspect in the purchaseing of the loue of God; novv the loue of God requireth of vs; that wee restrayne our feelings and feares, and that wee mortifie, and annihilate thē; wherefore it doeth not require, that wee should manifest thē and make thē knowen to others; Therefore it is not want of Simplicie, to sett a good countenāce on it, whē wee are moued in the interiour; But should not this deceaue those who should see vs, say you; for so much as although we should be verie vnmortified, they would beleeue that wee are very vertuous? This reflectiō, my deare sister, vpō what they will say, or what they will thinke of you, is contrarie to simplicitie; for as wee haue sayed, she hath no other eye, then to cōtēt God, ād not creatures, but onely as the loue of God requireth it. After that the simple soule hath done an actiō that she iudgeth is her dutie to doe, she thinketh no more thercō, and if it cōmeth into her mind to thinke what they will say, or what they will thinke of her, she prōptly cutteth of all this, because she cānot endure any stop or stay, to diuerte her in her designe, which is to keepe her selfe attentiue to her God, to increase in her selfe his diuine loue; the cōsideratiō of creatures moueth not her for any thing, for she referreth all to the Creator. The same is to be sayed of that which one may say: whether it bee not permitted to make vse of Prudence, for the not discouering to superiours, that which wee shall thinke may trouble thē, or our selues, in speaking of it: for Simplicitie regardeth onely if it bee expediēt to speake, or doe such a thing, & thē she putteth her selfe to the woorke, not loosing time to cōsider, if the superiour bee troubled, or my selfe. If I haue declared some thought I haue had of her; or if she be not troubled, nor I neither; if it bee expediēt for mee to speake it, I will not omitt simply to declare my minde; let it happen after as God will. when I shall haue done my dutie, I will not put my selfe to payne for any other thing: wee must not allwaies feare trouble so much, whether it be for our selues, or for another; for the trouble of ones selfe is not a sinne; if I knovve that goeing into some cōpanie, one will speake some woordes that will trouble and moue mee, I ought not to auoyde the goeing amōge thē; but I ought to carrie my selfe armed with the confidence vvhich I ought to haue in the diuine protectiō, that it will fortifie mee to ouercome and vanquish my nature, against which I will make warre; This trouble is not made but in the inferiour part of our soule, wherefore wee must not bee astonished, when it is not obeyd; I would say, when wee doe not cōsent to that, which it suggesteth to vs: for that must not bee done. But from whence cōmeth this trouble, but for want of Simplicitie; forsomuch as wee muse oftentimes to thinke what one vvill say, and what one will thinke, in steed of thinking on God, and of that which may make vs more pleasing to his diuine bountie and goodnes; but if I speake such a thing, I shall remayne in more payne thē I was before I spake it: vvell, if you will not declare it, and that it be not necessarie, hauing no need of instruction in this act, resolue your selfe readilye, and loose not the time to consider, vvhether you ought to declare it, or not. For there is no reason to make an hovvers consideration vppon all the triffling actions of our life: Moreouer I thinke in my opinion, that it is better and more expedient to tell our Superiour the thoughts which mortifie vs most, thē many others which serue for nothing, but for to prolong the discourse wee haue vvith her, and if you remayne in payne, it is nothing but immortification that causeth it; for to vvhat purpose vvill I speake of that, which is not necessarie for my profitt, and omitt that which may more mortifie mee.-Simplicitie, as vvee allreadie sayed, seeketh nothing but the pure loue of God, the vvhich is neuer found so vvell, as in the mortification of our selues, and according to the measure that mortification encreaseth, so much the more neere vvee approche vnto the place vvhere wee shal find his diuine loue. Moreouer the Superiours ought to bee perfect, or att least they ought to doe the vvorkes of the perfect: and therefore they haue their eares open, for to receaue and vnderstand all that wee vvill say to them, vvithout putting themselues to much payne. Simplicitye intermedleth not with what others doe or vvill doe. She thinketh of her selfe, yet not for her selfe doth she thinke but what is truelie necessarie, for as for other things she allwaies speedilie turneth away her thoughts. This vertue hath a great affinitye with humilitye, which permitteth vs not to haue a vvorse opinion of any, then of our selues.

§. 4. You aske, hovv Simplicitye must bee obserued in cōuersations and recreations? I aunswere you as in all other actions, although in this there must bee had a holy freedome & libertie for to entertayne our selues vvith discourse, vvhich serue the spiritt for matter of ioy, & recreation. VVee must bee verie reall in conuersation, yet wee must not therefore bee inconsiderate, for so much as simplicitye allwaies followeth the Rule of the loue of God; but it may happen that you shall speake some little thing, which may seeme not to bee so vvell taken of all as you would desire: you must not for all this bee musing to make reflections vppon all your vvordes; No! For it is without all doubt, selfe-loue that causeth vs to make these inquiries, whether that vvhich wee haue sayed or done bee well taken; Holy simplicitie runneth not after her vvordes, nor her actions, but she leaueth the euēt of them to the diuine prouidence, to the which she is souueraignelie vnited: she tourneth not her selfe to the right hand, or to the left: but followeth simply on her way: so that if she encounter therein any occasion to practise some vertue, she serueth her selfe carefully thereof, as of a meanes proper to attayne to her perfection, vvhich is the loue of God, but she presseth not her self too earnestly to search them; neither doth she contemne them, she troubleth her selfe vvith nothing, she houldeth her selfe quiet and peacefull, in the confidence she hath, that God knoweth her desire vvhich is to please him, & this sufficeth her. But how may wee accord two things so contrarie? you say on the one side, that wee must haue a great care of our perfection and aduancemēt, and on the other, you forbidd vs to thinke thereon. Marke heere, if you please, the miserie of humayne spiritt; for it neuer stayeth, or resteth it selfe in a mediocritie; but it runneth ordinarilie into extremities; VVee haue this defect from our good mother Eue, for she did euen as much, when the wicked spiritt did tempt her to eate of the forbidden fruite. God hath forbidden, sayed she, that wee should touch it, in stead of saying hee had forbidden them to eate it. VVee doe not say, that you may not thinke of your aduancemēt: but that you thinke not thereon with too much eagernes and trouble.

§ 5. It is also want of simplicitie that wee make so many considerations, vvhen wee see the faultes one of another, to knovve whether such things are necessarie to acquaint the Superiour withall, or no. For, tell mee, is not the Superiour capable of this, and

and to iudge whether it bee requisite to correct it or not; but what knowe I, for what intentiō this sister shall haue done such a thing, say you? it ma verie well bee her intention is good: Therefore you ought not to accuse her intention, but her exteriour action, if there bee any imperfection: neither may you say. The matter is of small cō sequence, and not worth the troubling of this poore sister; for all this is contrarie to Simplicitye. The Rule which commaundeth to procure the amendment of the sisters by the meanes of aduertismēts, cōmaundeth vs not to bee so cō'ideratiue in this point: as if the honour of the sisters did depend vppon this accusatiō; Truely vvee must obserue, and expect a conuenient time to giue correction: For to doe it sodaynelie, or passionatelie is somewhat daingerous: but this excepted, wee ought in simplicitie to doe that, which wee are obliged to doe according to God, and that without scruple. For although it may bee this persō is in passion, and troubled after the aduertisment, that you shall haue giuen her, you are not the cause of it, but her immortification. And if she committ any fault vppon the sodayne, this wil be the cause that she will auoyd many others, that she would haue cōmitted in perseuering in her defect. The Superiours ought not to omitt to correct the sisters because they haue an auersion to correctiō: for it may bee so, that as long as wee liue wee shall allwaies haue itt: For so much as, it is a thing totally cōtrarie to the nature of man, to bee misesteemed and corrected; but this auersion ought not to bee fauoured of our vvill, the vvhich ought to loue humiliation.

§. 6. You desire that I speake a worde of the Simplicitye vvhich wee ought to haue, to leaue our selues wholie to bee guided according to the interiour, as well by God, as by our Superiours. There are soules which will not, as they say, bee guided but by the spirit ſpiritt of God, and it ſeemeth vnto them, that all things they imagin bee inſpirations, and motions of the holye Ghoſt, who taketh them by the hand, and leadeth thē in all they deſire to doe, as childrē, wherein truely they deceaue thēſelues verie much: For I praye you, was there euer any had a more ſpeciall vocatiō then that of S. Paul, in which our Lord himſelfe did ſpeake to cōuert him? ād notwithſtāding hee vvould not instruct him, but hee ſent him to Ananias, ſaying: Goe, thou shalt find a man who vvill tell thee vvhat thou shalt doe? and although Sainct Paule might haue ſayed, Lord, and vvherefore wilt not thou thy ſelfe? notvvitſtanding hee ſayed not ſo, but vvent verie ſimply to doe as hee vvas commaunded: and should vvee thinke our ſelues to bee more fauoured of God, then Saint Paul, beleeuing that hee vvill guide vs himſelfe vvithout the meanes of any creature. The guid of God, for vs (my deare childrē) is no other then Obedience, for, out of it there is nothing but deceate. It is a verie certayne thing, that vvee are not all guided by one and the ſelfe ſame vvay: yet it is not ſo, that each of vs knovveth by which way God calleth vs, this appertayneth to the Superiours, vvho haue light from God to doe this. wee muſt not ſay, that they doe not knovve vs vvell; For vvee ought to beleeue that Obediēce and ſubmiſſiō are allvvaies the true markes of a good inſpiration, and althoug it may happen, that wee haue not any conſolation in the exerciſes that they apooint vs to doe, and that vve haue manie in the others, it is not by conſolation that they iudge of the goodnes of our actions; Therefore vvee muſt not be tyed to our proper ſatisfaction; for this should bee to cleaue to the flovvers, and not to the fruite. You shall dravve more profitt from that vvhich you shall doe, follovving the direction of your Superiours, then you

you shall in followving your interiour instincts, which ordinarilie doe not proceede but from selfe-loue, vvhich vnder the coullour of good, seeketh to please it selfe, in the vaine esteeme of our selues. It is a most certayne truth, that our good dependeth of leauing our selues to bee cōducted, and gouerned by the spiritt of God, vvithout any reseruatiō, and this is that vvhich the true simplicitie, that our Lord hath so much recommended, doth pretend, Bee simple as Doues, sayed hee, to his Apostles; He stayed not there, but added further more; if you become not simple as a little child, you shall not enter into the kingdome of my Father. A child, vvhiles hee is verie little, is held in so great simplicitie, that hee hath no other knovvledg then of his mother, hath but one onely loue, vvhich is for his mother, and in this loue one onely desire, vvhich is the bosome of his mother, being placed in this vvelbeloued breast, hee desires no other thing. The soule vvhich hath perfect simplicitie, hath but one loue, vvhich is for God: and in this loue she hath but one onely pretence, vvhich is to repose vpon the breast of her celestiall Father, and as a child of loue to make her aboade there, leauing intirelie all the care of her selfe to her good Father, neuer more troubling her selfe for any thing, but still retayning this holy confidence, so that neither the desires of vertues and graces themselues doe disquiet her; and indeed vvherefore serue the importune and vnquiet desires of vertues, the practice vvhereof is not necessarie to vs? gratiousnesse, mildnesse, loue of our ovvne abiection, Humilitie, Svveete Charitie, cordiall freindshipe tovvards our neighbour, and Obedience, are the vertues vvhich vvee ought to practice most commonlie, because they are necessarie for vs, and the encounter of such occasions is frequent vvith vs; but for Constancie, Magnificence, and such

such other vertues, that it may bee vvee shall neuer haue occasion to practice, let vs not trouble our selues, wee shall not bee for this the lesse Magnanim ous or generous.

§.7. You aske of mee, hovv the soules, vvho in prayer are dravvne to this holy simplicitie, and this perfect forsaking all in God, ought to guide themselues in all their actiōs? I aunsvvere, that not onely in prayer, but in the conduct of their vvhole life, they ought inuariably to vvalke in the spiritt of simplicitie, and abnegation, remitting their whole soule, their actions and successes to the good pleasure of God, by a loue of perfect and most absolute confidence, leauing themselues to the mercie and care of the eternall loue, vvhich the diuine prouidence hath of them, and therefore they must hould themselues constant in this course, not permitting any alteratiō or reflection about themselues, to see vvhat they doe, or vvhether they bee satisfied; Alas, our satisfactions and consolations doe not satisfie the eyes of God: but they onely content this miserable care, and loue that vvee haue of our selues, out of God ad his consideration. Certaynely the children, vvhich our Lord noteth vnto vs to bee the modle of our perfection, haue not ordinarilie any care, aboue all in the presence of their Fathers and Mothers, they keepe themselues neere to them, neither regarding their satisfactions, nor cōsolations, vvhich they take in good part, and enioy in simplicitye, vvithout any curiositie of considering the causes, or the effects, loue so much imploying thē, that they can doe no other thing. Hee vvho is verie attentiue to please louingly the celestiall louer, hath neither hart nor leasure to reflect vppon himselfe, his spiritt continually tending thether vvhere loue carrieth it.

§. 8. This exercise of the continuall abandoning

ning of himselfe into the hands of God, doth excellently comprehend all the perfection of other exercises: its most perfect puritye, and simplicitie, and whiles God permitteth vs to vse it, vvee ought not to change it. The spirituall louers, spouses of the celestiall king, truely doe viewe thēselues, from time to time as Doues, who are neere the most pure waters: to see if they bee well accommodated to the liking of their Louer, and this is performed in the examens of their Conscience, whereby they cleanse, purifie, and adorne themselues; the best they may, not for to bee perfect, nor to satisfye thēselues, nor for the desire of their progress in wel-doing, but to obey the spouse; for the reuerence they beare vnto him, and for the exceeding desire they haue to giue him contentemēt: Is not this a verie pure Loue, vnspotted, and verie simple, since they doe not purifie themselues to bee pure, they adorne not themselues to bee fayre, but onelie to please their Louer, to whom if deformitie were as acceptable, they would loue it as much as beautie? And so these simple Doues, doe not imploye care or time, nor any eagernes to wash and trimme themselues: For the confidēce that their Loue giueth them of being much beloued, although vnworthy (I say the Confidēce that their Loue giueth them, in the Loue and bountie of their Louer) taketh from them all solicitude, and diffidence, of not being sufficiently fayre, and the desire to Loue, rather then to adorne and prepare themselues to Loue, cutteth of from them all curious care, and maketh them content with a sweete and faythfull preparation, made Louinglye, and Cordiallye.

8. And to conclude this point, St. Francis sending his Religious into the world in a iourney gaue them this aduise, in steed of monye, and for all their prouision: Cast your care on our Lord, and hee will feede

feede you; I say the same to you(my most deare daughters)cast all your pretensions,your solicitudes and affections, within the fatherlie breast of God, and hee vvill guide you; nay hee vvill carrye you wheere his loue vvill haue you. Lett vs heare and imitate our blessed Sauiour, vvho as a most perfect psalmist singing the soueraigne sonnets of his loue, vppon the tree of the crosse,concludeth them thus; My Father,I commend and committ my spiritt into thy hands;hauing sayed this,(my deare daughters) vvhat remayneth but to expire,and to dye the death of loue, not liuing any more to our selues but IESVS CHRISTE liuing in vs? Thē shall cease all the vnquietnesse of our hart, vvhich proceedeth frō the desire that selfe loue suggesteth, and from the tendernesse,that wee haue in and for our selues;which causeth vs secretly to bee verie busie in the search of the satisfactions and perfections of our selues. And being imbarqued vvithin the exercise of our vocation vnder the vvinde of this simple and loueing confidēce, vvhithout perceauing our progresse wee shall doe verie much, not goeing vvee shall gett forvvard,and not mouing from our place,wee shall dravve neere our country, as those doe vvho sayle on a full sea, vnder a prosperous vvinde. Then are all the euents and varietie of accidents vvhich happē receaued svveetly and mildlye;For hee who is in the hands of God, and reposeth vvithin his breast,vvho is abandoned to his loue, and committed to his good pleasure, vvhat is it, that may bee able to shake and moue him? Certaynelie in all occurrances, vvithout studying like a Philosopher, vppon the causes, reasons, and motiues of euents, hee pronounceth from his hart,this holy acceptatiō and consent of our Lord: yeas, my father,for so it hath bene pleasing in thy sight; Then vvee shalbe all imbrued in svveetnesse and mildnesse towardes our sisters and neighbours; for vvee shall see these soules vvithin the breasts of our Sauiour; Alas! Hee that regardeth his neighbour out of it, runneth hazard to loue him neither purelie, constantlie, nor equallie; But therein vvho vvould not loue him? vvho vvould not support him? vvho vvould not suffer his imperfections? vvho vvould find any defect in him? vvho vvould find him distastfull or burdensome? Novv this neighbour (my most deare daughters) as hee is vvithin the breast of our sauiour, is there so welbeloued, and so amiable, that the louer dyed for loue of him. Furthermore the naturall loue of consanguinitie, good countenances, vvelbeseemings, correspondences, sympathies, and other graces shall then bee purified, and reduced to the perfect obedience of the most pure loue of the good diuine pleasure: and truelie the greatest good & happinesse of soules vvho aspire to perfection, should bee, not to haue any desire to bee beloued of creatures, but by this loue of Charitie, vvhich affectionateth vs to our neighbour, and each one in their degree, according to the desire of our Lord.

§. 10. Before I end, I must speake a vvord of the prudence of the serpent; for I haue considered, that if I did speake of the simplicitie of the Doue; you vvould quicklie obiect vnto mee the Serpent. Many haue demaunded vvhat serpent it vvas of vvhom our Lord vvould haue vs learne Prudence: omitting all other aunsvveres that may bee made to this question vvee vvill novv take the wordes of our Lord: bee Prudent as the serpent, vvho, vvhen hee is taken, exposeth all his bodie to saue his head; in like manner ought vvee to doe, exposeing all to dãger, vvhen it is requisite for to conserue our Lord and his loue vvhole and intire vvithin vs: For hee is our head, and vvee are his mem-

members: and this is the Prudence that vvee ought to haue in our Simplicitie. Furthermore you must remember, that there are tvvo sortes of Prudence vvherevvith vvee must be furnished, to vvitt naturall, and supernaturall. Touching the naturall, it must bee vvell mortified, as not being vvholie good, suggesting vnto vs many considerations, and vnneceſſarie preuentions and foresights, vvhich hould our spiritts verie farr of from Simplicitie.

The true vertue of Prudẽnce ought indeed to bee practiced, for so much as it is a spirituall salte, vvhich giueth tast and sauour to all the other vertues: But it ought so to bee practiced by the Religious of the Visitasion, that the vertue of simple confidence surpaſſe all; for they ought to haue an entire simple confidence, vvhich may cause them to remayne in repose, betvveene the armes of their celestiall Father, and their most deare mother our Bl. Ladie, being before aſſured they vvill allvvaies protect them; vvith their most amiable care, since they are aſſembled for the glorie of God, and the honour of the most holy Virgin. God bee bleſſed. Amen.

THE THIRTEENTH ENTERTAYNMENT.

OF THE RVLES AND SPIRITT *of the Visitation.*

§. 1. It is a verie difficult thing which you demaũd of mee, to witt what is the sp iritt of your Rules, and how you may vnderstand them; Now before wee speake of this spiritt: You must knowe what it meaneth to haue the spiritt of a Rule; for wee heare it ordinarilie spoken, such a Religious hath the true spiritt of his Rule. VVe will take out of the holie Gospell two examples, which are verie proper for to make you comprehend this. It is sayed that St. Ihon Baptist was come in the spiritt and vertue of Elias, and therefore hee did reprehẽd sinners bouldly and rigourously, calling them vipers-broode, and such other wordes; But what was this vertue of Elias? It was the zeale which proceeded of his spiritt, for to annihilate and punish sinners, making fire fall frõ heauen to ouerthrowe and cõfund those who would resist the Maiesty of his Maister. This was then a spiritt of rigour that Elias had. The other example that wee find in the Gospell, which serueth to our purpose is: That our Lord desiering to goe to Ierusalem, his disciples diswaded him from it, because some had affection to goe into Carphanaum, & others into Bethania; and so they endeauoured to leade our Lord to the place whither they vvould goe. It is noe new thing to haue inferiours guid their maisters according to their vvill; But our Lord, vvho vvas facill to condescend, notwithstanding setled his face (for the Euangelist vseth the same vvordes) to goe

goe vnto Ierusalem, to the end that the Apostles should not presse him further, not to goe thither. Then goeing towards Ierusalem, hee desired to passe through a towne of Samaria; but the Samaritans would not permitt him; wherupon Saint Iames and Saint Ihon being in choler, were so angry against the Samaritans, for the inhospitalitye shewed towards their Maister, that they sayed vnto him: Maister, wilt thou that wee make fiere fall from heauen to consume them and punish them for the outrage they haue done thee? And our Lord aunswered them, you knowe not of what spiritt you are; as who would say, doe you not knowe, that wee are no more in the time of Elias, who had a spiritt of rigour, and although hee were a verie great seruant of God, and did well in doeing that which you would doe, notwithstanding you should not doe well to imitate him: For so much as I am not come to punish and confound sinners; but to drawe them sweetlye to penance and to follow mee.

§.2. Now Lett vs see what the perticuler spiritt of a Rule is. The better to vnderstand this, exāples must bee alleaged of Religion in general; and afterwardes we will retourne to our selues. All Religions and all assemblyes of deuotion haue one spiritt, which is generall, and each one hath one which is his in particular. The generall, is the pretence that they all haue to aspire to the perfection of Charitie; but the particular spiritt is the meanes to attayne to this perfection of Charity: that is to say, to the vniō of our soule with God, and with our neighbour for the loue of God; the which is made with God, by the vnion of our will with his, and with our neighbour by meekenesse, which is a vertue immediatlie depending of charitie. Lett vs now come to this particular spiritt: Truelie it is verie different in diuers orders, some vnite themselues to God and to their neighbour by Contemplation, and for this cause they haue verie great solitude, and conuerse as little as may bee vvith the vvorld, no not one vvith another but att certayne times: They also vnite themselues vvith their neighbour, by the meanes of prayer, praying to God for him. On the contrarie the particular spiritt of others is, truely to vnite themselues to God and their neighbour; but it is by the meanes of action although spirituall. They vnite themselues to God; but this is in reconcileing their neighbour vnto him, by studie, preachings, Confessions, conferences, and other actions of pietie; and the better to performe this act tovvards their neighbour, they conuerse vvith the vvorld, allthough they vnite themselues to God by prayer; yett notvvistanding their principall ende is that vvee speake of: to vvitt, to endeauour to conuert soules, & vnite them to God. Others haue a seuere and rigoerous spiritt, vvith perfect contempt of the vvorld, and of all its vanities and sensualities, desireing to induce others by their example to cōtemne earthlie things, and for this serue the asperities of their habitts and exercises. Others haue another spiritt, and it is a verie necessarie thing to knovve vvhat is the peculier spiritt of each Religion, and pious assembly.

§. 3. For to knovve this vvell, vvee must consider the end vvherefore it hath bene begun, and the diuers meanes to attayne to this end. There is a generall spiritt in all Religions, as vvee haue sayed: but it is the particuler of vvhich I speake: and to which vvee must haue so great a loue, that there is not any thing vvhich vvee may knowe that is conforme to this end, that vvee vvould not embrace vvith all our hart. Knovve you vvhat it meaneth, to loue the

the end of our Institute? it is to bee exact in the obseruance of the meanes to attayne to this end, which are our Rules and Constitutions, and to bee verie diligent to doe all that belongeth and helpeth to obserue them the more perfectly: this is to haue the spirit of our Religion. But this exact and punctuall obseruance must bee vndertaken in simplicitye of hart, I vvould say vvee must not desire to goe beyond it, by pretences to doe more then is appointed vs in our Rules; For it is not by the multiplicitie of things that vvee doe that vvee gaine perfection; but it is by the perfection and puritie of intention vvith the vvhich vvee performe them. You must therefore regard vvhat is the end of your Institute, and the intention of your Institutour, and settle your selues to the meanes vvhich are appointed you to attayne thereunto. Touching the end of your Institute, you must not search into the intention of the three first sisters that began it, no more then the Iesuitts did into the first designe that Saint Ignatius had: for hee thought nothing lesse then to doe that vvhich hee did aftervvards; as likevvise Saint Francis, Saint Dominicke and others, vvhich haue begun Religious Orders. But God to vvhome it appertayneth to make such assemblyes of pietie, causeth them to florish, in this fashiō that vvee see they doe, for vvee must not beleeue, that this is the vvorke of men, vvho by their inuention haue begun this kind of life so perfect, as this of Religion is, It is God by vvhose inspiration, Rules haue bene composed, vvhich are the proper meanes to attayne to this generall end of all Religions, that is, to vnite themselues to God, and to their neighbour for the loue of God. But as each Religion hath his peculier end, and also particular meanes to attayne to this end, and generall vnion, so all haue a generall meanes to attayne thereunto, vvhich is by the three essentialle vowes of Religion. Euerie one knoweth, that riches and the goods of the earth, are powerfull attracts, to dissipate the soule, asvvell for the ouer great affection she hath vnto them, as for the solicitudes she must haue to keepe them, yea to increase them; for so much as man neuer hath enough of them as hee desireth. A Religious person cutteth of all this at once by the vowe of pouertie. And doth the same to the flesh, and to all his sensuallities, and pleasures, aswell lawefull as vnlavvfull, by the vowe of Chastitie. VVhich is a very great meanes to bee vnited to God most peculiarlie; for so much as sensuall pleasures doe verie much vveaken, and depresse the forces of the spiritt, dissipate the hart and the loue vvee ovve to God, and hinder vs from giuing our selues intirelie vnto him: by this meanes vvee doe not content our selues to goe out of the vvorld, but furthermore vvee goe out of our selues, that is to say renouncing the terrestriall pleasure of our flesh; But much more perfectlie doe vvee vnite our selues to God by the vowe of Obedience, for so much as vvee renounce our vvhole soule, and all her povvers, her vvills, and all her affections, to submitt and subiect our selues, not onely to the vvill of God, but to that of our Superiours, vvhich vvee are allwaies to regard, as the will of God himselfe. And this is a verie great renounciation, because of the cõtinuall productions of the little wills that selfe-loue causeth. Then being thus sequestred from all things, vvee doe retire into the intime of our harts, to vnite our selues the more perfectlie to his Diuine Maiestie.

§. 4. Novv to come in particular to the end for which our Congregation of the Visitation hath been erected, and thereby to comprehend more

easilie

easilie vvhat is the spiritt of the Visitation, I haue allwaies iudged that it vvas a spiritt of a profound humilitie tovvards God, and gentlenesse tovvards our neighbour: For so much as hauing lesse rigour for the bodie, there must bee so much more meeknes of hart. All the auntient Fathers haue determined, that vvhere corporall mortifications, and austerities are vvanting, there they ought to haue more perfection of spiritt: Humilitie then tovvards God, and mildnes tovvardes your neighbour in your houses must supply the austeritie of others. And allthough austerities are good in themselues, and are meanes to attayne to perfection, yet they will not bee so good in your house, in as much as this should bee against your Rules. The spiritt of svveetnesse is so the spiritt of the Visitation, that vvhosoeuer vvould introduce more austeritie therein then novv there is, should incontinently destroy the Visitation: for this should bee to doe against the end, for which it hath bene erected, vvhich is to bee able for to receaue therein infirme wœmen and maydens, that haue not sufficient strenght of bodie to vndertake i, or which are not inspired and dravvne to vnite themselues to God, by the vvay of austerities which they vse in other Religions. It may bee you will say to mee, if it happen that a sister hath a strong complexion, may not she vse more austerities then others, vvith the permission of the Superiour, in such sort that the other sisters doe not perceaue it? I aunsvvere to this, there is no secrett, that passeth not secreatlie to another; and so from one to other, they come to make Religions in Religions; & from little combinations, in the end all is dissipated. The Bl. Mother S. Teresa foretould admirable well the hurt which these little enterprises bring, of desiering to doe more then the Rule ordayneth, and vvhich the communitie doth not exercise, and particularlie, if it bee the Superiour, it vvill bee greater. For euen so soone as her Religious shall perceaue them, they vvill incontinentlie doe the same; and they shall not vvant reason, for to perswade themselues that they doe vvell, some thrust forvvards vvith zeale, others to please the Superiour, and all this vvill serue for a tentation to those vvho cannot, or vvill not doe the same.

§. 5. VVee must neuer introduce, permitt, nor suffer these particularities in Religion. Neuerthelesse excepting certayne particular necessities, as if it should happen, that a sister vvere oppressed vvith some great vexation, or tentation, then it should not bee an extraordinarie for to aske of the superiour to doe some penance more then others: For wee must vse the same simplicitie that the sicke doe, vvho ought to aske the remedies, vvhich they thinke may comfort them: So that if you had a sister heere, that vvere so generous and couragious, as to haue a vvill to attayne perfection in a quarter of an hovver, doing more then the communitie, I vvould councell her that she should humble and submitt her selfe, and not haue a desire to bee perfect but vvithin three dayes, vvalking the traine of others. And if vvee meete vvith sisters vvho haue strong and able bodies, in good time bee it, notvvithstanding they must not desire to goe faster then those that bee vveake. Behould in Iacob an example vvhich is admirable, and verie proper for to shewe vnto vs, hovv vve ought to accommodate our selues vnto the vveake, and to stopp our force, to subiect our selues to goe euen vvith them, espetiallie vvhen we haue obligatiõ therevnto as the Religious haue to follovv the cõmunitie, in all that is of perfect obseruance. Iacob departing from the house of his Father-in-lavve Laban, vvith all his wiues, children, seruantes, and flockes of catell to retourne into his ovvne house, feared extremelie to meete vvith his brother Esau, for so much as hee did thinke his brother vvas allwaies irritated against him, vvhich vvas not so: being then in the way, poore Iacob vvas greatlie afraide, for hee mett Esau very vvell accompayned, vvith a great troupe of souldiers. Iacob hauing saluted him, found him very gentle tovvards him; for hee sayed to him, my brother, lett vs goe in companye, and end our iourney together; to vvhom holy Iacob aunsvvered, My Lord and my brother, not so if you please, for so much as I leade my children, and their little pace should exercise, or abuse your patience; but for mee vvho am obliged ther vnto, I measure my pace to theirs, likevvise my sheepe haue lately brought forth their young lambes, vvho are yett tender, and not able to goe so swift, and those occasions vvill stay you verie much in the way. Mark I pray you the milde beauiour of this holy Patriarcke. Hee accommodated himselfe vvillinglie not onely to the pace of his little children; but also to his lambes. Hee vvas on foote, and this vvas a happie voiage to him, as is sufficientlie knovvne, by the blessings vvhich hee receaued from God all the vvaye long, for hee savv and spake manie times vvith the Angells, and vvith the Lord of Angells and men; and in fine hee had a better part then his brother vvho vvas so vvell accompayned. If vvee desire our voyages should bee blessed of the diuine goodnes, lett vs submitt our selues vvillinglie, to the exact and punctuall obseruance of our Rules, and that in simplicitie of hart, not desireing to double exercises, vvhich vvould be to contradict the intention of the Institutour and the end for vvhich the Congregation hath bene erected. Lett vs then vvillinglie accommodate our selues to the infirme, vvhich which may be receaued therein, and I assure you, wee shall not arriue to perfection the later for this; but on the contrarie, this vvil be a meanes to leade vs thereunto the sooner, because not haueing much to doe, wee shall apply our selues to performe our dutie with the greatest perfection that shal be possible for vs. It is this wherein our workes are most pleasing to God; for so much as hee hath not regard to the multiplicitie of things which wee doe for his loue: (as wee haue sayed euen novv) but to the feruour of Charitie vvherewith wee effect them. I find if I bee not deceaued, that if wee determine with our selues to obserue our Rule perfectlie, wee shall haue busines enough, vvithout charging our selues vvith more, for so much as all that which concerneth the perfection of our estate is comprised therein. The blessed mother Sainct Teresa sayeth that her Religious vvere so exact, that it was expedient that the Superiour had a verye great care to speake of nothing, but what was verie fitt to bee doe: because that vvithout any other bidding, they would sett themselues to doe it; and for to obserue their Rules more perfectlie, they were punctuall in the least little. She reporteth that one time, there was one of her Religious, who hauing not well heard a Superiour cõmaund her, sayed to her, that she did not well vnderstand what she sayed, and the Superiour aunswered her verie rudely and inconsideratlye: Goe put your head into the well (sayed she to her) and you shall vnderstand it. The Religious vvas so readie to depart, that if they had not stayed her, she was goeing to cast her selfe into a vvell. Truelie there is lesse to bee done to bee exact in the obseruance of the Rules, then to bee willing to obserue them but in part.

§. 6. I cannot sufficientlie declare of what impor-

tance

cance this point is, of being punctuall in the least thing, which serueth to obserue the Rule more perfectly, as also of not desyreing to vndertake any thing more, vnder what pretext soeuer it be. For so much as this is the meanes to conserue Religion in her integritie, and in her first feruour; & the cōtrarie to this is that, which destroyeth it, and maketh it to fall from her first perfection. You will aske of mee, if there should bee more perfection to conforme ones selfe so to the communitie, that euen they should not aske to cōmunicate extraordinarie by? who doubteth it, my deare daughter? except it bee in a certayne case, as on the Feaste of our Patron, or Sainct to whom wee haue had deuotion all our life, or some vrgent necessitie. But touching certayne petty-feruours that vvee haue sometimes, which are ordinarilie the effect of our nature which causeth vs to desire the holie Communion; Wee must not haue regarde to this, no more then the mariners haue to a certayne winde, which riseth at the breake of day which is produced of vapours, that are exhaled from the earth, and continueth not; but ceaseth so soone as the sayed vapours are a little ascended and dispersed, and therefore the Maister of the shipp who knoweth it, calleth not vpō the mariners, nor displaieth the sayles to sett forward in fauour of it; likewise wee must not esteemee euerie wind for a good wind; that is to say, so many pettie motions or wills for inspirations; to witt novv to aske to cōmunicate, by and by to pray, thē some other thing. For selfe loue which allwaies seeketh her satisfactions, would remayne intirelie content with all this, and principallie with these little inuentions, and will not cease to furnish vs allvvaies with new: this day when the communitie doth communicate, she will suggest to vs, that for humilitie you must aske to abstayne,

and

and vvhen the time of humbling our selues shall come, it vvill perswade vs to reioice, and to aske the holie Cõmunion to this effect; and so vvee shall neuer haue done. vvee must not hould those things vvhich are out of the Rule for inspirations. if it bee not in extraordinarie cases, vvhich perseuerance maketh vs to knovve, that it is the vvill of God, as it is found touching the sacred Communion, in two or three great Saints whose directours vvould haue them daylie to communicate. I find this to bee an act of verie great perfection, to conforme our selues in all things to the communitie, and neuer to omitt the practice thereof by our ovvne election. For besides that this is a verie good meanes to vnite vs vnto our neighbour, it doth hide moreouer from vs our ovvne perfection. There is a certayne simplicitie of hart, vvherein consisteth the perfection of all perfections; and it is this simplicitie which maketh our soule haue no other aspect then towardes God; and that she keepe her selfe closelie recollected wholie vvithin her selfe, for to apply her selfe vvith all fidelitie that is possible for her to the obseruances of her Rules, not povvring out her selfe to will nor desire to vndertake to doe more then this. She vvill not exercise excellent and extraordinarie things, vvhich may cause her to bee esteemed of creaturrs; and therefore she houldeth her selfe verie lovve (or) abiect in her selfe, and hath no great satisfactions; for she doth nothing of her ovvne will, nor any thing more then others, and so all her sanctitie is hidden from her eyes. God onelie seeth it who delighteth himselfe in her simplicitie, by the vvhich she rauisheth his hart, and vniteth her selfe to him. She cutteth of at a blovve all the inuentions of selfe-loue, vvhich taketh a singuler delight to enterprise great and excellẽt things, and such as may cause vs to bee much esteemed

abouc

aboue others. Such soules doe totallie enioy great peace and tranquillitie of spiritt. VVee must neither thinke nor beleeue, that doing nothing more then others, and followving the communitie, vvee haue the lesse meritt. O no! For perfection consisteth not in austerities. Allthough they bee a good meanes to attayne thereunto, and that they bee good in themselues, notvvithstanding for vs they are not: because they are not conforme to our Rules, nor to the spiritt of them, it being more perfection to keepe our selues vvithin their simple obseruance and to followve the communitie, then to desire to exceede it. The person vvho vvill keepe her selfe vvithin these limitts, I assure you she shall finish a great iourney in short time, and shall bring much fruite to her sisters by her example. In fine vvhen wee are to rovve it must bee done by measure: the gally-slaues who rowe vppon the sea, are not so soone beaten for rovving a little lazilie, as if they guide not the stroke of the are by measure: wee ought to endeauour to aduance all the Nouices verie equallie, in doing the same things, to the end they rovve equallie, and although all doe it not vvith equall perfection, wee cannot remedie it, the like is seene in all communities.

§. 7. But you say it is for mortification that you stay a little longer in the quire on festiuall dayes then others, because that the time that you haue alreadie indured there, hath succeeded vvell with you during the space of tvvo or three hovvers together, all haue remayned there. To this I aunsvvere you, that it is not a generall rule, that vvee must doe all those things from which vvee haue repugnance, no more tken to abstaine from things to vvhich vvee haue inclination. For if a sister haue an inclination to say the diuine office, she must not omitt to assist thereat vnder pretext of mortifying her selfe.

Moreouer

Moreouer on feastiuall dayes the time that remay-ueth, which is left free to doe what they please, each one may imploy her selfe according to her de-uotion: yet it is true notwistanding that haueing bene three howers yea more in the Quire with the communitie, it is much to bee feared, that the quarter of an hovver that you stay there longer, is but a little morcell that you vvill giue to selfe-loue.

§. 8. In fine (my deare daughters) vvee must loue our Rules verye much, since they are the meanes by which wee should attayne vnto their end. VVhich is for to guid vs with facillitie to the perfection of Charitie, which is the vnion of our soules with god, and with our neighbour: and not onelie this; but also to revnite our neighbour with God, the which wee doe by the way that wee pre-sent vnto him, the which is verie sweete and facille. No womā must bee reiected for want of corporall strenght, prouided that she haue a will to liue ac-cording to the spiritt of the Visitation, which is (as I haue sayed) a spiritt of humility towardes God, and of Svveetnes of hart towards our neighbour; and it is this spiritt which causeth our vnion as well with God as with our neighbour. By humilitie wee vnite our selues with God, submitting our selues to the exact obseruance of his wills, which are signified to vs in our Rules: for wee ought piouslie to be-leeue, that they haue bene composed by his inspira-tiō being receaued by the holie church and approu-ed by his Holines, which are most euident signes thereof. And therefore wee ought to loue them so much the more tenderly, and to bind thē fast euerie day vppon our breasts many times, in forme of ac-knowledgment towards God who hath giuen thē vs. By sweetnes of hart wee vnite our selues with our neighbour, by an exact punctuall cōformitie of life, māners, and exercises doeing neither more nor

lesse

lesse then those with whō wee liue, and that which is marked vnto vs in the way wherein God hath placed vs together, imploying and settling all the forces of our soule to performe them vvith all the perfection that shal be possible for vs. But note this which I haue sayed manie times, that wee must bee verie punctuall in the obseruance of our Rules euē in the verie least little, it ought not to bee vnderstood as punctualitie of Scruple: O no! for this is not my meaning, but a punctualitie of chast spouses who content not themselues to auoyd the displeasure of their celestial spouse, but would doe all that they can, how little soeuer it may bee, that is most pleasing vnto him.

§.9. It shalbe much to the purpose that I propose some remarkable example, vnto you, to make you comprehend how acceptable to God the conforming of our selues to the cōmunitie in all things is. Hearkē thē to this that I will say to you: wherefore thinke you did our Lord ād his blessed Mother submitt themselues to the lavve of the presentatiō and purification, but because of the loue they beare to the communitie. Truelie this example should bee sufficiēt to moue Religious persons to follow their communitie exactlie, neuer seuering themselues frō it. For neither the sonne nor the Mother were in any sorte obliged to this lavve, not the sonne because hee was God; not the Mother because she was a most pure Virgin; they could easilie haue exempted themselues whiout the knowledg of any person; for might she not haue gone to Nazareth, in guisse of goeing to Ierusalem? But she did not so: but verie simply followed the communitie: she might verie vvell haue sayd: The lavve is not made for my most deare sonne nor for mee, it doth not oblige vs at all: But since all men are obliged thereVnto, and obserue it, vvee vvill submitt our

our selues verie vvillinglie, for to conforme our selues to euerie one of them, and not to bee singuler in any thing. The Apostle Sainct Paul sayeth verie vvell, that our Lord in all things must bee like to his brethren, sinne excepted: But tell mee vvas it feare of preuarication, vvhich rendred the mother and her sonne so exact in the obseruance of the lawe? No truelie it vvas not that, for there vvas not any preuaricatiō for them; But they were drawne by the loue they carryed to their eternall Father. No man can loue the commaundement, except hee loue him that made it. According to the measure that vvee loue, & esteeme him that made the lawe, wee shall render our selues exact in the obseruance thereof. Some are tyed to the lavve vvith chaines of iron, and others vvith chaines of gould, I vvould say seculars. vvho obserue the commaundements of God, for the feare they haue of being damned, obserue them by force, and not for loue. But Religious, and those who haue care of the perfectiō of their soules, are tyed therevnto vvith chaines of gold, that is to say by loue: they loue the commaūdements and obserue them louinglye, and to obserue them the better, they embrace the obseruance of the councells: and Dauid sayed that God hath commaunded, that his commaundements should bee verie well keept; Behould how hee willeth that wee bee punctuall in obseruing of them: Certainlie all true louers doe so: for they auoyd not onely the preuarication of the lavve: but also they auoyd the verie shadovve of the preuarication, and for this cause the espouse sayeth that his spouse resembled a Doue, vvho keepeth her selfe besides the riuers, that runne svveetlie, and vvhose waters are christaline. You knowe well that the doue houldeth her selfe secure neere to the waters, because that she seethe there the shadowes of the praying fou-

les

les that she feareth, and so soone as she seeth them she taketh her flight, and so she cannot bee surprised. In like sort (vvill the Sacred espouse say) is my beloued: for whiles she flyeth before the shadovve of the preuarication of my commaundements, she feareth not to fall into the hands of disobedience. Truelie that person vvho depriueth himselfe of himselfe voluntarilie, by the vowe of obedience, not to doe his will in indifferent things, sheweth sufficientlie that hee loueth to bee subiect in those that are necessarie, and of obligation. VVee must then bee exceeding punctuall in the obseruance of the lavves and Rules, vvhich are giuen vs by our Lord: but aboue all in this point of follovving of the communitie, and wee must take heede of saying that vvee are not bound to obserue this Rule, or particular commaundement of the Superiour, for so much as it is made for the weake and vvee are strong and healthfull; nor on the contrarie, that the commaundment is made for the strong and vvee are weake and infirme: O God! there must bee nothing lesse then this in a communitie. I coniure you if you bee strong, that you weaken your selues for to yeald your selues conforme to the infirme; and if you bee weake, I say to you strenghten your selues to march fitly vvith the strong. The great Apostle Sainct Paul sayeth that hee made himselfe all to all, for to gayne all: vvho is infirme vvith vvhom I am not? vvho is sicke with whom I am not sicke? With the strong I am strong. Behould hovv S. Paul, whē hee is vvith the infirme, is infirme, and taketh willingly the commodities necessarie to their infirmities to giue them confidence to doe the same; but when hee findeth himselfe with the strong, he is as a gyant to giue them courage, and if hee can perceaue his neighbour to bee scandalized with any thing that hee doth, allthough it were lawefull for him

him to doe it, notwithstanding hee hath such a zeale of the peace and tranquillitie of his hart, that hee willingly abstayneth from the same.

§. 10. But you will say to mee, novv it is the houre of recreation, I haue a verie great desire to goe praie to vnite my selfe more immediatlie with the diuine goodnes, may I not verie well thinke, that the lawe which ordayneth recreation, doth not oblige mee, since I haue a spiritt Iouiall enough of my selfe? No! wee must neither thinke it, nor speake it. If you haue not neede to recreate your selfe, notwithstanding you must make recreatiō for those vvho haue neede thereof; Is there not any exceptiō in Religiō? The Rules oblige then all equally: yeas without doubt: but there are lavves vvich are iustly vniust, for example: The fast of Lent is commaunded for euerie one, seemeth it not to yon that this lavve is vniust, since that the church moderateth this iniust Iustice, giuing dispensations to those that cannot obserue it? in like sort it is in Religion· the commaundement is equally for all, and none of themselues can dispence therewith: but the Superiours moderate the rigour according to the necessities of euerie one. VVee must take heede of thinking, that the infirme are lesse profitable in Religion then the strong, or that they doe lesse, or haue lesse meritt, because they doe all equallie the will of God. The Bees shewe vs an exāple of that which wee say. For some of them are imployed to keepe the hiue, and others are perpetuallie in labour to gather hony; notwithstanding those that remayne in the hiue, eate not lesse hony, then those that take the paynes to picke it out of the flowers. Doth it not seeme to you that Dauid made an vniust lawe, when hee cōmaunded that the souldiers that did garde the baggage, should part the bootie equallie with those that went to battaill, and who retourned all loaden with blowes?

blowes? No truelie) it was not iniust, for so much as those that kept the baggage, kept thē for those that did fight, and those who were in the battaile, did fight for those that kept the baggage, so they deserued all one recompence, since they all obeyed equallie to their King. God bee Blessed.

LIVE JESVS.

THE FOVRTEENTH ENTER-TAINEMENT.

AGAINST SELFE-IVDGMENT AND THE tendernes vvee haue ouer our selues.

§. 1. THe first question is: If it bee a thing verie contrarie to perfection, to bee subiect to ones selfe-opinion: whereunto I aunswere, that to bee subiect to haue selfe-opiniōs or not to haue thē, is a thing that is neither good nor euill, for so much as it is naturall to euerie one to haue selfe-opiniōs, but this doth not hinder vs from attayning to perfection, prouided that vvee tye not our-selues thereunto, or that vvee loue them not; for it is onely the loue of our ovvne opinions which is infinitly contrarie to perfection, and this is that vvhich I haue so oftentimes sayed, that the loue of our proper iudgment, and the esteeme wee make of it, is the cause that there are so fevve perfect; there are found many persons, vvhich renounce their proper will, some for one subiect, and others for another: I say not onely in Religion; but amongst seculers, and in the Courts of Princes themselues: If a Prince commaund a courtier any thing, hee vvill neuer refuse to obey; but to auowe

auowe that the commaundement is well made, this arriueth rarelie. I vvill doe vvhat you commaund mee in the manner you desire, will hee aunſwere; but they allwaies pauſe vpon their, but; which is as much as to ſay, that they knovve vvell it should bee better othervviſe. None can doubt (my deare daughters) but that this is verie contrarie to perfection: for it produceth ordinarilie vnquietneſſe of ſpiritt, variances, murmurations, and in fine it nourisheth the loue of proper eſtimation; And therefore proper-opinion and ſelfe-iudgment ought neither to bee eſteemed nor loued! But I muſt tell you that there are perſons, vvho ought to forme their opinions, as Bishops, and Superiours are to doe, vvho haue charge of others, and all ſuch as haue gouerment: Others ought not to trouble themſelues, vnleſſe obedience ſo ordayne: For otherwiſe they should looſe their time, vvhich they ought to imploy faythfully in retayning themſelues with God; and as the inferiours should be eſteemed little attentiue to their perfection, if they would ſettle themſelues to conſider their ſelfe opinions; ſo likevviſe the Superioures should bee held incapable of their charges, if they did not forme their opinions, and would not take ſinall reſolutions, although they ought not to content themſelues therein, nor to tye themſelues therevnto: for this should bee contrarie to their perfection. The great Saint Thomas, who had one of the greateſt ſpiritts that a man could haue, vvhen hee formed any opinions, hee did ground them vpon the moſt pregnant reaſons that hee could: and neuertheleſſe if hee found any one who did not approue that which hee had iudged good, or contradicted him therein, hee would not diſpute nor bee offended in himſelfe? but ſuffered it willglye. VVherein bee manifeſted verie well, that hee did not loue his ovvne opinion yet

yet so that hee did not disapproue it neither; leauing it so as others should find it good or no; after hee had performed his part hee troubled himselfe no further. The Apostles were not addicted to their owne opinions, no not euen in things appertayning to the gouerment of the Holy church vvhich was an affayre of so great importance, so that after they had determined the cause by the resolution which they had takē, they were not offended if any did censure the same, and if any did refuse to agree to their opinions, although they were verie well grounded; they did not seeke to make them to bee receaued by contesting nor by disputes. If then the Superiours would change opinions at all encounters, they vvould bee esteemed light, and imprudēt in their gouernments: so also if those vvho haue no charges, would tye themselues to their opiniōs, desyring to mayntaine them, and cause them to bee receaued, should they not be held for obstinate? yes truelie. For it is a most assured thing, that the loue of selfe-opinion degenerateth into obstinacie, if it bee not faythfully mortified and cut off. VVe see an example of it euen amongst the Apostles: It is an admirable thing that our Lord hath permitted many things that the Apostles haue done, vvorthy truelye to haue bene written, to lye hidden vnder a profound silence, and that the imperfectiō, which the great Sainct Paul and Sainct Barnaby committed together, hath bene vvritten: It is vvithout doubt a spetiall prouidēce of our Lord, who would haue it so for our particular instruction: they went both together to preach the holy Gospell, and tooke with them a young man called Iohn Marke, vvho was kinsman to Sainct Barnabee; These two great Apostles fell into dispute whether they should take him with them or leaue him, and finding themselues of a contrarie opinion vpon this fact, and not being

being able to agree, they separated themselues one from the other? Now therefore tell mee, ought we to bee troubled, when wee see some defect amongst our selues, since the Apostles did also committ them?

§. 2. There are certayne great spiritts that are verie good, but who are so subiect to their opiniõs, and esteeme them to bee so good, that they will neuer forgoe them, and good heed must bee taken not to aske it of them incircumspectlie and vnawares: For after wards it is almost impossible, to make them acknowledg and confess, that they haue fayled, for so much as they thrust thẽselues so farr into the search of reasons, to mayntane that which they haue once sayed to bee good, that there is no meanes, vnlesse they giue themselues to an excellẽt perfection, to make them vnsay vvhat they haue sayed. There are also found great spiritts, and verie capable, that are not subiect to this imperfection: but verie vvillinglye dismisse their opinions, although that they bee verie good; they arme not themselues to the defence of them, vvhen any contrarietie, or contrarie opinion is opposed to that which they haue indged for good and well assured, euen as vvee haue sayd of the great Saint Thomas: vvhereby you see it is a naturall thing to bee subiect to opinions; ordinarilie melancholie persons are more giuen therevnto then those that are of a iouiall and pleasant humour; for these are easilie tourned at euerie hand, and facile to beleeue that which is sayed to them. The great Saint Paula was obstinat in mayntaining the opinion that she had formed to her selfe, of exercising great austerities, rather then she vvould submitt herselfe, to the aduise of many that did councell her to abstaine; and likevvise many other Saints vvho thought they must macerate their bodies verie much to please God, in such sort that they therefore refused to obey

obey the phisition, and to performe that which was requisite to the conseruation of their perishing and mortall bodies; and although this was an imperfection, they leaue not for this to bee great Saints and verie acceptable to God; the vvhich teacheth vs, that vvee ought not to trouble our selues, vvhen wee perceaue in our selues imperfections, or inclinations contrarie to true vertue, prouided that wee become not obstinate to perseuere willinglie in them: For Saint Paula and others rendring themselues stifneckt, although it was in a small matter, haue bene reprehensible in the same. Concerning our selues wee must neuer omitt so to forme our opinions, but that wee will vvillinglie depose them vvhen it is needfull, vvhether vvee bee obliged or not obliged to forme them. Therefore to bee subiect to esteeme of our ovvne iudgment, and to seeke out reasons to mayntaine that vvhich vvee haue apprehended and found to bee good, is a verie naturall thing: but to permitt our selues to goe thereafter, and to bee fastned thervnto vvould be a notable imperfection. Tell mee, is it not time vnprofitably lost, espetiallie in those that haue not charge, to muse on this?

§. 3. You say, vvhat must vvee doe then to mortifie this inclination? we must cutt of that vvhich nourisheth it; it commeth into your mind that your Superiour erreth in commaunding this or that to bee done in such manner, and that it vvould bee better done so as you haue conceaued? turne from you this thought, saying to your selfe, Alas! what haue I to doe vvith it since it is not committed to mee? It is allwaies much better to vvithdravve our thought simply, then to search reasons in our mind to make vs beleeue that vvee haue done vvrong: for in steed of doing it, our vnderstanding vvhich is preoccupated of her particular Iudgment will

giue vs the change; in such sort that in steed of annihilating our opinion, it will giue vs reasons to maintayne it, and acknovvledg it for good. It is allvvaies more profitable to contemne it vvithout regarding it, and to chase it away so promptly vvhen vvee perceaue it, that vvee knovve not vvhat it was that it vvould say. It is verie true that wee are not able to hinder this first motion of complacence vvhen our opinion is approued and followed; for this cannot bee auoyded: but wee must not muse vpon this complacence, vvee must blesse God and passe it ouer, not troubling our selues more vvith this contentment then of a little feeling of greife, vvhich vvould come to vs if our opinion vvere not followed or found good. VVee must vvhen it is required, either for Charitie or of obedience to propose our aduise vpon the subiect vvhereof the question is, doe it simply; but for the rest wee must yeald our selues indifferēt, vvhether it bee receaued or not. VVee may somtimes argue vpon the opinions of others, and shevv the reasons vvhervppon our reasons doe depend: but wee must doe this modestly and hūbly, not dispising the aduise of others, nor contesting to make ours to bee receaued. It may bee you vvill aske, if it be not to nourish this imperfection, to seeke aftervvards to speake vvith those vvho haue bene of your opinion, vvhen there is no more question of takeing resolution, it being alreadie determined what ought to bee done; vvithout doubt this vvould bee to nourish, and maintayne our inclination, and consequentlie to commit an imperfectiō. for it is a true marke that one submitteth not her selfe to the aduise of others, and that she allvvaies preferreth her ovvne particular iudgment. The thing being determined which hath bene proposed, vvee must not so much as speake nor thinke thereof, vnlesse it vvere a thing notably
wicked;

vvicked : for then if vvee could yet further find some inuention to alter the execution, or to remedye the businesse, wee ought to doe it the most charitably that could bee, and the most innocently, to the end not to trouble any person, nor to contemne that vvhich they should haue found to bee good.

§. 4. The sole and onelie remedie to cure proper iudgment, is to neglect that vvhich commeth into our thought, applying our selues vnto some better thing : for if wee will permitt our selues to make reflection vpon all the opiniõs that diuers encounters vvill suggest vnto vs ; what will arriue but a continuall distraction , and an impeachment of things more profitable, and vvhich are proper for our perfection , making vs become incapable to make holie prayer? For hauing giuen leaue to our spirit to muse it selfe in the consideration of such deceates, it vvill allvvaies thrust it selfe more forwards, and vvill produce thoughts vpon thoughts, opinions vpon opinions, and reasons vpon reasons which vvill maruelouslye importune vs in prayer: For prayer is no other thing then a totall application of our spirit vvith all her faculties vnto God, Novv being vvearied out in the poursuite of vnprofitable things, it becommeth so much lesse able and apt for the consideration of the mysteries, on vvhich vvee vvould make our prayer. Consider then this that I had to say vpon the subiect of the first questiõ, by the vvhich wee haue bene taught, that to haue opinions is not a thing contrarie to perfection, but to haue the loue of our ovvne opinions and consequentlie to esteeme them. For if vvee did not esteeme them, vvee should not bee so amorous of them : and if vvee did not loue them, wee should little care to haue them approued, and wee should not bee so readie to say, lett others beleeue vvhat they vvill, but as for my selfe : doe you knowe what that is you would say (as for my selfe) verilie no other thing but I will not submitt my selfe, but rather I wilbe constant in my opinion and resolution. This is, as I haue manie times sayed, the last thing that wee leaue; and notwithstanding this is one of the most necessarie things to bee quitted and renounced for the attayning of true perfectiō, for otherwise wee shall neuer gaine holie humilitie, which hindreth and forbiddeth vs to make any esteeme of our selues or of all that depēdeth thereon; and therefore if we haue not the practice of this vertue in great recommendation, wee shall allwaies thinke our selues to bee better then wee are, and that others come short of vs, & ovve vs respect.

§. 5. Novv enough is sayed vppon this subiect. If you aske me nothing more wee will passe to the second question, vvhich is; If the tendernes that wee haue ouer our selues doe not hinder vs verie much in the way of perfection: That you may vnderstand this the better, I must put you in mind of that which you knowe verie well, to witt, that we haue two loues in vs, the affectiue loue, and the effectiue loue: and this is aswell in the loue that wee beare tovvards God, as in that vvhich wee haue towardes our neighbour, and furthermore tovvardes our selues: but wee will speake heere but of that of our neighbour, and then wee will retourne to our selues. The diuines to make the difference of these tvvo loues to bee the better comprehended, are accustomed to serue themselues vvith the comparison of a Father vvho hath tvvo sonnes, the one of them is a little minion, as yet a verie childe, of good grace: And the other is a perfect man, a braue and generous souldier, or of some other condition. The Father exceedingly loueth these tvvo sonnes, but vvith a different loue; For hee loueth the

the little one vvith an extreame tender and affe-ctiue loue; marke I praye you, What is there that hee doth not permitt this little infant to doe vnto him? He dandels him, hee kisseth him, hee setts him vpon his knees, houldeth him in his armes, vvith exceeding delight asvvell to the child as to him-selfe; if the child bee stung vvith a Bee, hee ceaseth not to blovve vpon the hurt, vntill such time as the greife be appeased; If his eldest sonne had bene stunge vvith a hundred Bees, hee vvould not haue vouchsafed to moue his foote, although he loue him vvith a great, strong, and solide loue. Consider I pray you, the difference of these tvvo loues; for although you haue seene the tendernesse that this Father hath to his little one, hee doth not therefore leaue his designe to send him forth of his house, and to make him a Knight of Malta, appointing his elder sonne to bee his heire, and inheritour of his estate: This elder then is loued with effectiue loue, and the other little one with affectiue loue; the one and the other are loued but differentlie; The loue that wee haue to our selues, is of this sort affe-ctiue and effectiue. The effectiue loue is it, that gouerneth great persons, ambitious of Honour and of Riches; for they doe procure to themselues as much goods as they can, and are neuer satisfied in getting: these loue thẽselues exceedinglie vvith this effectiue loue: But there are others that loue them-selues more vvith the affectiue loue, and these are those, vvho are verie tender of themselues, and who doe nothing but bemoane, dandle, cherish, and con-serue themselues, and who feare so much all that may hurt them, that it is a great pittie to behould them: If they bee sicke, vvhen they haue no more payne then in their fingers end, there is no-thing more hurt then they are; they say they are most miserable, no euill, how great soeuer it bee, is comparable to that they suffer, and they cannot find medicines sufficient to cure them, they cease not to medicine themselues, and in thinking to conserue their health they loose it and ruinate it altogether: if others are sicke it is nothing; in fine there is none but they vvho are to bee bemoaned and are subiect to weepe tēderlie ouer themselues, endeuoring thereby to moue those that see them to compassion; They take little care, vvhether others esteeme them patient or no, so that they beleeue them to bee verie sicke and afflicted: imperfections certainlie proper to children, and, if I durst say it, to vvoemen, and furthermore amongst men, to those that are of an effeminate hart and little couragious: for amongst the generous this imperfection is not mett vvith all, for vvell made spirits stand not vpon these childish toyes and sottish delicacies, vvhich are proper for nothing but to stopp vs in the way of our perfectiō: and yet for all this, vvee cannot endure that one esteeme vs delicate; is not this verie much tendernes?

§.6. I remember a thing that hapned to mee retourning from Paris. I encountered in a house of Religious vvoemen vvith this accident vvhich serueth to my purpose, and truelie I had more consolation in this encounter, then I had in all my iourney, although I had mett vvith manie verie vertuous soules, but this one did comfort mee aboue all. There vvas in this house a maide vvho made her triall or nouitiate: she was meruelouslie gentle docile, subiect, and obedient: in fine she had all the most necessarie conditions to bee a true Religious vvoeman: in the end it hapned by misfortune, that her sisters did marke in her a corporall imperfectiō vvhich vvas cause that they began to bee in doubt, whether they ought not to dimisse her for this cause. The mother Superiour loued her verie much and vvas troubled to doe it: but notwithstanding the sisters did stronglie ground themselues vpon this corporall incommoditye: Novv vvhen I was there, the matter vvas referred to mee touching this good poore soule, vvho is vvell descended, she vvas brought before mee, being there she placed her selfe vpon her knees, It is true my Lord, sayed she, that I haue such an imperfection, vvhich truelie is so shamefull (naming it alovvde vvith great simplicitie) I confesse that our sisters haue verie great reason, not to bee willing to receaue mee, for I am insupportable in my defect; But I beseech you to bee fauorable vnto mee, assuring you if they receaue mee exercising their charitie tovvards mee, that I vvill haue a great care not to trouble them, submitting my selfe vvith all my hart to keepe the garden or to bee imployed in other offices vvhatsoeuer they bee, that may keepe mee farr of from their companie, to the end I may not molest thē. Truelie this maydē touched my hart, O she vvas not much tender of her selfe: I cannot hould my selfe from saying, that I vvould vvith all my hart haue the same naturall defect, and vvithall haue the courage to declare it before the whole world vvith the same simplicitye that she did before mee; she had not so much feare of being disesteemed as manie others haue, neither vvas she so tender ouer her selfe; she did not make any of these vaine and vnprofitable considerations, vvhat vvill the Superiour say if I declare this or that to her? if I aske her any helpe or reliefe, she vvill say or thinke, that I am verie delicate: and if it bee true, vvhy vvould you not that she should thinke so? But vvhen I tell her my necessitie she maketh mee so cold a countenāce, that it seemeth that she is not pleased vvith it: It may verie vvell bee, my good daughter, that the Superiour hauing other things enough in her head, hath not

 allvvaies

allvvaies attention to smile or speake verie gratiouslie, when you delare to her your greife, and this is it you say which troubleth you, and taketh from you the confidence to speake to her of your infirmities: O God! my deare daughters these are childish toyes, wee must goe simply: If the Superiour or the mistrisse haue not entertayned you as you desire, one time, yea many; you must not bee disgusted therefore, nor iudg they doe allwaies the same: O no: Our Lord will touch them it may bee with his spiritt of sweetnes, for to yeald themselues more pleasing at our next retourne; so wee must not bee so tender as to desire allwaies to speake of all the infirmities wee haue, when they are not of importance: a little head ache, or a little tooth ache, which will quicklie passe perchance if you would beare it for the loue of God, there is no neede to goe speake to make your selfe to be beemoaned a little; it may bee you will not speake to the superiour, or to her that may take care to ease you, but with more facillitie to others: because say you that you would suffer this for God; O my deare daughter, if it were so that you would suffer it for the loue of God, as you thinke: you would not goe to tell it to another that you knovve well, will find her selfe obliged to declare your greife to the Superiour, and by this meanes fetching a cōpasse you shall haue yonr cōtentment, but in good earnest you had better make your demaūd simply to her that can giue you leaue to take it; for you knowe well, that the sister that you speake to of your headache, hath not povver to bidd you goe lye downe on your bed; this thē is no other designe or intētiō (although wee thinke not so expresslie) but to the end to bee bemoaned a little by this sister, and this doth greatlie satisfie selfe-loue; Now if it happē by encoūter that you speake it (the sister it may be asking you how you doe at that time) me) there is no harme, so that you tell it simply, without aggrauating it or bewailling your selfe; But more then this, must not be spokē but to the Superiour, or to the mistrisse; you must no more bee afraid, although they bee a little rigorous in correcting such a fault; For, my deare daughter, you take not frō thē the cōfidēce and libertie to correct you, goe simply then, tell thē of your greife: I beleeue well that you take more pleasure, ād are more cōfidēt to tell your payne to her who hath not the charge to cōfort you, thē to her that hath care ād power to doe it: whiles you doe so, euerie one bemoaneth you, and all sett thēselues a worke to prouide you remedies, whereas if you told it to the sister who hath charge of you, you must enter into subiectiō to doe that which she should ordayne, ād whiles with all your hart you auoyd this blessed subiectiō, selfe-loue seeketh to be your gouernesse ād yet mistrisse of your will, But if I tell the Superiour (you reply) that I haue the headache, she will bidd mee take my rest; well: what is that to the purpose? If your necessitie be not such, it will cost you little to say, mother or sister I thinke I am not so ill as to laye mee downe on my bedd, and if she say, you shall doe it notwithstanding, goe your waies simply: for wee must allwaies obserue great simplicitie in all things; to walke simply is the true way of the Religious of the visitation, which is exceeding pleasing to God and most assured. But seing a sister that hath some trouble in her mind, or some other incommoditie, not to haue the confidence or courage to ouercome her selfe to declare it to you, and you perceaue verie well that the want thereof doth carrye her into some melancholie humour, ought you to call her to you, or to lett it come of her selfe? In this, consideration must gouerne vs: for sometimes, wee must condescend to informing our selues what the

 matter

matter is, and at other times vvee must mortifie these humours, in letting the alone, as vvho would say, you vvill not ouercome your selfe to aske remedie for your payne, suffer it then in good time, you deserue it vvell.

§.7. This delicacie is much more insupportable in things of the spirit then in corporall: and yet it is most infortunatlie practiced and nourished by spirituall persons, vvho vvould bee Saints in an instant, desiering notvvithstāding that it should cost them nothing, no not the sufferinge of the combatts the inferiour part causeth them, by the feeling that it hath in things contrarie to nature, and yet vvill wee or vvill vvee not vvee must haue courage to endure it, and consequentlie to resist these schirmishes all the time of our life in many encounters, if vvee vvill not become bankrupt in the perfectiō that vvee haue vndertaken. I allvvaies desire verie much that vvee distinguish the effects of the superiour part of our soule, from the effects of the inferiour part, and that vvee bee neuer astonished at the productions of the inferiour part of our soule hovv euill soeuer they bee. For that is not capable to stopp vs in the way, prouided that vvee hould our selues constanc in the superiour part, to aduāce our selues allvvaies forvvard in the vvay of perfection, vvithout studying and loosing our time, to bevvaile our selues, that vvee are vnperfect, and vvorthy of compassion, as if vvee vvere to doe no other thing, then lament our miserie and misfortune, for being so backvvard to come to the topp of our enterprise: This good virgin of vvhom vvee haue spoken vvas nothing tender or reserued in speaking to mee of her defect: but she tould it me with a hart and countenance verie assured, vvherein she pleased mee much. But for vs it doth vs so great good to vveepe vpon our defects to content selfe loue,

loue. VVee must (my deare daughthers) bee verie generous, ād not astonished to see our selues subiect to a thousand sorts of imperfections, and yet haue a great courage to contemne our inclinations, our humours, fantasticallnesse, and delicacies, faythfully mortifying all this at euerie occasion: and if notvvithstanding vvee happen to committ defects novv and then, vvee must not therefore bee at a stay, but must raise our courage vp againe to bee more faythfull at the next occasion, and so passe further, making progresse in the way of God, and in the renuntiation of our selues.

§. 8. You demaund moreouer, if the Superiour seeing you more sadd then ordinarie, aske you what is the matter: and you seeing many things in your head that molest you, cannot tell vvhat it is, hovv must you doe then? you must say simply, I haue many things in my head, but I knovve not vvhat it is. You feare say you, the Superiour vvill thinke you haue not confidēce to tell her; But vvhat ought you to care, vvhat she thinketh or thinketh not; prouided that you doe your dutie, vvhereof doe you trouble your selfe? so that to say, vvhat wil she say if I doe this, or that, or vvhat vvill the Superiour thinke, is exceeding contrarie to perfection, vvhen vvee settle our selues therein. For you must allvvaies remember in all that I say, that I intend not to speake of that vvhich the inferiour part of the soule doth: for I make no reckoning of it, it is then the superiour part that must contemne this what will they say? or vvhat will they thinke? this hapneth to you, vvhen you haue rendred an account of your conscience because you haue not sufficientlie told particular faultes, you say you thinke the superiour vvill say, or thinke that you vvould not tell her all: it is the same of this rendring of account, as of confession: VVee must haue an equall simpli-

simplicitye in the one and in the other. Novv tell mee, should I say, if I confesse such a thing, vvhat will my confessour say, or what will hee thinke of mee? Let him thinke and say vvhat hee vvill, prouided that hee hath giuen mee absolution, and that I haue done my duty, it sufficeth mee: and as after confession it is not time to examine our selues, to see if wee haue tould all that wee haue done: but it is the time to keepe our selues in trãquillitye closely attentiue to our Lord, vvith vvhom wee are reconciled, and to giue him thankes for his benifitts, it being nothing necessarie to make a search of that which wee haue forgotten: in like manner it is vvhen wee haue rendred our accompt: That which commeth to our mind must bee simply told, after it must no more bee though of: But euẽ as it would not bee a good preparation to goe to confession, not to bee willing to examine our selues, for feare of finding somthing worthy to bee confest: in likesort wee must not neglect to enter into our selues before the rendring of accompt, for feare of finding somthing, which should be troublesome to speake. Nether must you bee so tender to speake all, nor to rũne to the superiour to crie hola for the least payne that you feele, the which it may be wilbe past within a quarter of an hower. wee may well learne to suffer sõwhat generouslie these small matters for which wee cannot procure remedie, being ordinarilie the productiõs of our imperfect nature, as are these inconstancies of humours, of wills, of desiies, vvhich produce sõtimes a little perplexity, sõtimes a desire to speake, and thẽ all of a sodayne a great auersiõ to doe it, and the like, to which wee are subiect, and shalbe as lõg as wee liue in this passing ãd decaying life. But touching this payne that you say you haue, and which taketh frõ you the meanes to keepe you attẽtiue to God, vnlesse you goe presẽtlie to declare

it to

ke to the superiour, I say to you, that you must note that it may bee it taketh not frō you the attentiō to the presence of God; but rather the sweetnes of this attentiō: Now if it bee but this, if you haue the courage ād the will as you say to suffer it without seeking of comfort, I tell you that you shall doe verie well to doe it, although that it doe bring you some little vnquietnesse prouided it bee not too great: but if it should take frō you the meanes to drawe neere to God, at that time you should goe to lett the Superiour knowe of it, not to seek comforte, but to gaine way in the presence of God, although there would be no great harme to doe it for your cōfort: moreouer the sisters must not bee so tyed to the kind entertaynment of the superiour: That if she speake not to them according to their content, presentlie they perswade thēselues by cōsequence that they are not beleeued. O no, our sisters doe loue humilitie and mortification too much, to bee frō henceforth melancholie vpon a light suspition (which may be without groūd) that they are not so welbeloued as their selfe-loue maketh them desire to bee.

§. 9. But (some one will say) I haue committed a fault against the superiour, and therefore I enter into these apprehensions that she is displeased with mee, & in a word that she will not haue mee in so good esteeme as she hath had. My deare sisters, all this discontent is made by the cōmaundment of a certayne spirituall Father who is called selfe loue, who beginneth to say, how? haue I failed in this manner? what vvill our mother say or thinke of mee? O! there is nothing to bee expected that is good of mee, I am a poore miserable creature, I shall neuer doe any thing that may content our mother, and the like wise lamentations: they doe not say, Alas! I haue offended God, I must haue recourse to his goodnes hopeing that hee vvill strenghthen

mee;

mee: They say O I knovv vvell that God is good, hee will not regard my vnfaythfullnes, hee knovveth verie vvell our infirmitye, Ah? but our mother. This wee renevve still to continue our complaints: without doubt care must be had to please our superiours: For the great Apostle Saint Paule declareth it and exhorteth thereunto, speaking to seruants and it may also bee attributed to children: Serue, sayeth hee, your Maisters to the eye, as if hee would say, haue a care to please them; but after hee also sayed. Serue not your maisters to the eye, as if hee had sayed, that they must looke vvell to themselues, for to doe nothing more in the sight of their maisters, then they would doe being absent, because the eyes of God doth allvvaies see them, to vvhom they ought to haue a great respect not to doe any thing that may displease him, and in so doeing, they must not trouble themselues, nor care to desire allvvaies to please men, for it is not in their povver, doe the best you can not to vex or anger any person: but after this if it happen, that by your infirmitye you discontent them sometimes, recurr persently to the doctrine that I haue so often preached to you, and vvhich I haue had so great a desire to graue in your harts, humble your selues instantlie before God, acknovvledging your frailty and weakenesse, and then repayre your fault with an act of humilitye, if it deserue it, tovvardes the person that you haue disquieted, and this done neuer trouble your selfe: For our spirituall Father which is the loue of God forbidds vs to doe so, teaching vs that after vvee haue made an act of humilitie euen as I haue sayed, vvee should re-enter into our selues, for to cherish tenderlye and dearelie this blessed abiection, vvhich hapneth to vs for hauing offended, and this vvelbeloued reprehension, that the Superiour vvill giue vs, wee haue tvvo

loues,

two Iudgments and two wills, and therefore wee must make no reckoning of all that selfe loue, selfe iudgment, or selfe will suggesteth vnto vs, prouided that wee doe make the loue of God to raygne aboue selfe loue, the iudgment of Superiours yea of Inferiours and equalls aboue our owne (which wee must annihilate as neere as wee can) not contenting our selues to subiect our will, in doeing all that they will haue vs doe, but subiecting our iudgment to beleeue that wee should haue no iudgment, if wee did not esteeme this to bee iustly and reasonably done, reiecting also absolutelie the reasons that it would bring to make vs beleeue that the thing which is commaunded vs, should bee better done otherwise, then as they haue bidden vs. We must with simplicitie alleage our reasons for once, if they seeme good; but then wee must yeald without more replies, to that which they say to vs, and by this meanes make our selfe-iudgment dye, which wee esteeme so wise and prudent aboue all others. O God! mother, our sisters are so resolued to loue mortification, that it wilbe a pleasing obiect to behould them, consolations wilbe nothing to them, in comparison of the price of afflictions, drinesses and repugnances, so much doe they desire to render themselues like to their spouse. Assist them therefore well in their enterprise, mortifye them well & couragiously, not sparing them: for it is that which they demaund, they will no more bee ty'ed to cherishings, since it is contrarie to the generositie of their deuotion, the which will make them heerafter, to sett themselues so absolutely to desire to please God, that they will no more regard any other thing, if it bee not proper to aduance them in the accomplishment of this desire. It is the marke of a dellicate hart, and a tender deuotion, to permitt our selues to bee carried

ried away with euerie little encounter of contradiction: bee not afraid, these childeshnesses of a melancholye and spightfull humour will neuer bee amongst vs. VVe haue so much courage, thankes bee to God, that we wil apply our selues to make so good progresse heereafter, that it willbe agreat contentement to behould vs. In the meane time, my Deare daughters, lett vs purifie our intention, to the end that doing all for God, for his Honour and Glorie, we doe expect our recompence onlie from him: his Loue shalbe our reward heere, and himselfe shalbe our recompence in all eternitie.

THE FIFTEENTH ENTERTAINEMENT.

IN VVHICH IS DEMAVNDED VVHEREIN consisteth the perfect determination of regarding, and follovving the vvill of God in all things: and vvhether vvee may find and follovv it in the vvills of Superiours, equalls, and inferiours vvhich vvee see to proceeede vpon their naturall or habituall inclinations, and of some notable points touching Confessours and Preachers.

§. 1. VVee must knowe that the determinatiō of following the vvill of God in all thiugs without exception, is contained in our Lords prayer in these words that wee say euerie day: Thy wille bee done in earth as it is in heauē. There is not any resistance of the will of God in heauen, all are obedient and subiect to him: euen so say vve that it may arriue to vs, and this vvee aske of our Lord to doe, neuer bringing any resistance there vnto: but remayning most obedient and subiect, in all occurrences to his diuine will:

But the soules thus determined haue neede to be inlightned, in what they shalbe able to know this will of God. Of this I haue spokē verie cleare ly in the booke of the Loue of God: Notwithstanding to satisfye the demaund which hath bene made mee, I will heer say something more. The vvill of God may bee vnderstoode in thvvo manners. There is the vvill of God signified, and the will of good pleasure. The vvill of God signified is distinguished into four parts, which are the commaundements of God, and of the Church, Counsells, Inspirations, Rules and constitutions. The commaundements of God, and of the Church necessarilie euery one must obey, because it is the absolute will of God, vvho willeth that in this, we should obey if wee wilbe saued. Hee willeth also that wee should obserue his Councells; but not with an absolute will, but onelie by vvay of desire; wherefore wee loose not Charitie, neither shall vve bee seperated frō God, for not hauing courage, to vndertake Obedience to his Councelles. Likewise wee ought not to desire to vndertake the practice of all, but of those that are most conforme to our vocation: For there are some of them which are so opposite to others, that it wilbe impossible without doubt to imbrace the practice of the one, and not to take avvay the meanes to practice the other. It is a coūcell to leaue all for to follovv our Lord naked void of all things: It is a councell to lend and giue allmes; tell mee, the person who hath once forsaken and giuen avvay all that hee had, of what can hee giue Almes, since that hee hath nothing? wee must then follovv the conuncells that God would we should follovv, and not beleeue that hee hath giuen them all, that wee should follovv them all. Now the practice of the councells that wee heere ought to practice, are those

that

that are conteyned in our Rules. Moreouer vvee haue, sayed that God signifieth his vvill to vs, by his inspirations; it is true: but notvvithstanding hee vvill not, that vvee should discerne of our selues, if this vvhich is inspired, is his vvill, much lesse that vvee should presumptiouslie follow his inspirations: neither will hee that vvee should expect that hee himselfe doe manifest his wills, or that hee send his Angells to teach them vs; But his vvill is that in doubtfull cases and of importãce wee should haue recourse to those, vvhõ hee hath established ouer vs, to guid vs, and that wee should yeald our selues totallie subiect to their councell and opinion, in this which regardeth the perfection of our soules. Behould then hovv God manifesteth his vvill, which wee call signified vvill. Moreouer there is the will of the good pleasure of God, the which vvee ought to behould in all euents, I would say in all that hapneth vnto vs, in sicknes, in death in afflictiõ, in consolatiõ, in aduerse and prosperouse things, in breif in all things vvhich are not foreseene. And according to this vvill, vvee ought alwaies to bee readie, to submitt our selues in all occurrences, in things disaggreable, in death, as in life; in fine in all that is not manifestlie against the signified vvill of God; for that is allvvaies to bee preferred.

9.2. This being so, vvee aunswere to the second part of the demaund. That you may the better vnderstand this, I must tell you what I haue read a fewe dayes past, in the life of the great Saint Anselme, where it is sayed, that during all the time that hee was Priour and Abbott of his Monasterie hee was exceedinglie beloued of euerie one; because hee vvas verie cõdescending permitting himselfe, to yeald to the vvill of all, not onely of the Religious, but also of strangers. One came to him

saying,

saying, Father, your Reuerence should take a little broth, hee tooke it; an other came to him and sayed, This vvill doe you hurt; instantlie hee left it: so hee did submiat himselfe (in all that where in there was no offence to God) to the vvill of his brethren who without doubt did follovv their owne inclinations: especially the Seculers, vvho did also make him turne at euerie hand according to their vvill. Novv this great gentlenesse and condescending of this Sainct was not approued of all, allthough hee vvas vvel beloued of all; so that one day some of his brethren desiring to shevve to him, that this vvent not vvell according to their iudgment, and that hee ought not to bee so gentle and condescending to the will of all the world, but that hee ought to make those whom hee had in charge, to yeald vnto his will. O, my children (sayed this great Saint) it may bee you doe not knovv with what intention I doe it: knovve then when I remember that our Lord hath commaunded, that vvee should doe to others as wee vvould they should doe to vs, I can doe no othervvise; For I vvould that God did my will, and therefore I doe vvillinglie that of my brethren, and of my neighbours, to the end it may please our good God to doe mine sometimes. Furthermore I haue an other consideration, which is that after that which is the signified will of God, I cannot knovve better the will of his good pleasure nor more assuredlie, then by the voice of my neighbour: For God doth not speake to mee, neither doth hee send his Angells, to declare to mee what is his good pleasure. The stones, brute beasts, and plantes speake not: there is no other then man, who can manifest the will of my God to mee, and therefore I bind my selfe to this as much as I can. God commandeth mee Charitie tovvards my neighbour: and it is a great Charitie to conserue ones selfe in

vnion

vnion one vvith another, and to preserue this, I doe not find a better meanes, then to bee gentle and condescending: Sweetnes and humble condescendence ought allwaies to beare svvay in all our actions. But my principall consideration is, to beleeue that God manifesteth his vvill to mee, by those of my brethren, and therefore I obey God as oftentimes as I condescend to them in any thing. Moreouer hath not our Lord sayed, that if wee become not as a little child wee shall not enter into the kingdome of heauen? doe not meruaill then if I bee sweete, and facill to condescend as a child; since in this I doe no other then that vvhich hath bene ordayned by my sauiour. There is not any great domage, whether I goe to bedd or remayne vpp, Whether I goe thither or remayne heere: but it should bee an imperfection in mee not to submitt my selfe to my neighbour. You see, my deare sisters, the great Sainct Anselme submitteth himselfe, to all that which is not contrarie, nor against the commaundements of God or holy church, or against the Rules, for this obedience is allwaies to bee preferred I doe not thinke that if they had desired any of this that hee would haue done it. O no! But this obserued, his generall Rule vvas in these indifferent things to condescend wholy to all. The Glorious Saint Paul, after that he had sayed, that nothing should separate him from the Charitie of God, neither death nor life, no not Angells themselues, nor all Hell if it should band against him, should bee able to doe it; I knowe nothing better (sayeth hee) then to yeald to all, to laugh vvith them that laugh, to weepe with those that weepe, and in fine to yeald my selfe to euerie one. Sainct Pachome one day making matts had vvith him there a child, vvho beholding what the Sainct did, sayed vnto him: O Father you doe not

not vvell this must not bee done so. The great Saint allthough hee did make these matts vvell enough neuerthelesse arose readily, and sett himselfe neere vnto the child, vvho shewed him how hee should make them. Novv there vvas another Religious man, vvho sayed to him: Father you committ two faults in condescending to the will of this child; For you expose him to the danger of vanitie; and spoile your matts, for they were better so as you did them; to whom the blessed Father aunswered: My brother, if God permitt that the child conceaue vanitie, it may bee that in recompence hee will giue mee humilitie, and when hee shall haue giuen it mee, I shall afterwards bee able to giue some to this child. There is not any great harme to dispose in this or that manner the bulrushes to make the matts; but it would bee verie great danger, if vvee haue not affection to this word so celebrated of our sauiour: if you become not as little children, you shall haue no part in the kingdome of my Father. O what a great good is this, my sisters, to bee so facill and pliable to bee turned by obedience at euerie hand!

§. 3. Now not onely the Saints haue taught vs this practice of the submission of our will: but also our Lord, asvvell by examplo, as by word: but how by word? the councell of abnegation of ones selfe, What other thing is it, but to renounce in all occasions his owne will, and his particular iudgment, to followe the will of another, and to submitt himselfe to all? allwaies excepting that wherein wee should offend God. But it may bee you will say, I see cleerlie, that this, which they vvould haue mee doe, proceedeth from a humayne vvil, and naturall inclination; and therefore God hath not inspired my mother, or my sister to make mee doe such a thing? No, it may bee God doth

doth not inspire this to her; yet truelie hee will, that you should doe it;and you fayling therein resist the determination of doing the vvill of God in all things;and consequently the care you ought to haue of your perfection; wee must then allwaies submitt our selues to doe all that they desire of vs, for to doe the will of God, prouided that it bee not contrarie to his will, which hee hath signified in the manner aforesayed.

§.4. Novv to speake a word of the will of creatures, it may bee taken in three kindes, by vvay of affection, by way of complacence, or else without intention, or besides their designe; according to the first, our will must bee verie strong, to embrace willinglie these wills, which are so contrarie to ours, vvhich would not bee contraried; & yet ordinarilye wee must suffer verie much in this practice of follovving the wills of others, vvhich are for the most part different from ours, wee ought therefore to receaue by way of sufferance the execution of such wills, and to serue our selues of these daylie contradictions for to mortifie vs, accepting them with loue and gentlenesse; By way of complacence ther is no neede of exhortation to make vs follow them: for wee obey most willinglie in delectable thing: yea wee runne before these wills to offer them our submissions. Therefore it is not of this kinde of will that you demaund, if wee must submitt our selues therevnto: for wee haue no doubt thereof: but of those that are farr from the purpose, and of vvhich vvee knovve not the reason wherefore one desireth this of vs: it is this wherein the difficultye lieth. For wherefore should I doe the will of my sister, rather then my ovvne? also, is not mine as conforme to the will of God as hers, in this slight occurrence? for what reason ought I to beleeue, that this, which she telleth mee that I should

should doe, is rather an inſpiration of God, then the will that moueth mee to doe another thing? O God, my deare ſiſters, heere it is where the Diuine Maieſtie vvould make vs to gaine the priſe of ſubmiſſion; for if wee did allwaies perceaue verie well, that they haue reaſon to commaund vs, or pray vs to doe ſuch a thing, vvee should not haue any great meritt in doeing it, neither any great repugnance, becauſe without doubt all our whole ſoule would willinglie grant this; but when the reaſons are vnknovve to vs, our ſoule repineth at it then our iudgment ſtormeth, and wee feele the contradiction. Now it is in theſe occaſions, that wee ought to ſurmount our ſelues, and with a childish ſimplicitie to put our ſelues to the buſines without diſcourſe, or reaſō, and ſay: I knovve verie well that the will of God is, that I should rather doe the will of my neighbour then my owne, and therefore I will ſett my ſelfe to the practice thereof not conſidering if this is the will of God, that I ſubmitt my ſelfe, to doe that which proceedeth of paſſion, or otherwiſe by an inſpiration, or motiō of reaſon: for wee muſt walke through all theſe ſmall matters in ſimplicitye: I pray you to what purpoſe should there bee an houre of meditation made, for to knowe if it bee the will of God that I drinke, When they praye mee, or that I abſtayne by penance or ſobrietye; and the like ſmall matters which are not worthy of conſideration; and principallie, if I ſee I shall content my neighbour how little ſoeuer in doeing them? in things of conſequence wee ought not to looſe our time in conſidering them, but wee muſt addreſſe our ſelues to our Superiours, to the end to knowe of them what wee haue to doe, after vvhich they are no more to be thought of: but whe muſt depend abſolutlie on their opiniō, ſince God hath giuen vs them, for the guid of our ſoules soule in the persection of his Loue. And if wee ought thus to condescend to the will of euerie one, much more ought vve to doe it to the will of Superiours, whom vvee ought to esteeme and regard amongst vs, as the person of God himselfe; for indeed they are his liefrenants; vvherefore, although vvee should knovve that they had naturall inclinations yea passions thē selues, by the motions whereof they should commaund somtimes, or reprehend the faults of their inferiours, it should in no sort astonish vs: for they are men as others, and consequentlie subiect to haue inclinations, and passions: but it is not permitted vs to iudg, that they commaund vs this out of their passion, or inclination: and this thing wee must bee verie watie not to doe; Notwithstanding if wee should knowe palpably that this was so, wee must not omitt to obey sweetlie and louinglie, & submitt our selues with humilitye to the correction. It is a thing truelie verie hard to selfe-loue to be subiect to all these encounters; it is true, but also it is not this Loue that we ought to cōtent nor hearken vnto but onely the most Holy Loue of our soules IESVS; Who demaūdeth of his Deare spouses, a holie imitation of the perfect Obedience that hee rendred, not onelie to the most iust and good vvill of his Father; but also to that of his parents, and which is more to that of his enimies, who without doubt did follovv their passions in the torments, which they imposed vpon him, and yet good Iesus submitted himselfe to vndergoe them sweetlie, humbly, and louinglie. VVe shall see sufficientlie that this vvord of our Lord, vvhich ordayneth that we take vp his Crosse ought to bee vnderstood of receauing cordially the contradictions, vvhich are made vs, in all encounters by holy Obediēce, hovv light and of how little importāce socuer they bee. I will giue

giue you further an admirable example, to make you comprehend the valwe of these little crosses; that is to ssay, of obedience, condescendance, and pliablenesse to follow the will of euerie one: but especially of superiours. Sainct Gertrude vvas religious in a monasterie, vvhere there vvas a superiour, vvho did knovv verie vvell, that the blessed Sainct vvas of a vveake and delicate complexion: wherefore she caused her to be entertayned more delicately then the other Religious vvœmen, not permitting her to vse the austerities, vvhich the custome vvas to doe in that Religion; vvhat thinke you then the poore virgin did to become holie? no other thing, then to submitt her selfe verie simply to the mother, and although feruour did make her desire to doe the same that others did doe, yet she made no shewe thereof, for when they commaunded her to goe to bedd, she went thither simply without reply, being assu red she should enioy the presence of her spouse, asvvell vvithin her bedd by obedience, as if she had bene in the quire vvith her sisters and companions. And for testimonie of the great peace and tranquillitie of spiritt that she gayned in this practice, our Lord reuealed to Sainct Mictild her companion, that if any vvould find him in this life, they should seeke him first in the most Holie Sacrament of the Alter, and then in the next place, in the hart of Sainct Gertrude; wee must not bee astonished at this, since the spouse sayeth in the Canticle of Canticles, that the place where hee resteth himselfe is in the midday: Hee sayeth not, that hee reposeth himselfe in the morning, nor in the Euening, but in the Midday, because that in the midday there is not any shadowe. The hart of this great Sainct vvas a true midday, vvhere there vvas not any shadovve of scruples nor selfe will; and therefore her soule did fully enioy her beloued, who did take his delights in her: In fine, obedience is the salt vvhich giueth tast and sauour to all our actions, & maketh them meritorious of eternall life.

§. 5. Furthermore, I desire this day to speake two or three words of Confessiō. First I desire you should beare a great respect to the Confessours: for (besides that wee are verie much obliged to honour Preisthood) wee ought to regard them as Angells that God hath sent vs, for to reconcile vs vnto his diuine maiestie: and not onelie this, but furthermore vvee ought to regard them as the liestenants of God vpon earth; and therefore although it happen somtimes, that they shevve themselues men committing some imperfections, as demaunding some curiositie, vvhich is not concerning confessiō: as, vvhat should bee your names? what penances you doe? if you practice vertues? and vvhat they are? if you haue any tentations? and the like; I would aunsvvere according to that they aske, although you are not obliged thereunto: for vvee ought not to tell them, that wee are not permitted to speake to them of any other thing then that vvhereof you haue accused your selfe: O no? wee must neuer vse this defect, for it is not true; you may say all vvhatsoeuer you will in Confession, prouided that you speake not, but of that vvhich concerneth your particular; and not of that vvhich concerneth the generall of your sisters. But if you feare to speake of somthing they aske you, for feare of intāgling your selfe, as shalbee to tell them if you haue any tentations; if you apprehend the disclosing of them, in case they vvould knovve the particulers thereof, you may aunswere them: I haue had some, Father, but by the grace of God I doe not thinke that I haue offēded his diuine goodnes therein, but neuer say, you haue bene forbiddē to confesse this or that. Tell in good truth to your cōfessour, all that which doth

doth breed you trouble, if you will: but I say againe to you, take heede to speake of a third nor of a fourth person.

§. 5. In the second place, wee haue some reciprocall obligation to the Confessours in the act of Confession to keepe silent that which they shall say vnto vs, vnlesse it bee something of good edificatiō, and more then so vvee ought not to speake. If it happen that they giue you any councell against your Rules and manner of life, heare them with humilitie and reuerence, and then you shall doe as your Rules shall permitt, and not otherwise: the Confessours haue not allwaies intention to oblige you vppon payne of sinne to that which they say to you: their councells ought to bee receaued by way of simple direction; notvvithstāding esteeme them much, and make a great account of all that they shall say to you in Confession: for you cannott beleeue the great profitt that there is in this Sacrament, for the soules that come therevnto vvith requisite humility. If they vvould giue you for penance any thing that were against your Rule, praye them verie gently to change this penance into an other, for so much as being agaynst your Rule, you feare to scandalize your sisters if you should doe it. Furthermore, you must neuer murmur against the confessour, if through his fault something happen in Confessiō, you may speake simply to the superiour that you are verie desirous if it please her to confesse to some other, vvithout saying any thing: for so doeing you shall not discouer the imperfection of the confessour, and also shall haue the commoditie to cōfesse to your cōtent: but this is not to bee done lightlie and for matters of nothing. wee must auoyde extremities: for as it is not good to support notable defects in confessiōs, so vve must not bee so delicate, that vvee cānot beare some small matters.

 §. 7. Thir-

§. 7. Thirdly, I desire verie much that the sisters of the Visitation take a great care to particularize their sinnes in Confession, I vvould say, that they who shall haue nothing remarkable which were worthy of absolutiō tell some particular sinne: for to say that they haue many motions of choler, of sorrovv, and the like, is not to the purpose: for choler and sorrovv are passions, and their motions are not sinne, for so much as it is not in our power to hinder them, choler must bee disordered or cause in vs some disorderlie actions to bee a sinne, wee must therefore particularize some thing that marketh a sinne. I desire moreouer that you should haue a great care, to bee verie true, simple, and charitable in Confession, (truth and simplicitie is one selfe same thing) telling verie clearelie your faults, vvithout vanitie & without cunning, making your account, that it is God to vvhom you speake, frō whō nothing can bee concealed, & verie charitable, not mingling anie thing of another in your Confessiō: for example, hauing to Confesse of what you haue murmured in your selues, or else with the sisters, that the superiour hath spoken verie drilie to you, doe not say you haue murmured at the harsh correction that the superiour hath giuen you: but simply that you haue murmured against the superiour. Tell onely the euill that you haue done ād not the cause and that which thrust you therevppon, and neuer directlie nor indirectlie discouer the offence of others in accuseing your selfe ād neuer giue willinglie occasion to the Confessour to suspect vvho it is that hath contributed to your sinne· also alleage not any vnprofitable accusations in Confessiō, as to say you haue had thoughts of the imperfectiōs of your neighbour, of vanitie, yea and worse, you haue had distractions in your prayers, if you haue stayed deliberatlie in them tell it in veritie, and content not

your

your selfe to say, that you haue not had sufficient care to keepe your selfe recollected, dureing the time of your prayer; but if you haue bene negligent to reiect a distraction say so, for these generall accusations serue for nothing in Confession.

§. 8. I desire moreouer, my deare daughters, that in this house you beare great honour to those who preach the word of God to you; truelie wee haue verie much obligation to doe it. For, it seemeth that these are celestiall messengers, who come as from God to teache vs the way of saluation, wee ought to regard them as such, and not as simple men; for although they speake not so well as celestiall men, wee must not therefore diminish the humility and reuerence wherewith wee ought to heare the Word of God, which is allwaies the same, as pure and as holie as if it were declared and pronunced by Angells. I marke how when I write to a person vpon ill paper, and in a bad character, he giues mee thankes with asmuch affection, as when I write vpon better paper, and in more legible Characters; and vvhy? because hee maketh not reflection vpon the paper (which was not good) nor on the character (vvhich vvas badd) but on mee vvho vvritt to him: in like sort ought vvee to doe of the vvord of God: not to regard vvho it is that declareth it to vs or preacheth it, it ought to suffice vs that God serueth himselfe of this preacher to teach it vs. And since vvee see that God honoureth him so much as to speake by his mouth, hovv is it possible that wee can bee Wanting to honour and respect his person?

THE SIXTEENTH ENTERTAYNMENT.

TOVCHING AVERSIONS: HOVV VVEE ought to receaue bookes: and that vve must not be astonished to see imperfections in Religious persons, no not in Superiours themselues.

§. 1. THe first Question is, vvhat it is that wee call auersion? Auersions are certayne inclinations, vvhich are somtimes naturall, vvhich are cause that vve haue a certayne grudge of hart at the approch of those tovvards vvhom wee haue them, vvhich hindreth vs that vvee loue not their conuersation, that is to say, vvee take no pleasure therein, as wee vvould doe in the companie of those towards vvhō vvee haue a svveete inclinatiō which maketh vs loue them vvith a sensible loue, because there is a certayne alliance & correspondance betvveene our spiritt and theirs. Novv to shevv that it is naturall to loue some by inclinatiō, ād not others, doe vvee not see, that if tvvo men enter into a tennis court, vvhere two others are playing at tennis, those vvho enter vvill at the first sight haue an inclination, that the one winne rather then the other, and vvhence commeth this? since they haue neuer seene the one nor the other; nor haue heard them spoken of; nor know not if one bee more vertuous then the other, vvherefore they haue no reason to bee affectionate more to the one thē the other. VVe must then confesse that this inclination of louing some better then others is naturall: wee see it in beastes themselues, vvhich haue no reason yet haue

haue this auersion, and this inclination naturallie. Experience makes this plaine in a little lābe newlie brought forth, shevv him the skinne of a woalfe (although hee bee dead) hee setts himselfe to flight, hee bleats, hee hides himselfe vnder the flanks of his damm; but shevv him a horse (which is a much greater beast) hee is nothing at all afrayd, but vvill playe with him: the reason of this is no other, but that nature giueth him sympathy with the one, and antypathy from the other. Now wee must make no great account of these naturall auersions, no more then of inclinations, prouided that wee submitt our selues vvholie to reason. I haue an auersion to conuerse vvith a person, vvhom I knovve to bee of great vertue, and vvith vvhom I may get much profitt; I must in no sort follow my auersiō, which maketh mee auoyd the encounter of him, but I ought to subiect this inclination to reason, which ought to make mee to seeke his conuersation, or at least to remayne there vvith a spiritt of peace and tranquillitie vvhen I meete with the occasion: but there are persōs vvho haue so great feare of hauing auersion from those they loue by inclination; that they auoyd their conuersation, for the feare they haue of meeting vvith some defect, vvhich might take from them the svvetnes of their affection & freindshipe. VVhat remedie for these auersions, since none can bee exempt hovv perfect soeuer hee bee? Those vvho are naturallie austere; vvill haue auersion from them that are verie svveete, & and vvill esteeme this svveetnes a very great remissenes, although this vertue of svvetnes bee more vniuersalie loued. The onlie remedie of this euill (as of all other kinds of temptations) is a simple diuersion, I meane, not to thinke thereon: but the miserie is that vvee vvould vvillinglie knovv vvhether vvee haue reason or not, to haue auersion from some person;

O! vvee must neuer muse to seeke this: our selfe-loue, vvhich neuer sleeps, vvill gilde the Pill so well for vs, that it will make vs beleeue that it is good, I vvould say, that it vvill make vs see, that it is true we haue certayne reasons vvhich vvill seeme good to vs, and then these reasons being approoued of our proper iudgment and selfe-loue, there wilbe no more meanes to hinder from finding them iust and reasonable. O! truelie wee ought to take great heede of this. I extend my selfe to speake somwhat heerein, because it is a matter of importance. VVee neuer haue reason to haue auersion, much lesse to haue a desire to nourish it: I say then, when these are simple naturall auersions, wee must make no account of them, but diuert our selues without making shew of any thing and so deceaue our spiritt: but wee must fight and beat them downe whē wee see that nature passeth further, and vvould make vs depart from the submission wee owe to reason, vvhich neuer permitteth vs to doe any thing in fauour of our auersions, no more then of our inclinations (vvhen they are wicked) for feare of offending God. Now vvhen vvee doe no other in fauour of our auersions, then speake a little lesse pleasinglie, then wee should doe to a person to whom wee should haue great feelings of affection, this is no great matter, for it is not allmost in our power to doe otherwise. And when wee are in the motion of this passion, they should doe vvrong to require that of vs.

§. 2. The second demaund is, hovv vvee ought to comport our selues in the receauing of bookes which are giuen vs to read? The Superiour vvill giue to one of the sisters a booke that treateth verie well of vertues: but because she loueth it not, she will not make profitt of her reading: but vvill read it vvith negligence of spiritt: and the reason is, that she allreadie knoweth at her fingers ends the contents there-of, and that causeth her to haue more desire they giue her another booke to read. Now I say that this is an imperfection, to haue a will to choose or desire another booke, then the same that they giue vs, and this is a marke that wee read rather to satisfie the curiositie of our spiritt, then to profitt by our lecture. If wee did read for our profitt and not to content our selues, wee should bee as equallie satisfied with one booke as with another; at least vvee vvould accept vvith a good will, all those our superiour should giue vs for to read. I say much more, for I assure you that if wee did neuer take pleasure to read but one onely booke, prouided that it were good and did speake of God: yea vvhen there should not bee in it, but onelie this name of God, vvee should bee content, since wee should find busines enough to doe, after the reading of it ouer and ouer agayne many times. For to desire to read to content curiositie, is a signe that vvee haue a little lightnes of spiritt, and that it doth not sufficientlie take care to performe the good which it hath learned in these little bookes of the practice of vertues, for they speake verie well of humilitie and mortification, therefore they doe not practice them when they accept not of them with a good will.

Now to say, because I loue thē not I shall make no profitt of thē, is no good consequence, no more then to say, I knovv allreadie all by hart, I can take no pleasure to read it. All these are childish toyes, doe they giue you a booke that you know alreadie, or allmost all, by hart? blesse God for it, for so much as you will more easilie comprehend the doctrine thereof. If they giue you one that you haue allreadie read many times, humble your selfe, and assure your selfe that God vvould haue it so; to the end you should bee more carefull to doe, thē to learne, and that his goodnes giueth it you for the second & third time, because you haue not made your profitt thereof at the first reading, But the miserie from vvhence all this proceedeth is, that vvee seeke allvvaies our ovvne satisfaction, and not our greater perfection. If peraduenture they haue regard to our infirmitie, and that the Superiour put vs to the choise of a booke, vvhat should vvee doe? then wee may choose it vvith simplicitie, but further then so, vvee must remayne allwaies humbly submisse to all that which the Superiour ordayneth, vvhether it bee to our liking or not, neuer making shew of the feelings vvee haue contrarie to this submission.

§. 3. The third Question is, if vvee should bee amazed to see imperfections amongst our selues, or in our Superiours? Touching the first point, it is vvithout doubt, you ought not at all to bee amazed if you see some imperfections heere vvithin, euen as in other houses of Religious vvœmen, hovv perfect soeuer they bee; for you shall neuer bee able to doe so much, as not to committ some defects heere and there, according as you shalbe exercised. It is no great meruaile to see a Religious, vvho hath nothing vvhich troubleth her, or exerciseth her, to bee verie gentle, and to committ fevve faultes: vvhen they say to mee, behould such a one, vvhom vvee neuer savve committ imperfection, I aske presentlie, hath she any charge? if they tell mee no, I make no great account of her perfection: for there is much difference betvveene the vertue of this one, and that of another vvho shalbe vvell exercised, bee it interiourlie by tentations, bee it exteriourlie by the contradictions that are giuē her. For the vertue of streinght, and the strenght of vertue are neuer

gotten

gottten in the time of peace, and vvhiles vvee are not exercised by its contrarie.

Those vvho are verie gētle vvhiles they haue no contradiction, and vvho haue not gotten this vertue at the point of the speare, as vvee say, they are truelie verie exemplar, and of great edification; but if you come to proue it, you shall see them presently moued, and vvitnesse, hovv their svvetnesse was not a strong and solide vertue; but imaginarie rather then true. There is much difference betweene hauing cessation from vice, and hauing vertue, vvhich is cōtrarie to it. Many seeme to bee verie vertuous, vvho neuerthelesse haue not vertue; because they haue not purchased it vvith labour. Very often it hapneth that our passions sleepe, and rest sencelesse, and if in this meane time vvee doe not make prouision of forces, to fight against them, and to resist them, vvhen they shall come to awake, wee shalbe ouercome in the battaill. VVee must allwaies remayne humble, and not beleeue that wee haue vertues, although wee committ not (at least that wee knovv) defects that are contrarie to thē. Trulie there are many, vvho gently deceaue themselues in this, that they beleeue, that the persons that make profession of perfection should not stumble into imperfections, and particularlie Religious: because it seemeth vnto them, that entring into Religion they cannot fayle to bee perfect, vvhich is not so; for, Religiōs are not made to gather perfect persons together, but persons who haue courage to pretend perfection.

§. 4. But vvhat shall vvee doe if vvee see imperfections in Superiours, asvvell as in others? wee ought not to bee amazed at it: But I hope you make not imperfect superiours, say you? Alas, my deare daughters, if vvee should make none Superiours vnlesse they were perfect, vvee must pray

to

to God to send vs Saincts or Angells to bee our superiours, for wee shall not find men capable: wee indeed seeke that they may not bee of wicked exã-ple: but not to haue imperfections, wee take no heede therein, prouided that they haue the conditions of spiritt which are necessarie, for so much as although there may bee found more perfect, yet notvvistanding they would not bee so capable to bee Superiours. Alas, tell mee, hath not our Lord himselfe shewed vs, that hee did not take this consideration in the election that hee made of Sainct Peter for Superiour of all the Apostles? For euerie one knows what this Apostle did in the death and passion of his Maister, standing to talke vvith a mayde seruant and so vnhappily denied his most deare Maister vvho had done him so much good hee made his brauado, and then in fine hee tooke his flight: but besides this, after hee vvas confirmed in grace by receauing of the holy Ghost hee did committ a fault vvhich vvas iudged of such importance, that Sainct Paul vvritting to the Galathians: sayeth to thẽ, that hee had resisted him in the face, because hee vvas to bee blamed. And not onely Sainct Peter, had his imperfections but moreouer Sainct Paul, and Sainct Barnabee also: for desiring to preach the Gospel they had a little dispute together, because S. Barnabee desired to take with them, Iohn Marke who was his Cosen: S. Paul was of a contrarie opinion, and would not that hee should goe with them, and Sainct Barnabee would not yeald to the will of Sainct Paul, and so they seperated themselues and went to preach, S. Paul into one country, and Sainct Barnabee into another with his Cosen Iohn Marke; It is true our Lord drevv good out of their variance, for else they had not preached but in one part of the world, & by this meanes they cast the seede of the Gospel in diuers places.

places. Lett vs not thinke whiles wee shalbe in this life, to bee able to liue without committing imperfections: for it cannot bee, whether wee bee Superiours or inferiours; since that wee are all men, and consequently wee haue all neede to beleeue this veritie as most assured, to the end that wee bee not astonished to see our selues, yea all of vs subiect to imperfectiõs; our Lord hath ordayned that vvee say euerie day these vvordes which are in the Pater Noster: Forgiue vs our offences as wee forgiue them that haue offended vs: and there is no exception in this ordinance, because wee haue all neede to make it; It is no good consequence to say, she is a Superiour, and therefore she is not cholerick, or she hath no imperfection. You wonder that comming to speake to the Superiour, she speaketh some word lesse svveet then ordinarie, it may bee she hath her head full of cares and affayres: your selfe-loue goeth away all troubled, in stead of thinking that God hath permitted this little drinesse in the Superiour to mortifie your selfe-loue, vvhich seeketh that the Superiour should make much of you, receauing amiably vvhat you would say to her; but in fine, it vexeth vs to meete with a mortification vvhere vvee looked not for it. Alas, vvee ought to goe and praye God for the Superiour, blessing him for this vvelbeloued contradiction. In a vvord, my deare daughters, Lett vs remember the vvords of the great Apostle S. Paul: Charitie thinketh not euill: as if hee vvould say, that she tourneth her selfe from seeing it, without thinking there-on, or staying to consider it.

§. 5. Moreouer you asked of mee touching this point: whether the superiour or directrice ought not to make shew of repugnance that the sisters doe see her defects, and what she ought to say vvhen a Religious cõmeth to accuse herselfe simply to her.

of some iudgment or thought that she hath had, vvhich noted her imperfectiō; as for exāple if some one haue thought that the superiour should haue vsed correctiō vvith passion. Now I say, that vvhich she is to doe in this occasiō, is to humble her selfe, and to runne to the loue of her abiection; but if the sister vvas a little troubled in speaking it, the superiour should not make semblance of any thing; but chang the discourse, yet notwithstanding hide the abiection in her hart. For wee ought to take good heade that our selfe loue cause vs not to loose the occasion of seeing our selues vnperfect and of humbling our selues: and although they forbeare the exteriour act of humility for feare of troubling the poore sister vvho is alreadie afflicted enough, they must not omitt to make the interiour: But if on the contrarie, the sister vvas not troubled in accuseing her, I should thinke it good that the superiour did freelye confesse that she had fayled, if it bee true: for if the iudgment bee false, it is good she declare it vvith humilitie, notvvithstanding allwaies reseruing the abiection pretiously, vvhich commeth to her of this that they iudg' her defectiue. You see hovv this little vertue of our ovvne abiectiō ought neuer to remoue one stepp from our hart; because wee haue need of it euerye houre, although wee be verie perfect, for as much as our passions will reuiue, yea somtimes after vvee haue liued in Religion many yeares, and haue made great progresse in perfection: euen as it hapned to a Religious of Sainct Pachome named Siluain, vvho in the vvorld vvas a player by profession, and being conuerted became Religious. Hee passed the yeare of his probation, yea manie others after, vvith verie exemplar mortification; they neuer hauing seene him exercise any act of his first occupation; twenty yeares after hee thought hee might doe well to make

make ſome merrimẽt, vnder pretence of recreating; his brethren, beleeuing that his paſſions were alreadie ſo mortifyed, that they had no povver to make him paſſe the limitts of a ſimple recreation: but the poore man vvas much deceaued, for the paſſion of ioy did ſo reuiue, that after his apish fopperies, hee betooke himſelfe to diſſolutions in ſuch ſort, that they reſolued to put him out of the monaſterie, vvhich they had done, but that one of his Religious brethren yealded himſelfe pledge for Siluain, promiſing that hee should amend himſelfe, vvhich he did, and became after a great Saint. Conſider then, my deare ſiſters, how vvee muſt neuer forgett what vvee haue bene, to the end wee become not worſe, and lett vs not thinke that vvee are perfect, vvhen vvee doe not committ manie imperfections: wee muſt alſo take head not to bee troubled if vvee haue paſſions, for vvee shall neuer bee vvholie exempt. Thoſe Hermitts vvho vvould avovv the contrarie, were cenſured by the ſacred councell, and their opinion condemned, and held for erroneous. VVee shall therefore allvvaies committ ſome faultes, but they ought ſo rarelie to bee committed, that tvvo bee not ſeene in fiftie yeares, euen as there were but tvvo eſpied in the lenght of time that the Apoſtles liued, after they had receaued the Holy Ghoſt, Neuertheleſſe if vvee should ſee three or four, yea ſeuen or eight, in ſo long a ſucceſſion of yeares, wee should not therefore be afflicted nor looſe courage, but rather take breath, and fortifie our ſelues to doe better.

§.6. Lett vs ſpeake furthermore one word for the ſuperiour; The ſiſters ought not to bee aſtonished, although the Superiour committ imperfections, ſince that Saint Peter, vvho vvas the paſtor of the vvhole church, and vniuerſall Superiour of all Chriſtians, fell into a defect, and ſuch a one, as

hee

hee deserued correction, euen as Saint Paul sayeth: Likevvise the Superiour ought not to make shevv of trouble that her faults are seene, but she ought to obserue the humilitie and gentlenesse, with which Saint Peter receaued the reprehension from Sainct Paul, notwithstanding hee vvas his Superiour. VVe know not which is more worthy of consideration, either the force of the courage of Sainct Paul to reprehend Sainct Peter, or the humilitie wherewith Sainct Peter submitted himselfe to the correction that was giuen him by S. Paul; yea for a thing wherein he thought hee did vvell, and had a verie good intention.

§.7. You demaund in the fourth place, if it should happen, that a Superiour had so much inclination to comply vvith secular persons, vnder pretence of profiting them, that she did omitt the particular care, vvhich she ought to haue of the Religious vvho are vnder her charge, or else that she had not time sufficient to execute the affayres of the house, because she vvould remayne too long at the parloy; if she should not bee obliged to cutt of this inclination although her intention were good? I vvill yeald this to you, that the Superiours ought to bee verie affable to seculars to profitt them, and they ought willinglie to giue them part of their time; but vvhat thinke you this little part ought to bee? it ought to bee the tvvelueth part, the eleauen remayning to bee imployed vvithin the house, in the care of the familie.

The Bees truelie goe forth of their hiue, but this is not but for necessitie or profitt, and they remayne but little vvithout, retourning backe againe; and principallie the king of Bees goeth but rarelie forth, but vvhen hee maketh a swarme of Bees that hee is inuironned vvith all his little people.

people. Religion is a misticall hiue full of cele-stiall Bees, who are assembled together to man-nage the honie of celestiall vertues, and there-fore the Superiour, who is amongst them as their king, ought to bee carefull to keepe them neere her, for to teach them the manner how to attayne and conserue these vertues. Notwithstanding, she must not bee wanting to conuerse with secular per-sons when necessitie or charitie requireth it; but further then so, the superiour must bee breife with seculars: I say besids necessitie and charitie, be-cause there are certayne persons of great respect who must not bee disgusted. But Religious men nnd vvœmen must neuer entertayne themselues vvith seculars vnder pretence of gayning freinds to their Congregation. O truelie! there is no neede of this; for if they keepe themselues vvith-in to performe that well which is their dutie, they ought not to doubt but our Lord vvill prouide their Congregation sufficientlie of freinds who are necessarie for them.

But if it trouble the Superiour to breake of companie vvhen the signe is giuen to goe to the diuine Office, for feare of discontenting those vvith vvhome she conuerseth, she must not bee so tender nor fearefull; For if they bee not per-sons of great respect, or othervvise vvho come not but verie rarelie, or vvho dwell farre of, she must not quit the diuine Office, nor prayer, if Charitie doe not absolutelie require it. Touching the ordi-narie visitts of persons whom they may freelie take leaue of, the Portresse should say, that our mother or sisters are in prayer, or at the Office, if they please to staye, or come another time. But if it happen for some great necessitie they goe to the parloy in these times, at the least lett them

take

take time after to remake their prayer, so much as they may or can possible: for of the Office none doubteth but they are obliged to say it.

§. 8. Novv in respect of the last question, which is if they ought not allvvaies to yeald some little particularitie to the Superiour, more then to the rest of the sisters, asvvell in garments, as in her diet, it shall soone bee resolued, for in a vvord I tell you, no; in no sort vvhatsoeuer, if it bee not of necessitie: euē as they doe to euerie one of the sisters, also, she must not haue a particuler chaire, if it bee not in the Quire, and in the Chapter; and in this chaire the assistant ought neuer to place her selfe, although in all other things they ought to beare her the same respect as to the Superiour. (vnderstand in her absence) In the Refectorie also she must onelie haue a seat as the others: although they all ovve her respect as to a particular person to vvhom they ought to beare a verie great reuerence, yet she must not bee singular in any thing, as little as she shalbee able; vvee allvvaies except necessitie, as if she bee olde or infirme; for then it shalbe permitted to giue her a chaire for her ease. VVee must carefullie auoyde all these things vvhich make vs appeare sōthing aboue others, I vvould say supereminent and remarkable. The superiour ought to bee acknovvledged and noted for her vertues, and not for her vnnecessarie singularities, espetiallie amongst vs of the Visitatiō, vvho desire to make a particular profession of great simplicity and humilitie: These honours are good for those Religious houses, vvhere the superiour is called Madame; but for vs there must bee none of all this.

§. 9. VVhat must vvee doe to conserue the spiritt of the Visitation vvell, and to hinder the dissipation thereof? The onelie meanes is, to keepe it locked and enclosed vvithin the obseruance of her

Rules:

Rules: but you say that there are some vvho are so iealous of this spiritt, that they vvould not haue it communicated out of the house: there is an excesse in this zeale vvhich must bee cutt of: for to vvhat purpose I praye you vvould you conceale from your neighbour that vvhich may profitt him, I am not of this opinion, for I vvould that all the good that is in the Visitation vvere acknovvledged and knovvē to euerie one, and therefore I haue allvvaies been of this iudgment, that it vvilbe good to cause the Rule and Constitutions to bee printed, to the end that manie seeing them may dravve some profitt thereof. VVould to God, my deare sisters, there might bee manie found that vvould practice them, they should see verie quicklie a great chang in themselues, vvhich vvould redound to the Glorie of God, and the saluation of their soules. Lett vs bee verie carefull to conserue the spirit of the Visitation, but not in such sort, that the care hinder vs from the communicating of it charitably, and vvith simplicitie to our neighbour, and to euerie one according to their capacitie, and doe not feare that it vvilbe dissipated by this communication: for Charitie neuer ruinateth any thing but perfecteth all things.

THE

THE SEAVENTEENTH ENTER-TAINEMENT.

VVHERE-IN IS DEMAVNDED: HOVV, and vppon vvhat motiue the Religious ought to giue their voice to those that they vvould admitt to Profession, as also to those they receaue into the Nouitiat.

§. 1. TVVo things are requisite for to giue their voice so as is befitting such persons: The first, that they admitt such persons, who haue a good call from God. The second that they haue requisite conditions for our manner of life. Touching the first point, that she must haue a good vocation from God, to bee receaued into Religion, you must knovv, that when I speake of this call and vocation, I intend not to speake of the generall vocation, such as that is by the vvhich our Lord calleth all men to Christianitie, nor yet of that vvhereof it is sayed in the Ghospell that many are called but fevv elect: For God vvho desireth to giue eternall life to all, giueth to them all the meanes to attayne thervnto, and therefore he calleth thē to Christianitie, and hath elected them correspondent to this vocation, follovving the attracts of God, and yet the number of those vvho are found therein is verie little in comparison of those vvho are called. But speaking more particulerlie of a Religious vocation, I say, that manie are vvell called of God into Religiō, but there are fevv vvho maintayne

tayne and conserue their vocation: for they begin vvell, but are not faythfull to correspond to the diuine grace, nor perseuerant in the practice of that vvich may conserue their vocation, and make it good & assured. There are others vvho are not vvell called, neuerthelesse being entred, their vocatiō hath been ratifyed and made good of God: euen as vve see in those vvho come through spleene & discontent into Religion, and although it seemeth that these vocations are not good, neuerthelesse vve haue seene that these being entred on such tearmes, haue succeeded verie vvell in the seruice of God. Others are incited to entrer into Religion for some disaster and missfortune, vvhich they haue in the vvorld, others for vvant of health or corporall beautie: and although that these persons, haue motiues vvhich of themselues are not good, notvvithstanding God serueth himselfe of them for to call such persons. In fine, the vvaies of God are incomprehensible, and his iudgments inscrutable, and admirable in the varietie of vocations, and meanes vvhich hee vseth to call his creatures to his seruice, to vvhich all honour and reuerence is due.

§. 2. Novv of this great varietie of vocations it follovveth, that it is a thing verie difficult to knovv true vocations, and yet this is the first thing vvich is requisite to giue their voice vvell, to vvitt, if the partye proposed bee vvell called, and if her vocation bee good: hovv then amongst so great a varietie of vocations, and of so different motiues, shall vvee bee able to knovv the good from the bad and not bee deceaued? This truely is a matter of great importance, and is verie difficult; notvvithstanding it is not so that wee are altogether destitute of meanes for to knovv the goodnes of a vocation. Novv amongst manie that I could alleage, I vvill speake of one onelie, as the best of all.

A good

A good vocation is no other thing then a firme and constant vvill, that the person called hath to serue God, in the manner and in the place to vvhich his diuine Maiestie calleth her, ād this is the best marke that vvee can haue to knovv vvhen a vocation is good: but note vvell that vvhen I say a firme and constant will to serue God, I doe not say that she must from the beginning doe all that is to be done in her vocation, vvith so great a stabilitie and constancye that she bee exempt from all repugnance, difficultie, or disgust in that vvhich dependeth thereon: no, I doe not say so, much lesse that this stabilitie and constancie bee such, that it exempteth her from committing faults, nor that therefore she bee so firme that she neuer happen to stagger or varie in the entreprise that she hath made, to practice the meanes vvhich may conduct her to perfection. O no truely; this is not that I vvould say: for euerie man is subiect to such a passion, alteration, and vicissitude, that hee vvho this day doth loue such a thing, to morrovv vvill loue another, in such sort that one day neuer resembleth another. Then it is not by the diuers motiōs & feelings, that vvee ought to iudg the stabilitie and constancie of the vvill, although vvee haue once embraced it; but if amongst this varietie of diuers motions, the vvill remaine firme, and quitteth not the good it hath embraced, allthough it feele some disgust, or coldnesse in the loue of some vertue, and that she doe not therefore omitt to serue her selfe of the meanes, that are appointed her: so that to haue a marke of a good vocation, a sensible constancie is not necessarie, but that vvhich is in the superiour part of the spiritt, vvhich is effectiue, is sufficient. Therefore to know if God vvill haue vs Religious, wee must not expect, that hee speake sensibly vnto vs, or that he send some Angell from heauen to signifie his will,

much

much lesse is it needfull to haue reuelations vpon this subiect; or to make an examine of ten or twelue Doctors to see if the inspiration bee good or badd, if it must bee followed or not. But vvee ought to correspond vvell, and cultiuate the first motion, and then not to bee afflicted if disgusts and luke-warmnes therein come vpon vs: for if vvee allvvaies endeuour to keepe our vvill verie constāt, to desire and search the good which is manifested vnto vs, God vvill not bee wanting to cause all to redound to his Glorie.

§. 3. And vvhen I say this, I doe not speake onelie for you, but more ouer for all wœmen that are in the vvorld, of whom truelie care ought to be had, in assisting them in their good designes. VVhē they haue the first motions a litle strong, nothing is difficult vnto them, it seemeth vnto them that they can breake through all obstacles. But vvhen they feele these changes, and that the former gusts are no more so sensible in the inferiour part, they thinke that all is lost, and that all must bee left, they vvill and they vvill not: that which they then feele is not sufficient to make them leaue the world I would willinglie, sayeth one of these virgins, but I know not if it bee the vvill of God that I bee Religious, for so much as the inspiration that I feele at this time is not strong enough me thinkes. It is true I haue had it much strōger then I haue at this time; but because it continueth not, it maketh mee beleeue it is not good. Truelie vvhen I meete with such soules, I wonder not at these disgusts, neither doe I beleeue them, that therefore their vocation is the lesse good: wee must onelie in this haue a great care to assist them, and learne them not to bee astonished at these changes in themselues; incouraging them to remayne constant in these mutations: Well, say I, to them, this is nothing, tell mee, haue you not

felt

felt a motion or inspiration in your hart to seeke so great a good? yeas, say they, it is verie true, but this quicklie passed: werie vvell say I to them, the force of this feeling passed, but not in such sort, that there remayneth not in you some affection therevnto: O no, sayeth she; for I feele alvvaies I knovv not vvhat, which maketh me yeald to this side: but that which troubleth me is, that I feele not the motion so strong, as it should bee for such a resolution. I aunsvvere them that they must not vex themselues for these sensible feelings, nor examine them so much, but that they content themselues with this constancie of their will, which in the midst of all this looseth not the affection of her first designe; Lett them onelie bee carefull to cultiuate it well, and to correspond well to this first motion: doe you not care thẽ (say I) of which side it cõmeth; for God hath many waies to call his seruants and handmayds to his seruice. Hee vseth somtimes sermons, other times reading of good bookes. Some haue been called by hearing the sacred words of the Gospel, as Sainct Francis and Sainct Antonie, vvho hauing heard these vvords: Goe sell all that thou hast, and giue to the poore and follovv mee, and vvhosoeuer vvill come after me lett him take vp his Crosse and follovv mee: left all. Others haue been called by troubles, disasters, and afflictions, vvhich befell them in the vvorld, vvhich gaue them occasion to sett themselues against it and abandon it. Our Sauiour often vseth such meanes to call diuers persons to his seruice, which hee could not gaine in any other sort.

§.4. For although God bee Allmightie, & can all that hee vvill, notvvithstanding hee vvill not depriue vs of the libertie, that hee hath once giuen vs, and vvhen he calleth vs to his seruice, his vvill is that it bee of our free election that wee goe therevnto

vnto and not by force or constraint: for although these doe come to God, as spightfull against the world, which hath vexed them, or else because of some labours and afflictions vvhich haue tormēted them: yet notwithstanding they omitt not to giue themselues to God with a free will: and verie often such persons doe proceede verie well in the seruice of God, and become great Saints, and somtimes greater then those, vvho haue entered into Religion by vocations more apparent. You haue read what Platus recounteth of a braue gentle man according to the world, who one day being well adorned and frisled, mounted on a fayre horse, vvith a goodly plume of feathers, endeauoring by all meanes to please the ladie that hee courted; as hee braued it, behould his horse threw him backward to the earth in the midst of the mire and durt, from whence hee came forth all foule and besmired with durt; This poore gentleman was so ashamed and confounded with this accident, that all in a chafe, hee resolued in that instant to become a Religious man, saying: O traiterous vvorld! thou hast mocked mee, but I will also mocke thee: thou hast played mee this tricke, but I will play thee another, for I will neuer haue part vvith the more, and at this instāt I resolue my selfe to become a Religious mān: and this done hee vvas receaued into Religion, vvhere hee ledd a holie life, notvvithstanding his vocation came vpon a disgrace.

§. 5. Furthermore there haue been others whose motiues haue been much more wicked then this, I haue credibly heard that a gētleman of our age, of a braue spiritt and bodye, and verie vvell descended, seeing the Father Capucins to passe by, sayed to the other Noble men vvith vvhom hee vvas; a desire taketh mee to knovv how these barefooted beggars doe liue, and to render my selfe amongst them, not with a determinatiō̄n to remayne allwaies there, but onelie for a month or three weekes, the better to marke what they doe, for thē afterwards I wilbe merrie, and make iestes vpon them with you. Hee so making his plot, pursueed it so stronglie and firmelie that hee vvas in fine receaued: but the diuine prouidence, vvho vsed this meanes to dravve him from the world, conuerted his end and wicked intention into good, and hee that thought to take others, was taken himselfe; for hee had not remayned but some few dayes vvith those good Religious, but hee was holie changed, perseuering faythfullie in his vocation, and hath been a great seruant of God. There are yet others, vvhose vocation in it selfe is not better then this, that is, of those vvho goe into Religion because of some naturall defect, as being lame, hauing but one eye, or being ill fauoured, or hauing some other like defect, ād moreouer that which appeareth worse is, that they are carryed thither by their parents, vvho verie often, when they haue children blind, lame or otherwise defectiue, sett them in a corner at the fire saying, this child is not vvorth anie thing for the world, wee must put him or her into Religion, vvee must procure some benifice for him, it wilbe a good discharge for our house: The childerē permitt themselues to bee conducted whither they please, vnder hope to liue of the goods of the altar: others haue a great nūber of children, vvell say they, vvee must discharge the house and send these into Religion, to the end the eldest hauing all may bee of vvorth and make a great shew in the world. But God verie often in this demonstrateth the greatnesse of his clemencie and mercie, imploying these intentions, which of themselues are in no sort good, to make these persons great seruants of his diuine Maiestie, and in this hee appeareth admirable: So this diuine Artisan

Artisan pleaseth himselfe to make beautifull buildings, vvith vvoode that is verie crooked, and which hath not any apparence to bee proper for any thing in the vvorld: Euen as a person vvho knoweth not what ioyners worke meaneth, seeing some crooked woode in the ioyners shopp, would wonder to heare him say that it to make some beautifull peace of worke: for hee would say if this bee as you say, how oftentimes must the planer passe ouer it, before it can bee made into such a worke? so ordinarilie the diuine prouidence maketh beautifull and principall peeces of vvorke with these crooked and sinister intentions; as hee made the lame and blind to enter into his feast, for to make vs see, that to haue two eyes and two feete serueth for nothing to goe into heauen, and that it is better to goe into heauen vvith one legg, one eye one arme, then for a man to haue two and loose himselfe. Novv such kind of poeple being thus come into Religion, wee see them oftentimes make great profitt, produce much fruit, and perseuere faythfullie in their vocation.

§. 6. There are others vvho haue been called verie well, vvho notvvithstanding haue not perseuered; but after they haue remayned in Religion some time, haue left all, & of this vvee haue an example in Iudas, of vvhose vocatiō wee cānot doubt but hee was vvell called; for our Lord did choose and called him to the Apostle-shipe with his owne mouth, from vvhence then came it that being so well called hee did not perseuere in his vocation? O this vvas because hee abused this libertie, and would not vse the meanes vvhich God had giuen him for this end, but in lieu of imbracing them, and vsing them for his profitt, hee tourned them into abuse, and in doeing this hee lost himselfe, by reiecting them; for it is a certayne thing, that vvhen

 God

God calleth any one to a vocatiō, hee obligeth himselfe consequentlie by his diuine prouidence, to furnish him vvith all requisite helpes, to become perfect in his vocatiō. Novv vvhen I say that our Lord obligeth himselfe, vvee must not thinke that it is vvee, vvho haue obliged him to doe this, in following his vocation; for vvee cannot oblige him: but God obligeth himselfe by himselfe, thrust forward, and prouoked to doe this by the entrailes of his infinit goodnes and mercie: so that decomming Religious, our Lord is of himselfe obliged to furnish mee vvith all that is necessarie for to bee a good Religious, not of dutie, but through his mercie and infinit prouidence: Euen as a great king, raising souldiers for warr, his foresight and prudence requireth, that hee prepare armour to arme them with all, for what likelihood were it to send them to fight without armes, which if he doe not prouide hee is taxed of great imprudence? Now the diuine Maiestie neuer wanteth care, nor foresight touching this: and to make vs the better creditt it hee obligeth himselfe there-vnto, in such sort that wee ought neuer to enter into conceat, that there is fault of his part, vvhen wee doe not well, yea his liberallitie is so great, that he giueth these meanes to those to whom hee is not obliged because hee hath not called them. Note also that when I say, that God is obliged to giue to those whom hee calleth, all the conditions requisite to bee perfect in their vocation, I doe not say that hee giueth them, to them all at once, at the instant that they enter into Religion, O no! vvee must not thinke that entring into Religion they can bee perfect so sodaynlie; it is sufficient that they come to tend to perfection, and to vndertake the meanes fitt to perfect themselues: and to doe this it is necessarie to haue this firme and constant will (of which wee haue spoken) of imbraceing all meanes proper for perfecting themselues in the vocation whereunto they bee called.

§. 7. Behold therefore how secreat and hidden the iudgments of God are, and as some who for despite, and by way of mockerie did enter into Religion, notwithstanding did perseuere well therein: so others being well called, and hauing begun with great feruour did make an euill end and leaue all: therefore it is a verie difficult thing to know if a wœmen haue a good vocation from God, for to giue her your voice; for although wee see her feruent it may bee she will not perseuere so: but so much the worse for her, you must not therefore if you see that she hath this constant vvill, to desire to serue God and perfect her selfe, deny to giue her your voice: for if she will receaue the helpes that our Lord vvill infaillibly giue her, she vvill perseuere: but if after some yeares she loose perseuerance to her damnation, you are not the cause but her selfe. And this bee spoken for the first part and knowledg of vocations.

§. 8. Tonching the second, that is to say, To know what conditions they ought to haue who offer themselues, first those wee receaue into the house, secondlie those wee receaue to the Nouitiat, and in the third place, those vvee receaue to profession. I haue little to say about the first reception, for vvee cannot know these much, vvho doe come with so good countenance, and outvvard shevv: speake to them they vvill doe all vvee vvill haue them: they resemble Sainct Iohn and Sainct Iames, to vvhom our Lord sayed: Can you drinke the Chalice of my passion? They bouldlie and freelie

 aunswered

aunſvvered I and yet the night of his paſſion they left and for ſooke him. Theſe women doe ſo, they make ſo manie prayers, ſo manie Reuerences, they shew ſo much good vvill that vvee cannot vvell deny them, and in effect in my opinion wee need not make verie great conſideration thereof. I ſay this for the interiour: for truelie it is verie difficult at this time, to bee able to knovv it, principallie of thoſe vvho come farr of, all that wee can doe to them, is to knovv who they are, and ſuch things as regard the temporall and exteriour, then open thẽ the gate, and put them to their firſt triall. If they bee of the place where wee dwell, wee may obſerue their behauiour, and by the conuerſation vvee haue vvith them, come to knovv ſomething of their interiour: but I find this verie difficulte notvvitſtanding: for they allwaies come in the beſt fashion and poſture they can. Now in my opinion for that which concerneth their corporall health, and infirmitie of bodie, there is no neceſſitie of making any great conſideration, for ſo much as in theſe houſes wee may receaue the weake and feeble aſvvell as the ſtrong and robuſt: ſince they haue beene built partlie for them, prouided that the infirmities bee not ſo great, that they make them wholie incapable of obſeruing the Rule, and vnable to performe that vvhich this vocation requireth: but excepting this, I would neuer refuſe them my voice, no not vvhen they should be blind, or should haue but one legg, if vvith this they should haue the other conditions requiſite to this vocation; and lett not humayne prudence ſay to mee, But if ſuch kind of poeple should allwaies bee preſented, muſt wee allvvaies receaue them, and if all vvere blind or ſicke vvho shall ſerue them? trouble not your ſelues vvith this for it vvill neuer arriue: leaue this in the care of the diuine prouidence, vvho knoweth vvell hovv to
prouide

prouide for it; and to call the strong necessarie for the seruice of the weake. VVhen the infirme shall present themselues, say, God bee blessed, and vvhen the strong come, in good time be it. In summe, the sicke vvho hinder not the obseruance of the Rule, ought not to bee reiected in your houses. Behould vvhat I had to say to you touching this first reception.

§. 9. Touching the second vvhich is of receauing any into the Nouitiat, I doe not yet find that there are any great difficulties, notvvithstanding vvee ought to haue more consideration then in their first receauing: for vvee haue had also more meanes to note their humours, actions and habitudes, vvee see vvell the passions that they haue; but for all this vvee ought not to hinder them from being admitted to the Nouitiat, prouided that they haue a good vvill to amend and submitt themselues, and to serue themselues of the medicines proper for to heale them. And although they haue repugnance against these remedies, and take them vvith great difficultie, their is nothing to bee sayed to this, prouided that they giue not ouer the practice of them; for medicines are allvvaies bitter to the tast, and it is not possible, that they receaue them, vvith the svveetnes they vvould doe if they were pleasing to the appetite: but for all this omitt not to haue their operation; and vvhen they haue it it is better then that they haue the more paine and labour: euen iust as a sister that hath her passions strong; she is cholericke, she committeth manie defects, if she wilbe cured of this, and desire that wee correct & mortifie it, and that wee giue her remedies proper for her cure, although the taking of them trouble and vex her, vvee must not therefore refuse her our voice, for she hath not onelie a will to bee healed; but furthermore she taketh the remedies which are giuen her for this purpose, although vvith payne and difficultie. VVe shall find those who haue been ill bredd, and not trained vp in ciuillitie vvho vvill haue a rude and lumpish nature: novv there is no doubt but these haue more payne and difficultie, then those who haue a more sweet and tractable disposition, and that they wilbe more subiect to committ faults then others vvho haue been better bredd: but neuerthelesse if they desire to bee vvell cured, and by their indeauours vvitnesse a firme vvill to seeke and desire to receaue the remedies, although it bee to their cost, to such as these I vvould giue my voice, notvvithstanding these relapses: For these after much labour produce great fruit in Religion becomming great seruants of God, and gayning strong and solide vertue; for the graces of God supplyeth the defect, and there is no doubt, that often vvhere there is lesse of nature, there is more of grace. Therefore vvee ought not to refuse to receaue such into the Nouitiat although they haue many euill habitts, prouided such persons vvil be cured. In summe to receaue one into the Nouitiat there is nothing to bee knovvne, but if she haue a good vvill, and if she bee deliberatelie resolued to receaue the vsage shal be giuen her for her cure, and to liue in great submission; hauing this I vvould giue her my voice: Behould! I thinke this is all that can bee sayed concerning this second reception.

§. 10. For the third it is a thing of great importance, to receaue any to professiō, and in this it seemeth to mee wee ought to obserue three things; the first that those vvee receaue to profession bee sound not of bodie (as I haue alreadie sayed) but of hart and spiritt, I vvould say, vvho haue their hart vvell disposed to liue in an entire flexiblenesse and sub-

and ſubmiſſion. Secondlie that they haue à good, ſpiritt; novv vvhen I ſay a good ſpiritt, I entend not to ſpeake of thoſe great ſpiritts, vvho are ordinarilie vaine, and full of ſelfe-iudgments, of imaginarie ſufficiencie, and vvho in the vvorld vvere ſhopps of vanitie, vvho come into Religion not to humble themſelues, but as if they vvould read there leſſons of Philoſophy and Theologie, haueing a vvill to guid and gouerne all. Of ſuch as theſe you muſt take great heede: I ſay there muſt bee good care taken of them, not that they muſt not bee receaued, if vvee ſee that they vvil bee chāged and humble themſelues: for they vvil be able in time vvith the grace of God to make this chang, vvhich will arriue without doubt, if they vſe faythfullie the remedies which shal be giuen them, for their amendment. Therefore when I ſpeake of a good ſpiritt, I intend iudicious and well made ſpiritts, and more-ouer of a moderate temper, who are not very great nor verie little, for ſuch ſpiritts allwaies doe much, vvithout knovving it themſelues. They applie thēſelues to worke, and giue thēſelues to ſolide vertues, they are tractable, and vvee haue not much trouble to guid them: for they eaſilie cōprehēd how good a thing it is, to leaue themſelues to bee gouerned by others. The third thing that is to bee obſerued is this, if she haue laboured vvell in the yeare of her Nouitiat, if she haue ſuffered vvell and profited vvith the medecines that haue been giuen her, if she haue made much of thoſe reſolutions that she promiſed entring into the Nouitiat of changing her euill humours and inclinations; for the yeare of Nouitiat hath bene giuen her for this. If vvee ſee she hath perſeuered faythfully in her reſolution, and that her vill remayneth firme and conſtant, and that she applyes her ſelfe to reforme her ſelfe, and behaue her selfe according to the Rule and constitutions, and that this vvill endure, yea allvvaies desireth to doe better, this is a good signe and a good conditiō, for to giue her your voice: although notvvithstanding she leaue not to commit faultes and also great enough, for although in the yeare of her Nouitiat she ought to labour for the reformation of her manners and habitts, it is not therefore to be sayed, that she must not make any relapse, nor that at the end of her Nouitiat she ought to bee perfect. For behold the Colledg of our Lord the Glorious Apostles, although they were called well, and had laboured much in the reformation of their liues, how often did they committ faultes not onelie in the first yeare; but also in the second and third? all did speake and promise maruelles, yea euen to follow our Lord into prison and death: but in the night of his passion, vvhen Iudas came to take their good Maister, all forsooke him. Therefore I will say that falles ought not to bee a cause that wee reiect one vvhen among all this, she remayneth vvith a verie strong will to redresse her selfe, and vvith a vvill to helpe her selfe by the meanes vvhich are giuen her for this purpose. This is that I had to say touching the conditions, which those ought to haue vvhom wee would receaue to profession, and vvhat the sisters ought to obserue to giue thē their voices: herevpon I will finish my discourse, if you demaund not any further question.

§.11. VVee demaund first, if any one be found, Who was subiect to bee troubled for small matters, and that her spirit was often full of melencholie and vnquietness, and that she did witness by this, little loue of her vocation: and yet notwithstanding this being past, she promiseth to doe maruailles, what should bee done to her? it is most certayne that such a person, being so changeable is not

propes

proper for Religiō: for in this she will not be cureed, wee must giue her leaue to depart. VVe doe not know, you say, whether this proceedeth from want of will to bee cured, or because she doth not comprehend wherein true vertue consisteth. But if after she hath bene made to vnderstand what she ought to doe for her amendment, she doth it not, but becommeth incorrigible, she must bee reiected; especially because her faults as you say, proceed not for want of iudgment, nor of abillitie to comprehend where-in true vertue consisteth, much lesse to know the meanes she ought to vse for her amēdment; but it is from the defect of the will which hath not perseuerance, nor cōstancie to execute and serue it selfe of that which she knoweth to be requisite for her amendment, although she say somtimes that she will doe better yet doth it not, but perseuereth in this inconstancie of will, I would not giue her my voice. Moreouer, you say, there are some so delicate that they cannot support correction without much trouble, and this maketh them often sicke: if this be so, open them the gate; for since they are sicke, and will not that wee treat them, nor apply to them the remedies fitt for their health, wee cleerlie see that doing so, they will become incorrigible, and giue not any hope to bee able to cure them: because this delicacie aswell of spiritt as of bodie, is one of the greatest hindrances which can bee in a Religious life, and therefore wee must haue an especiall care, not to receaue such who are vnmeasurably tainted therewith; because they will not bee cured, refusing to vse those things, which are giuen them for their health.

§. 12. Secondlie, wee demaund what wee ought to iudg of her, who withnesseth by her words, that she repenteth her selfe of entring into Religion? Trulie if she perseuere in these disgusts of her vo-

cation

cation and repentāce, and that vvee see that this maketh her remisse and negligent to behaue her selfe according to the spirit of her vocation, she must bee put forth; neuerthelesse vvee must consider that this may happen, either by a simple tentation, or for her exercise and triall: and this may bee knovvne, by the profit she shall make of such thoughts, disgusts or repentance, vvhen vvith simplicitie she shall discouer her selfe of such things, and that she vvil be faythful to vse the remedies that shal be giuē her for itt, for God neuer permitteth any thing for our exercise, but that hee vvould vvee should drayve profitt thereby, the vvhich is allvvaies done, whē vvee are faythfull to discouer our selues, and as I haue sayed, simple to beleeue and to execute that vvhich is appointed vs, and this is a marke that the exercise is of God: but vvhen vvee see that this person vseth her selfe-iudgment, and that her vvill is seduced and corrupted, perseuering in her disgusts, then her case is in ill estate, and as it vvere vvithout remedie: she must bee dismissed.

§. 13. Thirdlie you demaund if vvee ought not to make consideration, of giuing our voice to one that is not cordiall, or vvho is not equall tovvards all the sisters, and who hath manifested that she hath more inclination to one then to another. VVee must not bee so rigourous for these small matters; Consider that this inclination is the last peece of our renuntiation: for before wee can arriue to this point, not to haue any inclinatiō to one more then to another, and that these affectiōs bee so mortified that they appeare not, there must bee time for it. VVee must obserue in this as in all other things, if this sister is become incorrigible.

§. 14. In fine you say, if the opinion of the other sisters were wholie contrarie to that you know, and that there came an inspiration to you to speake

something

something that you haue knowne, which is to the aduātage of the sisters hould it bee ommitted to bee spaken of? no: allthough the conceate of others be wholie contrarie to yours, and that you bee onelie in this opinion: for this may serue for others to resolue thēselues what they ought to doe. The Holie Ghoste ought to preceede in the communitie, and they are to resolue themselues according to the varietie of opinions, for to doe as they iudg most expedient for his Glorie: Now this inclination that wee haue that others giue their voice, or that they giue it not, although we giue, or doe not giue ours, ought to bee contemned and reiected as another tentation: but wee must neuer make shew among the sisters of our inclinations or auersions in this occasion. In fine, for all the imperfections that woemen bring out of the world, this rule must bee regarded; when wee see that they amend themselues, although that they leaue not to committ faultes, wee must not reiect them; for by the amēdment they make it appeere that they will not remayne incorrigible.

THE EIGHTEENTH ENTERTAINEMENT.

HOVV VVEE OVGHT TO RECEAVE THE Sacraments, and recite the diuine Office vvith other pointes touching prayer.

§. 1. BEfore that wee know how wee ought to prepare our selues to receaue the Sacraments, and what fruit wee should receaue by thē, it is necessarie to knovv vvhat the Sacraments and their effects are. The Sacraments then are the conduits (so to speake) vvhereby God descendeth to vs, as by prayer vvee ascend to him, since prayer

prayer is no other thing then an eleuation of our spiritt vnto God. The effects of the Sacraments are diuers although they haue all but one and the selfe same end and pretention, which is to vnite vs with God. By the Sacrament of Baptisme, wee vnite our selues to God, as the sonne with the Father; by that of Confirmation, wee vnite our selues to him as a souldier with his Captayne, receauing strenght to fight and vanquish our enimies in all tentations. By the Sacrament of Pennance wee are vnited to God as reconciled freinds: by that of the Eucharist, as foode with the stomacke: by that of Extreame-vnction, wee vnite our selues to God as a child who comming from a farr country, alreadie putting one of his feete into the house of his father, to revnite himselfe with him, his mother, and all the familie. Now these are the effects of the Sacraments: but notwithstanding which demaunde all the vniō of our soule with her God. VVee will speake now but of two of thē, to witt of Pennance, and of the Holie Eucharist. And first it is most necessarie, that wee should know wherefore it is, that so often receauing these two Sacraments, wee doe not also receaue the graces, which they are accustomed to bring to soules which are well prepared; since these graces are ioyned to the Sacramēts. I will declare it in a word, it is for want of due preparation, and therefore wee must know how wee ought to prepare our selues well to receaue these two Sacraments, and so like-wise all the others.

§. 2. Therefore, the first preparation is puritie of intention; the second is attention, the third is hulitie. Touching puritie of intention, it is a thing totallie necessaire, not onelie in the reception of the Sacraments: but further more in all that wee haue to doe. Now the intention is then pure when wee receaue the Sacraments, or doe any other thing

whatsoeuer

vvhatsoeuer it bee, for to vnite vs vvith God, and to bee more pleasing to him, without any mixture of proper interest. You shall knovv this; if vvhen you desire to communicate, your Superiours vvill not permitt you, or othervvise if after the holie Communion you haue not had consolation, and notvvithstanding this you remayne in peace, not consenting to the assaultes vvhich may come to you: but if contrarivvise you consent to vnquietnesse, because they refuse yon to communicate, or because you haue not had consolation, vvho seeth not that your intention vvas impure and that you sought not to vnite your selfe to God, but to consolations, since that your vnion with God ought to bee made vnder the vertue of holie Obedience? and euen so likevvise if you shall desire perfection vvith a desire full of vnquietnesse, vvho seeth not that it is selfe-loue, vvhich vvould not that others should see imperfections in you? If it vvere possible, that vvee could bee as pleasing to God being imperfect as being perfect, vvee ought to desire to bee vvithout perfection, to the end to nourish vvithin vs by this meanes most holie humilitie.

§. 3. The second preparation is attention. Truelie vvee ought to goe to the Sacraments with verye much attention asvvell for the greatnesse of the vvorke, as concerning that vvhich each Sacrament requireth of vs. For exemple going to Confession, vvee ought to carrie thither, a hart louinglie dolorous, and to the holie Communion, wee ought to beare a hart ardentlie louing. I doe not say by this great attention that vvee should not haue any distractions, for this is not in our povver, but I intend to say that vvee must haue a verie particular care, not to settle our selues therein vvillinglie.

§. 4. The third preparation is humilitie, vvhich is a

is a vertue verie necessarie to receaue the graces abundantlie, vvhich flow vnto vs by the conduits of the Sacraments, because waters are accustomed to glide more swiftlie and stronglie, when the conduits are placed in bending places, and tending down-wards.

But besides these three preparations, I desire to speake a word to you about the principall end of all, which is the totall abandoning of our selues to the mercie of God, submitting our will and all our affection to his dominiō without any reseruation. I say without reseruation, for so much as our miserie is so great that wee alwaies reserue something to our selues. The most spirituall persons ordinarilie reserue to thēselues the will of haueing vertues, and when they goe to the holie cōmuniō; O Lord, say they, I abādō my selfe intirelie without reseruatiō into thy hādes; but lett it please thee to giue mee prudēce to know how to liue honourably, but they neuer demaunde simplicitie. O my God! I submitt my selfe absolutelie to thy diuine will; but giue mee fortitude to thy diuine will: but giue mee fortitude to performe excellent workes for thy seruice; but of sweetnes aud mildnes of spiritt to liue peaceably with their neighbour, they speake not off at all. Giue meee, will another say, that humilitie which is proper for to giue good example: but humilitie of hart vvhich maketh vs loue our owne abiection, they haue no neede thereof as they thinke. O my God, since that I am wholie thine lett mee haue allwaies consolation in prayer. Yea, is this that vvhich is necessarie for to bee vnited vvith God, vvhich is the pretention that vvee haue? But they neuer aske tribulations or mortifications. O! It is not the meanes to make this vnion, to reserue to themselues all these vvills, for the fayre shevv that they make: for our Lord desireth

to giue

to giue himselfe vvholie vnto vs, and his will is that reciprocally vvee should giue our selues entirelie vnto him: to the end, that the vnion of our soule vvith his diuine maiestie might bee more perfect, and that vvee might bee able truelie to say, follovving the great Apostle: I liue no more in my selfe, but it is Iesus that liueth in mee.

§. 5. The second part of this preparation consisteth in emptying our hart of all things, to the end our Lord himselfe may vvholie replenish it: trulie the cause vvherfore vvee doe not receaue the grace of sanctification (since that one onelie Communion vvell receaued, is capable and sufficient to make vs holie and perfect) proceedeth not, but of this that vvee permitt not our Lord to raigne in vs, as his goodnes desireth to doe. This vvelbeloued of our soules cometh into vs, and hee findeth our harts topp full of good affections and desires, but this is not that vvhich hee seeketh: for hee desireth to find them empty, that hee may make himselfe maister ād gouerner thereof: And to shevv hovv much hee desireth it, hee sayeth to his sacred spouse, that she should put him as a seale vppon her hart, to the end that nothing might enter there but by his permission, and according to his good pleasure. Novv I knovv that the midst of your harts is emptie (othervvise it should bee a verie great infidelitie) I vvould say that you haue not onelie reiected, and detested mortall sinne, but all kindes of vvicked affections: but alas all the nookes and corners of our harts are full of a thousand things, vnvvorthy to appeare in the presence of this Soueraygne King: VVee seeme to bind his hands and to hinder him from distributing the benefits and graces, vvhich his goodnes hath desire to be-

stovve

ſtovve vpon vs, if hee found vs prepared. Lett vs therefore on our part doe vvhat is in our povver, to prepare our ſelues vvell to receaue this ſuperſubſtantiall bread, abandonning our ſelues totally to the diuine prouidence, not onelie for that vvhich concerneth temporall goods, but principallie the ſpirituall, povvring forth in the preſence of the diuine goodnes, all our affections, deſires and inclinations, for to bee intirelie ſubiect vnto him, and lett vs aſſure our ſelues, our Lord vvill accomplish on his part, the promiſe that hee hath made of transforming vs into himſelfe, raiſing our baſenes vntill it bee vnited to his greatnes.

§. 6. VVe may communicate vvell for diuers ends, as to demaunde of God to bee deliuered of ſome tentation or affliction, bee it for our ſelues or for our freinds, or to begg ſome vertue, prouided it bee vnder this condition, for to vnite vs by this meanes more perfectlie vnto God, the vvhich arriueth not verie often, for in the time of affliction, vvee are more ordinarilie vnited vnto God, becauſe vvee remember him more often. And for as much as concerneth vertues, ſomtimes it is more to the purpoſe, and better for vs not to haue them in habitt, then if vvee had them, prouided notvvithſtanding that vvee doe acts of vertue, according to the meaſure that the occaſions doe preſent themſelues: for the repugnance that vvee feele to practice ſome one vertue, ought to ſerue vs to hūble our ſelues, and humilitie is allvvaies more vvorth then all this. In fine it is neceſſarie that in all the prayers and demaunds you make to God, you make them not onelie for your ſelues, but that you allvvaies obſerue to ſay vs, as our Lord hath taught vs in the Dominicall prayer, vvhere there is neither mee nor mine, nor I, that is to ſay, that you haue intention to pray to God, that hee giue the vertue

or grace

or grace that you aske of him for your selfe, to all those that haue the same necessitie: and lett this bee allwaies vvith intention to vnite your selfe more vvith him: for othervvise vve ought not to aske or desire any thing, neither for our selues nor for our neighbour, since this is the end, for vvhich the Sacraments are instituted: therefore vvee ought to correspond to this intention of our Lord, receauing them for this end, and vvee must not thinke, that communicating or praying for others, wee loose any thing thereby; except vvhen vvee offer to God this communion or prayer, for the satisfaction of their sinnes: for then vvee doe not satisfie for our ovvne, but notvvithstanding the meritt of the Communion, and prayer shall remayne to vs: for vvee cannot deserue grace one for the other, there is none but our Sauiour vvho can doe it; wee may indeed impetrate graces for others; but vvee are not able to deserue them. The prayer which wee haue made for them augmenteth our merit, aswell for the recompence of grace in this life, as of glorie in the other. And if any one did not make her attention to doe somthing for the satisfaction of her sinnes, the onelie attention that she should haue, to doe all that she doeth for the pure Loue of God should suffice to satisfie for them, since it is most assured, that vvhosoeuer should be able to make an excellent act of Charitie, or an act of perfect contrition, should satisfie fully for all his sinnes.

§. 7. You vvould it may bee informed, hovv you should know, if you doe profit by the meanes of receauing the Sacraments. You shall knovv it if you aduance your selfe in the vertues, which are proper to them; as if you dravve from Confession the loue of your owne abiection, and humilitie: for these are the vertues that are proper to it, and it is allwaies is allvvaies by the measure of humilie that vvee knowe our aduancement; See you not that it is sayed that whosoeuer humbleth him selfe shalbe exalted; to be exalted is to bee aduanced. If by the meanes of the holie Communion, you become verie gentle(since that this is the vertue which is proper to this Sacrament, vvhich is altogether svveete, delectable and mellifluous) you reap the fruit that is proper vnto it, and so you aduance your selfe: but if on the contrarie you become not more humble, nor more gentle, you deserue not your bread, since you vvill not labour for it.

§. 8. I desire verie much that vvhen the desire to communicate shall come into our mind, vvee goe simply to aske it of our Superiours, vvith resignation to accept humbly the refusall, if they giue it vs, and if they grant vs our request, to goe to the Cummunion vvith loue, although there bee mortification in the demaunding of it, vvee must not therefore omitt to doe it; for those vvho enter into the congregation, enter not there-in but to mortifie themselues, and the Crosse vvhich they carrie, ought to put thē in mind thereof. VVhat if the inspiratiō did come to some one not to communicate so often as the others, because of the knovvledg she hath of her indignitie? She may aske the Superiour expecting the iudgment she vvill giue, with great svveetnes and humilitie.

I vvould also that vvee did not disquiet our selues, vvhen vvee heare some fault that vvee haue, spoken of, or some vertue that vvee haue not, but lett vs bless God, because hee hath discouered to vs the meanes to attayne the vertue, and to correct in our selues the imperfection, and then to take courage to serue our selues of these meanes. VVee ought to haue generous spiritts, vvhich are not fastened but to God onelie, vvithout any attention to what to vvhat our inferiour part vvilleth, makeing the superiour part of our soule to raigne, since it is intirelie in our povver vvith the grace of God neuer to consent to the inferiour. Consolations and tendernesses ought not to bee desired, since that this is not necessarie vnto vs to loue our Lord the more. Therefore it is not necessarie to pause and consider if vvee haue good feelings: but vvee must doe that vvhich vve vvould doe if vvee had them. Also it is not necessarie to bee so Scrupulous to desire to confess so many small imperfections, since that vvee are not obliged to confess vs of veniall sinnes at all if vvee vvill not: but when one confesseth them, hee ought to haue a resolute vvill to amend: it vvil be othervvise an abuse to confesse them. Likevvise vvee must not torment our selues vvhen vvee doe not remember our faultes to confess them: for it is not credible, that a soule that maketh her often examine; doth not sufficientlie enough remember her selfe of those faultes that are of importance. As for so manie small and lighte faults, you may speake vvith our Lord about them euerie time that you perceaue them, one humiliation of spiritt, one sigh sufficeth for this.

§. 9. You aske hovv you may make your act of Contrition in little time, I tell you that there is allmost no necessitie of time to doe it vvell: since it is no other thing then to prostrate ones selfe before God in the spiritt of humilitie, and repentance for hauing offended him. Secondlie you desire that I speake to you of the diuine Office: I vvill vvillinglie; and first I say to you, that vvee ought to prepare our selues to say it, from that instant that vvee heare the bell that calleth vs thereunto, and vvee ought in imitation of Sainct Bernard, to aske of our hart vvhat it is that

it goeth

it goeth to doe; and not onelie in this occasion, but also in the entrance to all our exercises, to the end vvee may carrie to euerie one of them, the spiritt that is proper for it; for it wilbe to no purpose to goe to the Office as to recreation; for to recreation vee must beare a spiritt amorouslie ioyfull; and to the Office a spiritt seriouslie louing; vvhen vvee say: *Deus in adiutorium meũ intende*; vvee must thinke that our Lord reciprocallie sayeth to vs: And bee you attentiue to mee: Lett those vvho vnderstand somevvhat of that vvhich they say in the Office, employ faythfullie this talent according to the good pleasure of God, vvho hath giuen it to helpe them to keepe themselues recollected, by the meanes of the good affections they may dravve there-of; and lett those vvho doe not vnderstand, keepe themselues simply attentiue to God, or else make darting amourous desires, vvhiles the other Quier sayeth the verse, and they make the pauses. It ought also to bee considered, that vvee doe the same office as the Angells, although in diuers language; and that vvee are before the same God, before vvhom the Angells tremble, and euen as a man vvho did speake to a king, should become verie attentiue, fearing to committ some fault; but if notvvithstanding all his care, hee did happen to faile, hee vvould blush incontinentlie: so likevvise ought wee to doe in the Office, stãding vpon our gaurd, fearing to faile: More-ouer it is requisite, to haue attention to pronunce vvell, and to say as it is ordayned, aboue all in the beginning: but if vvee happen to committ some defect therein, vvee must humble our selues for it vvithout astonishment, since it is no strang thing, for vvee doe it elswhere: but if vvee happen to doe it manie times, and that this continue, there is a signe that vvee haue not conceaued a true displeasure of our first fault; and it is it is this negligence vvhich should bring vs verie much confusion, not because of the presence of the Superiour; but for the respect of God, and of his Angells vvho are present vvith vs. Novv it is allmost a generall rule, that vvhen vvee committ so often one and the selfe same fault; it is a signe vvee vvant affection to amend it, and if it bee a thing vvhere-of vvee haue been oftentimes aduertised, there is apparence that vvee neglect the aduertisment.

§. 10. More-ouer you ought not to haue a scruple of omitting in the vvhole office tvvo or three verses by mistake, prouided that you did it not of purpose, but if you slumber a good part of the office, although you say your verses on your quire, you are obliged to say it againe; but vvhen you doe things that are necessarie to bee done in the Office, as to cough or to spitt, or that the Mistris of the ceremonies speaketh for matter of the office, then you are not obliged to say it againe.

VVhen they enter into the Quire, the Office being begun, they must place themselues in their ranke vvith the others; and follovv on the Office vvith them, and after that it is sayed, you must retake that which the Quire had sayed before you were there, ending vvhere you had taken it; if not you must say vvith a lowe voice, that vvhich the Quire hath sayed, then hauing ouertaken it, cōtinue there-vvith in case your assistance there bee truelie necessarie. You must not say your Office againe for hauing been distracted in saying of it, prouided it bee not, voluntarie and althoug you should find your selues at the end of some psalme not being vvell assured that you haue sayed it because that you haue bene distracted not thinking there-on, omitt not to pass forvvard humbling your selues before God;

for vvee

for vve must not allvvaies thinke that vvee haue been negligent vvhen the distraction hath been long; for it may verie vvell bee it vvill endure the length of an Office vvithout any fault of ours, and hovv bad soeuer it vvere vvee should not bee troubled; but make simple refusalls of it from time to time before God: I desire that vve should neuer bee troubled for the bad motions that vve haue, but that vve faythfullie and couragiouslie imploy our selues not to consent there-vnto, since there is verie great difference betvveene, to feele, and to consent.

§. 11. You desire that I speake something of prayer; manie are verie much deceaued, beleeuing that much method is necessarie to doe it vvell, and they trouble themselues to find out a certayne art, vvhich they thinke is necessarie to bee knovvne therein, neuer ceasing to subtilize, and pry about their prayers to see hovv they haue made them, or hovv they shalbe able to doe it according to their likeing, thinking they must not cough nor moue dureing the time, for feare that the spiritt of God vvithdravve it selfe. A verie great follie truely; as if the spiritt of God vvere so nice, that it depended of the methode and countenāce of those vvho praye; I doe not say that vve must not vse those methodes vvhich are appoynted vs; but vvee ought not so tye our selues vnto them, as those doe vvho neuer thinke they haue made their prayer vvell, if they haue not made their considerations before the affections that our Lord giueth them, vvhich is notvvithstanding the end for the vvhich vvee make considerations; such persons resemble those vvho findeing themselues in the place vvhither they pretended to goe, retourne backe againe because they are not come by the vvay that hath been taught them; Neuerthelesse it is requisite vvee behaue our selues

vvith

great reuerēce speaking to the diuine Maiestie since the Angells who are so pure tremble in his presence: but good God! will some soules say, I cannot allwaies haue this feeling of the presence of God, which causeth so great an humiliation to the soule, nor this sensible reuerence, which annihilateth mee so sweetlie and acceptably before God: Now it is not of this that I entend to speake, but of that which the superiour part, and the topp of the spiritt worketh, houlding it selfe abiect, and in humilitie before God, in acknowledgmēt of his infinitt goodnes and our profoūnd littlenesse & indignitie.

§. 12. VVee must also haue a great resolution, neuer to abādon prayer, for any difficultie that may bee found there-in, nor to goe with any preoccupation of desires, to bee comforted and satisfied there-in: for this will not bee to yeald our will vnited and ioyned to that of our Lord, whose will is that entring to prayer wee bee resolued to suffer the payne of continuall distractiōs, drinesse and disgust which shall come vpō vs there-in, remayning as cōstant as if wee had had much consolation and trāquillitie, since it is certayne that our prayer shall not bee less acceptable to God nor lesse profitable to vs, for being made with more difficultie: prouided that vvee allvvaies place iustlie our vvill with the vvill of the diuine Maiestie remayning in a simple attētiō, and dispositiō to receaue the euēts of his good pleasure with loue, bee in it prayer, or other occurrāces: hee will cause that all things shal be profitable to vs, and acceptable to his diuine goodnes. Therefore this shall be to pray vvell, my deare daughters, to keepe your selues in peace and tranquillitie neere our Lord, or in his sight vvithout any other desire, or pretentiō but to bee vvith him, and to content him.

§. 13. The first methode thē for to entertayne our sel-

ues in prayer, is to take some point, as the misteries of the death, Life and passion of our Lord, the which are the most profitable; and it is a verie rare thing, that wee cannot bee able to profit by the consideration of that which our Lord hath done, who is the soueraygne Maister, whom the eternall Father hath sent into the world to teach vs what wee ought to doe: and therefore besides the obligation that wee haue, to forme our selues according to this diuine modell, we ought to bee verie exact to consider his actions, for to imitate them, because it is one of the most excellent intentions that wee can haue, for all whatsoeuer wee doe, to performe it because our Lord hath done it, that is to say, to practice vertues, because that our Father hath practiced them, and as hee hath practiced thē; The better to comprehend this, wee ought faythfullie to ponder, see, and consider them in prayer; for the child that loueth his Father well hath a great affection to conforme himselfe to his humours, & to imitate him in all that hee doeth. That which you say is true, that there are soules, who cannot settle themselues, nor busie their spiritts vpō any misterie, being drawne to a certayne sweete simplicitie, which houldeth them in great tranquillitie before God, without any other consideration, then to know that they are before him, who is all their good: they may remayne so profitably, and this is good; but generallie speaking, we ought to prouide that all the sisters begin by the methode of prayer, which is the most sure, & which carrieth them to the reformation of life and mãners, which is this wee speake of, which is made about the mysteries of the Life and death of our Lord; there wee walke in securitie. Therefore wee ought to apply our selues sweetlie and simply about our Maister to learne that which hee would wee should doe,
and

and likevvise those that can vse their imagination ought to doe it; but it must bee vsed soberlye, verie simply & breiflie. The holie Fathers haue left many pious and deuout considerations, which wee may vse for this subiect, for since the great sancts and holie men haue composed them, who shall dare to refuse piouslie to beleeue that which they haue piouslie beleeued? VVee must goe assuredlie after these persons, of so great authoritie: But not contenting themselues vvith that vvhich they haue left; many men haue made numbers of other imaginations, and it is of these vvhereof vvee must not serue our selues for meditation, for so much as it may bee preiudiciall.

VVee ought to make our resolutions in the feruour of prayer, vvhen the sunne of iustice shineth vppon vs and inciteth vs by his inspiration. I vvill not say therefore, that vvee must haue great feelings and consolations, although vvhen God giueth them vs vvee are obliged to make our profitt of them, and to corespond to his loue, but vvhen hee doth not giue them vs, vvee ought not to vvant fidelitie; but to liue according to reason and the diuine vvill, and to make our resolutions vvith the point of our spiritt and superiour part of our soule, not omitting to effectuate and putt them in practice for any drynesse, repugnance or contradiction that can or may present it selfe. Behould then heere, the first manner of meditating, vvhich manie great saincts haue practiced, vvhich is verie good vvhen it is made as it ought.

§. 14. The Second manner of meditacting is, not to vse the imagination; but to hould themselues to the foote of the Letter, that is to say, to meditate purelie and simply the Gospell, and the misteries of our fayth, entertayning themselues familiarlie and verie simply vvith our Lord, of that vvhich hee

hath done and suffered for vs, vvithout any representation. Novv this manner is much more high
and better thē the first, and so it is more holie and
more assured, vvherefore vvee ought to bee carried
easilie by the least attract that vvee haue there-vnto;
obseruing euerie degree of prayer, to keepe our
spiritt in holie liberty, for to follovv the lights and
motions that God vvill giue vs; But for other kinds
of prayer more eleuated, vnlesse that God send them
absolutelie, I praye you that you vndertake them
not of your selfe, and without the aduise of those
vvho guide you.

LIVE IESVS.

THE NINETEENTH INTER-TAINEMENT.

VPON THE VERTVES OF Sainct Ioseph.

1. THe iust man is made like to the Palme-tree, as the holie Church causeth vs to sing in euerie feast of holie Confessours. But as the palme-tree hath a verie great varietie of particulier properties aboue all other trees, as being the prince and king of trees, as well for the beautie as goodnes of his fruit: euen so there is verie great varietie of Iustice, although that all the iust bee iust, and equall in Iustice: notvvithstanding there is a great disproportion betvveene the particular acts of their Iustice: euen as the garment of the Patriarke Ioseph doth represent vnto vs, vvhich vvas long euen vnto the heeles, imbrodered vvith a goodlie varietie of flovvers: euerie iust man hath a garment of iustice, vvhich couereth him euen to the heeles, that is to say, all the povvers & faculties

culties of his soule are couered vvith iustice, and his interiour and exteriour represent no other thing then iustice it selfe, being iust in all his actions and motions, asvvell interiour as exteriour; but notvvithstanding it must bee confessed that euerie garment is embrodered vvith varietie of diuers fayre flovvers, vvhereof the inequallitie maketh them not the less delightfull, nor lesse commendable. The great Sainct Paul the Hermitt vvas iust with most perfect iustice, and yet neuerthelesse, it is not to bee doubted, that hee did neuer exercise so much Charitie tovvards the poore as Sainct Iohn, vvho therefore vvas called the Almes-giuer, nor had hee euer the occasions to practice Magnificence, and therefore hee had not this vertue in so high a degree as manie other Saincts: hee had all vertues, but some of them not in so high a degree as the others: the Saints haue excelled some in one vertue, others in another, and although they are all Sainctts yet verie differentlie, there being asmuch difference in Sainctitie as there is in Saincts. This therefore being presupposed, I note three particular properties that the Palme-tree hath among all others, vvhich are in verie great nũber; vvhich properties appertayne best to the Sainct whose feast vvee celebrate, who is (as the holy Church ordayneth vs to say) like to the Palme tree. O vvhat a Sainct is the glorious Sainct Ioseph! vvho is not onelie a Patriark, but the cheife of all the Patriarcks; hee is not simply a Confessour but more then a Confessour: for in his Confession are contayned the dignities of Bishops, the generositie of Martyres, and of all the other Saincts. Therefore it is with iust reason that hee is compared to the Palme-tree which is the king of trees, and which hath the propertie of virginitie, of humilitie, and of constancie and valour. Thre vertues vvhere-in the Glorious Sainct Ioseph hath excee-dinglie excelled, and if vvee durst make compari-sons, there vvould bee manie vvho vvould mayn-taine that hee passed all the other Saincts in these three vertues. Among the Palmes is found the male and feemale. The male beareth not fruit, and neuer-thelesse hee is not vnfruitfull, for the Palme female vvould not beare fruit vvithout him and his aspect: in such sort that if the Palme female bee not plant-ed neere to the male-Palme tree and in his aspect, she remaineth vnfruitfull, & bereth not dates, vvhich is her fruit; and on the contrarie if she bee regarded of the male Palme and bee in his aspect, she produceth and bringeth forth much fruit, but notvvithstanding she produceth it virginallie, for she is not touched of the male, though hee looke on her there is no vnion made betvveene them, and though she produce her fruit in the shadovve and aspect of her Palme, yet this is verie purelie and virginallie; The male Palme tree contributeth nothing of his substance for this production, neuer-thelesse none can say, that hee hath not a great part of the fruit in the Palme female, since vvithout him she should not beare, but remayne barren and vnfruitfull. God hauing from all eternitie in his di-uine prouidence decreed, that a virgin should con-ceaue a sonne, vvhich should bee God and man together, notvvithstanding vvould that this virgin should bee maried; but o God! For vvhat reason say the Holie doctours did hee ordayne tvvo so dif-ferent things, to bee a virgin and maried together. The greater part of Fathers say, that this vvas to free our Bl. Ladie of the calūniations of the Ievves, vvho had not exēpted our Ladie frō calūnie and re-proach but thēselues, would haue become examiners of her puritie, and that to conserue this puritie and virginitie, it vvas necessarie that the diuine prouidē-ce should cōmitt her to the charge, & into the gard of amã vvho vvas a virgin, & that this virgin might conceaue, and bring forth this svveet fruit of life our Lord Iesus, vnder the shadovve of holie Mariage. Saint Ioseph vvas then as a Palme tree, vvho not bearing fruit, notvvithstanding is not vnfruitfull; but hath a great part in the fruit of the female Palme, not that Saint Ioseph contributed any thing, to this holie and Glorious production, but the onelie shadovve of Mariage, vvhich did free our Ladie & Glorious Mistrise from all sorts of calumnies, and censures, that her being big vvith child might haue caused her, and although hee did contribute nothing of his, hee had notvvithstanding a great part in this most holie fruite of his sacred spouse: For she did appertayne vnto him, and vvas planted neere vnto him, as a glorious Palme neere to its vvelbeloued Palme Tree; vvho according to the order of the diuine prouidence could not, nor ought not to haue produced but vnder his shadovve and by his aspect, I vvould say, vnder the shadovv of holie mariage that they had contracted together, a mariage that vvas not, according to the ordinarie fashion, so much for the communication of exteriour goods, as for the vnion and coniunction of interiour goods. O vvhat a diuine vnion vvas there betvveene our Blessed Ladie and Saint Ioseph! a vnion vvhich did cause this tresure of eternall riches, vvhich is our Lord to bee and appertayne to the glorious Saint Ioseph, euen as hee did appertayne to our Bl. Ladie not according to the nature that hee had taken in the bovvels of our Glorious Mistris, (nature which had been framed by the Holie Ghost of the Most pure bloud of our B L. Ladie) but according to grace, vvhich made him become participant of all the goods of his deare spouse, and the vvhich did cause that hee vvent meruelouslie increasing in perfectiō, and this by the cōtinuall cōuersation that hee had with our Bl. Ladie, who did possesse all vertues in so high a degree, that no other pure creature can bee able to attayne there-vnto: Notvvithstanding Sainct Ioseph was the man vvho did neerest approch to her; and euē as vvee see a looking-glasse opposed to the beames of the sunne, receaue the beames most perfectlie, and another looking-glasse being put iust against that which receaueth the beames, although the latter looking glasse take not or receaue the beames frō the sunne but by reflectiō, notvvithstāding it representeth thē so liuelie, that wee cannot allmost iudge which it is that receaueth thē immediatlie frō the sunne, either that vvhich is opposite to the sūne, or that vvhich receaueth them by reuerberatiō: of like sort was it in our Bl. Ladie, who vvas as a pure mirrour, opposed to the beames of the sunne of Iustice, beames that did bring into her soule all vertues in their perfection, perfectiōs and vertues, vvhich did make so perfect a reflection in S. Ioseph, that allmost it seemed that hee vvas as perfect, or that hee had the vertues in as high a degree, as the glorious virgin our Mistris had them.

§. 2. But in particular (to retayne vs in our matter begun) in vvhat degree had hee virginitie thinke vvee, vvhich is a vertue that maketh vs become like Angells? If the holie virgin vvas not onelie a virgin most pure and vvhite; but (as the holie Church singeth in the Response of the Lessons at Mattins) holie and immaculate virginity ccc. She vvas virginitie it selfe, hovv much thinke vvee did hee excell there-in; vvhose charge from the eternall father vvas to bee guardian of her virginitie; or to say better, companion, since that she had not any need to bee guarded by any other then her selfe, hovv excellent say I, ought hee to bee in bee in this vertue? They had both of them vovved to keepe virginity all there life time, and behould God vvill that they bee vnited by the band of a holie Mariage, not for to make them vnsaye and repent them of their vovve, but fot to reconfirme them, and to fortifie one the other to perseuere in their holie enterprise; wherefore they did renevv it, vovving to liue virginally together all their life. The spouse in the Canticle of canticles vseth admirable tearmes, for to discribe the bashfulnes or shamefastnes, the chastitie, and most innocent cādor of his diuine lover with his deare and welbeloued spouse. Hee sayeth thus; Our sister this little young virgin, alas! that she is little, she hath no breasts, vvhat shall wee doe to her in the day that she must bee spoken vnto? if she bee a vvall, lett vs build vpon it bulwarkes of siluer, and if shee bee a gate or dore, lett vs ioyne it together with boords of Cedar to strenghthen it, or with some incorruptible vvood. Behould hovv the diuine spouse speaketh of the puritie of the most holie Virgin: of the Church: of the deuout soule: but principallie this is addressed to the most holie Virgin, who vvas this diuine Sunamite by excellencie, aboue all others. Our sister, she is little, she hath no breasts: that is to say, she thinketh not of mariage, for she hath neither breasts nor care therefore. VVhat shall vvee doe to her in the day she is to bee spoken vnto? what meaneth this? In the day she is to bee spoken vnto? Doth not the diuine spouse speake vnto her alvvaies vvhen it pleaseth him? In the day she shalbe spoken vnto, tovvit, of the principall vvorde, that is vvhen vvee speake to maydes of their mariage: for so much as it is a vvord of importance, since it is in their choise to make election of a vocation and estate, vvhere-in they must allvvaies re-

remayne; if she bee a dore, vvee vvill double it or couer it ouer vvith boords of Cedar that is an incorruptible vvood, to make it stronger. The most Glorious virgin was a tower compassed with verie high walls, within the which inclosure the enimie could not enter, nor any kind of other desires then of liueing in perfect puritie and virginitie: vvhat shall vvee doe to her? For she is to bee vvedded, hee vvho hath giuen her this resolution of virginitie haueing so ordayned it? If she bee a tovver or vvall, lett vs fasten vpon it bulvvarks of siluer, vvhich in steed of beating dovvne the tower shall fortifie it more: vvhat is then the Glorious Sainct Ioseph, but a strong bulvvarke, vvhich hath been ordayned ouer our Blessed Ladie? since beeing her spouse she vvas subiect to him, and hee had care of her; Therefore Sainct Ioseph vvas not appointed ouer our Bl. Ladie, for to make her breake her vovv of virginitie, but contrarivvise he vvas giuen her for a companion there-of, and to the end that the puritie of our Ladie might more admirably perseuere in its integritie, vnder the vaile and shadovv of Mariage, and of the holy vnion they had together. If the most holie virgin be a dore (sayeth the eternall father) vvee will not haue it opened, for it is the orientall gate, whereby none can enter nor goe forth, but contrarivvise it must hee doubled and fortified vvith incorruptible vvodde, that is to say, giue her a companion in her puritie, vvhich is the great Sainct Ioseph, who ought for this office to surpasse all the Saincts, yea the Angells, and the Cherubins themselues in this so recommendable vertue of virginitie, a vertue vvhich made him become like to a Palme tree, as vvee haue sayed.

§. 3. Lett vs passe to the second propertie and vertue that I find in the Palme, I say to my purpose.

purpose, that there is made a iust resemblance and cōformitie betvveene Sainct Ioseph and the Palme tree in their vertue, vvhich is no other then holie humilitie; for althoug that the Palme, bee the prince of trees, it is notvvithstanding the most hū-ble, the vvhich it vvitnesseth in this, that it hideth his flovvers in the spring time, vvhen all other trees sett them forth to the shevve, and lets them not appeare but in the great heates. The Palme keepeth itt flovvers vvithin pouches or purses vvhich are made in forme of sheaths, or sizzarcases, vvhich doth represent verie vvell vnto vs the difference of soules vvho tend to perfection, from others, and the presēce of the iust from those vvho liue according to the vvorld; for the vvorldlings and earthlie men, who liue according to the Lawes of the earth, assoone as they haue some good thought, or some good cogitation, vvhich in their opinion is vvorthy to bee esteemed, or if they haue some vertue, they are neuer in rest, vntill such time as they haue manifested it, and made it knovvne to all those they meete vvithall; vvhere-in they runne the same hazard, that the trees that are forvvard to budd forth their flovvers in the spring time, as the Almonde trees are; for if peraduenture the frost ouertake them, they perish and beare no fruit: these vvorldlie men vvho are so light to make their flovvers bloome and sprout out, in the spring of this mortale life, by a spiritt of pride and ambition, allvvaies are in danger to rūne hazard to bee taken by the frost, vvhich maketh them loose the fruit of their actions: contrarivvise the iust hould allvvaies all their flovvers close vvithin the case of most holie humilitie and permitt them not to appeare as much as they can, vntill the great heates, vvhen that God the diuine sunne of Iustice, shall come povverfullie to vvarme their hart in eternall life,

vvhere

vvhere they shall beare for euer the ſvveete fruit of felicitie and immortallitie. The Palme permitteth not its flovvers to bee ſeene, vntill ſnch time as the vehement heat of the ſunne come to make its sheaths,caſes,or buggetts vvherin they are encloſed to cleaue or riue aſunder, after the vvhich its fruit appeareth ſuddenlie to the vevve: in like mãner doth the iuſt ſoule:for she keepeth her flowers,that is to ſay her vertues,hidden vnder the vaile of holie humilitie vntill death, vvherein our Lord cauſeth them to bee diſcloſed, and letteth them appeare outvvardlie, for ſo much as the fruits are not to withhould there apparence long after. O how excellently faythfull heerin vvas this great Sainct of vvhom vvee ſpeake! it cannot bee ſufficientlie declared according to its perfection, for notwithſtãding being ſuch as hee was, in what pouertie, and in vvhat abiection did hee not liue all the time of his life?vnder the vvhich pouertie and abiectiõ, hee kept hidden and couert his great vertues and dignities;but vvhat dignities my God?to be gouernour of our Lord,and not onelie this, but furthermore to bee his ſuppoſed father,and to bee the ſpouſe of his moſt holie Mother;O!truelie I doubt not at all that the Angells rauished vvith admiration did come in troopes after troopes to cõſider him,and to admire his humilitie, vvhen hee did retayne this deare child in his poore shopp, vvhere he laboured in his trade, to nourish the ſonne & the Mother vvho were committed to him. There is no doubt, my deare ſiſters, but that Sainct Ioſeph was more valiant then Dauid, and had more wiſdome then Salomon: Notvvithſtanding behoulding him reduced vnto the exercise of a carpenter, who could haue iudged ſo much of him,if he had not beẽ illuminated with celeſtiall light? ſo faſt did hee shut vp and keepe all the ſi gulergiftes, wherwith God had

grati-

gratified him: for vvhat wisdome had not hee, since that God gaue him in charge his most glorious sonne, and that hee was chosen to bee his gouernour? If the Princes of this vvorld haue so much care, as being a matter of importance, to giue to their children gouerners who are most capable; then God being able to make that the gouerner of his sonne should bee the most accomplished and cōpleat man of the world in all perfectiōs, according to the dignitie and excellencie of the thing gouerned, which was his most glorious sonne; the vniuersall prince of heauen and earth: hovv should it bee, that haueing povver to doe it, hee vvould not, or hath not done it? Therefore there is no doubt but that Sainct Ioseph was endovved with all the graces and giftes, which did deserue the office that the eternall father vvvould impose vppon him, giueing him the temporall, and domesticall stevvardshipp of his sonne, and conduct of his familie, which was composed but of three, which doth represent vnto vs the misterie of the most holie and most adored Trinitie: not that there is any comparison, but in that which respecteth our Lord, who is one of the Persons of the most holy Trinitie; for touching the others they are creatures: but notwithstāding wee may say euen so, That it is a Trinitie on earth, which in some sorte doth represēt the most holie Trinitie, Marie, Iesus and Ioseph: Ioseph, Iesus, and Marie: a Trinitie merueloushe recōmendable and vvorthy to bee honoured. You vnderstād thē how exceedinglie the dignitie of S. Ioseph was exalted, & how excellētlie hee was replenished with all sortes of vertues. On the other side you see neuertheless, how much hee was brought lowe and humbled, more then can bee declared or imagined. This one example sufficeth for the better vnderstanding of it; hee tooke his iourney tovvards his ovvne country, and vnto his tovvne of Bethlem, and none is refused of all lodging but himselfe (at least that vvee knovve of) so that hee was constrayned to retire himselfe, and to lead his chast spouse into a stable among the oxen and asses: O into vvhat extremitie vvas his humilitie and abiection reduced! his humilitie vvas the cause (euen as S. Bernard explicateth it (that hee thought vpon leauing our Bl. Ladie, vvhen hee savve her great vvith child: For Sainct Bernard sayeth that hee made this discourse within himselfe, VVhat meaneth this? I knovv that she is a virgin, for vvee haue made a vovv together to keepe our virginitie and puritie, vvherein she vvould in no sorte bee wanting, notwithstanding I see that she is great vvith child, and that she is a Mother, how can it bee that maternitie is found in virginitie and puritie, and that virginitie doth nott hinder Maternitie. O God? (sayed hee to himselfe) it may bee this is that Glorious virgin, of whom the Prophets doe assure vs, that she shall conceaue and bee the mother of the Messias? O! If this bee so, God forbidd that I should remayne with her, I that am so vnworthy of it, it wilbe much better that I secreetlie forsake her because of my indignitie, and dwell not auy longer in her companie: this was a feeling of an admirable humilitie, and the which did make S. Peter to cry out in the vessell, where hee vvas vvith our Lord, vvhē hee did see his Almigthie power manifested in the great draught of fishes that hee tooke, at his onlie commaundement, willing them to cast their netts into the sea: O Lord (sayed hee (being wholie trāsported, with the like feeling of humilitie as Sainct Ioseph) with drawe they selfe from mee: for I am a sinfull man, and therefore I am not worthy to bee with thee: I knovv well (vvould hee say) that If I cast my selfe into the sea I shall perish: but thou who art Allmighty canst walke

walke vppon the waters without danger: for this cause I beseeth thee to retyre from mee, and not that I withdrawe my selfe from thee: If Sainct Ioseph were so carefull to shutt vp all his vertues vnder the shadowe of most holie humilitie, hee had a most particular care to hide the pretious pearle of his virginitie, this was the cause hee consented to bee maried, to the end that none might know it, and because that vnder the holie vaile of mariage hee could liue vnknowne: whereby virgins, and those who will liue chastlie are taught that it is not sufficient for them to bee virgins, vnless they bee humble, and shut vp their puritie within the pretious box of humilitie: for othervvise it will happē vnto them as it did to the foolish virgins, vvho for vvāt of humilitie and mercifull Charitie, were repelled from the Mariage of the spouse, and therefore were constrained to goe to the wedding of the world, wher the councell of the Celestiall spouse is not obserued who sayeth that hee who will enter to the Mariage feast must bee humble, I would say that hee must practice humilitie: for (sayeth hee) going to a wedding, or being inuited to a Mariage, take the last place; wher-in wee see how necessarie humilitie is for the conseruation of virginitie, since vndoubtedlie not any one shalbee at the celestiall banquet and Nuptiall feast which God hath prepraed for virgins in the celestiall habitation, vnlesse that hee shalbe accompained with this vertue. VVee doe not keepe pretious things, especially odoriferous oyntments in the ayre, for not onelie these sweete sauours would euaporate themselues, but moreouer the flyes would corrupt them, and make them loose their price and worth: in like manner the soules of the Iuste fearing to loose the price and valour of their good workes, shut or locke them vp ordinarilie in a box, but

not

not in a cōmon box, no more then pretious oyntments, but in a box of Allabaster (such as S. Marie Magdaleine powred forth, (or emptied) vpon the sacred head of our Sauiour, when that hee reestablished her in virginitie, not essentiall but repared, the which is somtimes more excellent being acquired and re-established by penance, then that which haueing not receaued blemish is accompained with lesse humilitie. This Allabaster Box then is humilitie, within the which vvee ought in imitation of our Bl. Ladie and Sainct Ioseph to locke vp our vertues, and all that which may make vs to bee esteemed of men, contenting our selues to please God, and to remayne vnder the sacred vaile of the abiection of our selues, expecting the time (as wee haue sayed) vvhen God comeing to dravve vs into the place of securitie, which is his Glorie, himselfe cause our workes to appeare for his honour and glorie. But vvhat more perfect humilitie can bee imagined thē that of Sainct Ioseph? (I except that of our Bl. Ladie: for wee haue alreadie sayed, that Sainct Ioseph did receaue a great increase in all vertues by vvay of reflection, of those that the most holie virgin did imprint in him.) hee had a verie great part in that diuine treasure that hee had neere him, which vvas our Lord and Maister, & yet for all that hee so hūbled and abased himselfe, that it seemed not that hee had any part in him, yet notvvithstāding hee did appertayne to him more then to any other, next to the most holie Virgin, and none may doubt there-of, since hee vvas of his familie, and the sonne of his spouse who did appertayne vnto him. I am accustomed to say, that if a doue (to make the comparison more conforme to the puritie of the Sainct of whō I speake) should carrie a date in his becke, and lett it fall into a garden, would wee not say that

the

the Palme which should come of it, did appertayne to him vvho did ovve the garden? novv if this bee so, vvho can doubt, that the holie Ghost haueing lett fall this diuine Date, as a diuine Doue, into the inclosed and locked garden of the most holy virgin, (a garden sealed and inuironed on euerie side with the hedges of the holie vovve of virginitie, and all immaculate chastitie) who did appertayne to the glorious Sainct Ioseph, as to her husband, who shall doubt I say, or vvho can say that this diuine Palme-tree, which beareth the fruit that nourisheth to immortalitie, doth not appertayne wholie to this great Sainct Ioseph? who notvvithstanding is not therefore the more puffed vpp, nor becommeth the more proude, but rather becometh allwaies the more humble? O God! what a goodlie sight vvas it to behould the reuerence and respect, wherevvith hee did conuerse asvvell with the mother as vvith the sonne. If hee had a desire to leaue the mother, not knowing at that time the greatnesse of her dignitie, into what profound annihilation and humiliation of himselfe was hee aftervvards brought, vvhē hee savve himselfe so much honoured, that our Lord and our Ladie did yeald themselues obedient to his vvill, and did nothing but by his commaundement? this is a thing that cannot be comprehended, therefore it is necessarie that vvee passe to the third propertie that I note to bee in the Palme, which is valour, constancie, and strength, vertues that are found in a verie eminent degree in our Sainct.

§. 4. The Palme hath strength and valour, and likevvise a verie great constancie, aboue all other trees, also it is the cheife of all. The Palme shevveth his strēgth and cōstancie in this, that the more its loaden, the higher it riseth, ād becōmeth more high, the vvhich is verie contrarie not onelie to all other

trees

trees, but to all other things, for the more they bee loaden, the more they bovve dovvne tovvards the earth; but the Palme shevveth his strenght and constancie, in not submitting it selfe, nor euer bowing dovvne for any burthen they can put vpon it, for it is its instinct to mount vpvvards, and therefore it doth so, none being able to hinder it: it shevveth its valour in this, that its Leaues are made like svvords and seemeth to haue as manie svvords to fight as it beareth leaues; it it truelie vvith verie iust reason that Sainct Ioseph is sayed to resemble the Palme: for hee vvas allvvaies verie valiant, cōstant, and perseuerant. There is much difference betvveene cōstancie and perseuerance, strenght and valour; vvee call a man constant, vvho keepeth himselfe, firme, and prepared to suffer the assaults of his enimies, vvithout astonishment or loosing courage during the combatt: but perseuerance regardeth principallie a certayne interiour vexation or irksomnes, vvhich arriueth to vs in the lenght of our paynes, vvhich is one of the povverfullest enimies that vvee can encounter vvithall, novv perseuerance maketh a man to contemne this enimye, in such sort that hee remaineth victorious by a cōtinuall equallitie, and submission to the vvill of God. Courage is that vvhich maketh a man valiāt-lie resist the assaults of his enimies: but valour is a vertu vvhich causeth, that vvee are not onelie readie to fight, nor to resist when occasion presents it selfe, but that vvee assault the enimie at the same time hee looketh not for it. Novv our Glorious Sainct Ioseph was indued vvith all these vertues, and hee did merueilouslie vvell exercise them: for as concerning his constancye, hovv much I pray you did hee make it appeare, vvhen seing our Blessed Ladie great vvith child, and not knovving how this could bee, (My God vvhat distresse, vvhat anguish,

guish, what payne did hee not feele? notwithstādding hee complayned not, hee was not more vnciuill, nor more displeased towards his spouse, nether did hee treat her the worse for this, remayning as sweet and respectiue in his behauiour as hee had wont to bee. But what valour and what force did hee not vvitness in the victorie that hee boore away against the tvvo greatest enimies of man the diuell and the world? and this by the most exact practice of profound humilitie as wee haue noted in the whole course of his life. The diuell is such an enimie of humilitie, because the wāt hee had there-of, was it that expelled him out of heauen, and thrust him into hell (from whence humilitie would haue kept him, if he had chosen it for his inseparable cōpanion) that there is no inuention nor art, where-of hee serueth not himselfe to make a man fall from this vertue, and so much the more, because as hee knoweth, it is a vertue which maketh him become infinitely pleasing to God, so that wee may well say, valiant and strong is the man, who like Sainct Ioseph perseuereth therein, because that he remayneth an absolute cōquerour of the diuell and the world, which is filled with ambition, vanitie, and Pride. Touching perseuerance contrarie to this interiour enimye, which is the anxietie, which commeth vpon vs in the continuation of abiect, humbling, and paynfull things, of euill fortunes, if wee may so say, or else in diuers accidents that happen vnto vs; O how was this Sainct proued of God and men, euen in his iourney! The Angell commaunded him to depart speedelie, and to carrie our Ladie and her most deare sōne into Egipt, behould hee departeth in an instant without speaking a worde, hee inquired not whither shall I goe, what way shall I take? wherewith shall wee bee mayntained; who will receaue vs there? hee departed at aduen-

aduenture with his tooles on his backe, for to gayne his poore liuing and his families with the sweate of his browes; O how much might this anxietie where-of wee speake haue troubled him, especiallie seeing the Angell had not tould him how longe hee should bee there, so that hee could not settle any assured dvvelling, not knowing when the Angell vvould commaund him to retourne! If Sainct Paul admired so much the obedience of Abraham vvhen God commaunded him to goe out of his country, for so much as God did not tell him into what coast hee should goe, neither did Abraham aske it of him, Lord you commaund mee to goe; but tell mee then if it shal be by the south gate, or on the North side; but hee put him selfe on the way, and went according as the spiritt of God guided him. How exceeding admirable then is this perfect obedience of Sainct Ioseph? The Angell did not tell him vntill vvhat time hee should remayne in Egipt, neither did hee inquire it, hee remayned there the space of fiue yeares, as the most part beleeue, without seeking to informe himselfe of his retourne, assureing himselfe that hee who had commaunded that hee should goe thither, would command him agayne when hee should retourne, wherein hee vvas alvvaies readie to obey; hee vvas in a country not onely of strangers but also enimyes of the Israelites; for so much as the Egyptians had yet in mind, hovv they had left them, what they had bereaued them of, and that they had been cause that a great number of the Egiptians had been ouervvhelmed vvhen they did pursue them, and this stuck in their stomacks. I leaue it to your consideration what desire Sainct Ioseph might haue of his retourne, because of the continuall

fears

feares that hee might haue amongst the Egiptians : the greife of not knovving vvhen hee
should come forth might vvithout doubt greatly afflict and torment his poore hart; notvvithstanding hee remaynes allvvaies himselfe, allwayes sweete, tranquill, and perseuerant in his
submission to the good pleasure of God, to
which hee left himselfe fully to bee guided; for
as he was iust, hee had his vvill allwaies squared,
ioyned and conforme to the will of God. To
bee iust is no other thing, then to bee perfectlie vnited to the vvill of God, and to bee allvvaies
therein conforme in all sorts of euents, prosperous
or aduerse. That Sainct Ioseph allwaies in all oc-
sions hath been perfectlie submisse vnto the diuine
will, none can doubt; doe you not see hovv the
Angell tourneth him at all essaies, he telleth
him, that hee must goe into Egipt, hee goeth
thither; hee commaundeth that hee retourne, &
hee retourneth: God would that hee should bee allvvaies poore, vvhich is one of the most forceable
proofes that vvee can haue, and hee submitteth
himselfe loueinglie therevnto, and not for a time,
for this vvas all his life: but vvith vvhat pouertie? vvith a contemptible, needye, and reiectable
pouertie. The voluntarie pouertie vvhere-of Religious make profession, is verie amiable, for so
much as it hindreth them not, from takeing
and receauing those things vvhich shalbe necessarie for them, onelie forbidding and depriuing
them of superfluities: But the pouertie of Sainct
Ioseph, of our Lord, and our Blessed Ladie vvas
not such: for allthough it vvas voluntarie, for
so much as hee did loue it dearelie, it did
not leaue therefore to bee abiect, reiected
and contemned, and in verie great necessitie:
for euerie one esteemed this great Sainct as a
poore

poore carpenter, who without doubt could not make such gayne, but that many necessarie things would bee wanting, although hee did take paynes with an exceeding affection, for the entertaynmēt of his whole familie, which done hee did submitt himselfe most humbly to the will of God, in the continuatiō of his pouertie and abiection, not permitting himselfe to bee ouerthrowne, nor vanquished by interiour disquietness, which vvithout doubt did make him manie assaults; but remayned allwaies constant in submission, the which (as all his other vertues) went continuallie increasing and perfectionating themselues, euen as that of our Bl. Ladie, who did gayne euerie day an ouer-growth of vertues and perfections, that she did learne of her most holie sonne, who could not increase in any thing, for so much as hee was from the instant of his conception such as hee is, and shalbe eternallie, which did cause that the holy familie wher-in hee vvas, went allwaies increasing and aduancing in perfection: Our Bl. Ladie drawing her perfection from his diuine goodnes, and Sainct Ioseph receauing it (as wee haue allreadie sayed) by the mediation of our Bl. Lady.

§. 5. Now what remayneth there more to bee sayed, but that wee ought not to doubt, but that this Glorious Sainct hath much creditt with him in heauē, who hath fauoured him so much as to assūpt him thither in bodie and soule, the which is so much the more probable, because wee haue not had any Relique of his heere belowe on earth, and it seemeth to mee that none can doubt of this veritie: for how could hee refuse this grace to Sainct Ioseph, who had been so obediēt to him all the dayes of his life? without doubt when our Lord descended into Limbus Patrum, hee was spoken vnto by Sainct Ioseph in this sort; My Lord, remember your

selfe

selfe if you please, that when you came from heaue to earth, I receaued you in-to my familie, and that when you were borne I receaued you into my armes; now that you must goe to heauen lead mee thither with you, I receaued you into my familie, receaue mee now into yours, since you goe thither: I haue carried you betweene my armes, now take mee vpon yours, and as I haue had care to nourish and conduct you, during the course of your mortall life, take care of mee and conduct mee to the immortall life: and if it is true, the which wee ought to beleeue, that in vertue of the most Bl. Sacrament that wee receaue, our bodies shall rise againe at the day of iudgment, how can wee doubt, that our Lord did cause the Glorious Sainct Ioseph to ascend with him into heauen asvvell bodye as soule, who had had the honour, and the grace to carrie him so often in his Bl. armes, the which did please our Lord so much: O how many kisses did hee tenderlie giue him from his Blessed mouth, for to recompence in some sorte his labour. Sainct Ioseph then is in heauen in body and soule without doubt. Hovv happie should vee bee if vvee could deserue to haue part in his holie intercessions; for nothing shalbe denied him neither of our Bl. Ladie nor her Glorious sonne, hee will obteyne for vs if wee haue confidence in him, a holie grovvth in all sortes of vertues, but espetiallie in those which vvee haue found, that hee had, in a more high degree then all others, vvhich are the most holie puritie of bodie and spiritt, and the most amiable vertue of humilitie, constancye, valour, and perseuerance: vertues vvhich make vs in this life become victorious ouer our enimyes, and vvhich vvill make vs deserue the grace to enioy eternall revvardes in the next life, vvhich are prepared for them vvho shall imitate the example that Sainct Ioseph hath giuen them

them being in this mortall life, a reward which shall bee no lesse the eternall felicitie; in the which wee shall enioy the cleare vision of the Father, the Sonne, and the Holie Ghost. God bee Blessed. Amen.

LIVE IESVS.

THE TVVENTITH ENTER-TAINEMENT.

IN VVHICH IS DEMAVNDED, vvhat pretention vvee ought to haue entring into Religion.

§. 1. THe questiō that our Mother proposeth vnto mee to declare vnto you, my deare daughters; to vvitt the pretēce which one ought to haue to enter into Religion, is truelie the most important, most necessarie, and profitable that can bee explicated. Verily, my deare daughters, many women enter into Religion, who knovv not vvherefore: they will come to a parloyr or speaking place, Where they shall see the Religious women with a cheerefull countenance, haueing a good gesture, verie modest, and much contented, and they vvill say within themselues, good God! It is good to bee there, Lett vs goe thither, the vvorld doth frowne vpon vs, wee meete not with our pretentions in it. Another will say: good God! how well they sing! others come thither to encounter peace, consolations, and all sortes of sweetnesses, saying in their thought; My God! how happie are Religious women! being out of the noise of father and mother; who doe no other thing then com-playne

playne and chide, vee can doe nothing which contenteth them, wee are allwaies to begin anew: Our Lord promiseth those vvho forsake the world for his seruice many consolations, lett vs goe then into Religion. Behould, my deare daughters, three sortes of pretentions which are worth nothing to make vs enter into the house of God. Of necessitie it must be God who buildeth the Cittie, or othervvise although it vvere built, it must bee ruined againe. I will beleeue, my deare daughters, that your pretentions are better grounded, and therefore that you haue all good courages; and that God vvill blesse this little companie nevv-begun.

§. 2. There commeth to my mind tvvo or three similitudes fitt to giue you to vnderstand vvhervppon, and hovv your pretentions ought to bee founded for to bee solide: but I vvill content my selfe to explicate one vvhich shall suffice: put the case that an architect vvould build a house, hee doth two things: first hee considereth if his building bee for some particular, as for a Prince, or a king: because hee must proceed there-in in different manner; then hee must reckon by himselfe if his meanes bee sufficient for it. For hee who would vndertake to build a high tovver, and had not vvherevvith to finish it, vvould hee not bee laught at, for haueing begun a thing in vvhich hee could not come of vvith his honour? then hee must resolue himselfe to ruine the ould building, which is in the place where hee vvould erect a nevv. VVee would make a great building, my deare daughters, which is to build a habitation for God within vs: therefore lett vs consider vvell and maturelie if wee haue sufficient courage and resolution to ruine and crucifie our selues, or rather to permitt God to mortifie and crucifie vs, to the end that hee reedifie

O vs, for

vs, for to bee the liueing temple of his Maiesty: Therefore I say, my most deare daughters, that our onelie pretention ought to bee to vnite vs to God, as Iesus Christ did vnite himselfe to God his Father, vvhich vvas in dying vpon the Crosse: for I intend not to speake to you, of that generall vnion vvhich is made by Baptisme, vvhere Christians vnite thẽselues to God in takeing this diuine Sacrament and caracter of Christianisme, and oblige themselues to keepe his commaundements, & those of his Holie Church, to exercise themselues in good workes, to practice the vertues of Fayth, Hope, and Charitie, vvhich vnion of theirs is auailable and may iustlie pretend heauen, For vniting themselues by this meanes to God, as to their God, they are not obliged any further, they haue attayned their end, by the generall and spatious vvay of the commaundements. But touching you my deare daughters, it is not so; for besides this common obligation that you haue with all Christiãs, God by a verie spetiall loue hath chosen you to bee his deare spouses. You ought then to knovv how and vvhat it is to bee Religious vvomen. It is; to bee bound to God by a continuall mortification of our selues, and not to liue but for God, our hart allvvaies seruing his diuine Maiestie: our eyes, our tounge, our hands, and all the rest serueing him continuallie. VVherefore you see that Religion furnisheth you vvith all meanes proper for this effect, which are, prayer, reading, silence, vvithdravving of your hart from creatures to rest it in God onelie by continuall darting of affections to our Lord. And because vvee cannot arriue to this, but by the continuall practice of mortification of all our passions, inclinations, humours, and auersions, vvee are obliged to vvatch continuallie ouer our selues, that vvee may make

all

all this to die. Knovv (my deare sisters) that if a graine of vvheat falling into the ground doe not dye, it remayneth alone: but if it corrupt, it vvill bring forth a hūdred fould: the vvord of our Lord heerein is verie cleare, his most blessed mouth haueing pronounced the same: consequentlie, you vvho pretend the habitt, and you also, vvho pretend the holie Profession, consider vvell more then once, if you haue sufficient resolution to die to your selues, and not to liue but to God. Consider all vvell, the time is long enough to ruminate there-on before your vailes bee dyed blacke: for I declare to you, my deare daughters, and I vvill not flatter you, vvhosoeuer desire to liue according to nature, lett them remayne in the vvorld: and those vvho are determined to liue according to grace, lett them come into Religion, vvhich is no other thing then the schoole of abnegation and mortification of ones selfe; vvherefore looke to it, that you bee furnished with many instruments of mortification asvvell interiour as exteriour. But good God! you will say to mee; This is not that, that I sought after; I thought it vvas sufficient for to bee a good Religious vvoman, to desire to praye vvell, to haue visions and reuelations, yea of Angells in forme of men, to bee rauished in extasie, to loue vvell the reading of good bookes, and vvhat else. I vvas so vertuous, as it seemed to mee, so mortified, so humble, all the vvorld did admire mee; vvas it not to bee humble, to speake so svveetlye of all things appertayning to deuotion to my companions, to recount the sermons by my selfe, to conuerse gentlye vvith those of the house, aboue all vvhen they did not contradict mee! certainelie, my deare daughters, this vvas good for the vvorld: But Religion vvilleth that vvee doe vvorkes vvorthy of her vocation: that vvee dye to all things, asvvell to that vvhich is good to our vvill, as to vnprofitall and euill things. Thinke you that the good Religious men of the desert, vvho attayned to so great vnion vvith God, arriued thereunto in following their inclinations? Truelie no, they vvere mortified in most holy exercises; and although they felt great gust to sing the diuine Canticles, to read, pray, and doe other things, they did it not to content them selues; no not so, but contrarivvise, they did voluntarilie depriue themselues of these pleasures, for to giue themselues to paynfull and labour some vvorkes. It is verie true certaynlie that Religious soules receaue a thousand suauities and contentments amidst the mortifications and exercises of holie Religion: for it is principallie to them that the holie ghost distributeth his pretious giftes: therefore they ought to seeke nothing but God, and the mortification of their humours, passions, and inclinationes in holy Religion, for if they seeke any other thing, they shall neuer find the cōsolation that they pretended. vvee must haue an inuincible courage not to bee vveary vvith our selues, because that vve shall allvvaies haue somvvhat to doe, and to cutt off.

§. 3. The office of Religious ought to bee to cultiuate their spirit, to roote out all the ill productions that our deprau'ed nature euerie day causeth to bud, so that it seemeth there is allvvaies somthing to bee done anevv, and as the labourer ought not to bee troubled, since hee is not to bee blamed for not hauing reaped a good cropp, prouided notvvithstanding that hee hath care to cultiuate the earth vvell, and to sovve it vvell: euen so Religious ought not to bee afflicted, if they gather not so soone the fruites of perfection and vertues, prouided that they haue great fidelitie to cultiuate the earth

earth of their hart vvell, cutting of that which they perceaue to bee contrarie to perfection, to the vvhich they are obliged to ayme, since vvee shall neuer bee perfectlie cured vntill vvee bee in heauē. VVhen your Rule telleth you, that you aske for bookes at the appointed houre, thinke you that those which content you most, shall ordinarilie bee giuen you? noe, this is not the intention of the Rule; and the like of other exercises. A sister vvill thinke, as it seemeth to her, that she is verie much inuited to prayer, to say her Office, to bee retyred, and the Superiours say to her; sister goe to the kitshen, or else, doe such or such a thing, this is ill nevves for a sisters that is verie deuout. I say then that vvee must die that God may liue in vs, for it is impossible to procure the vnion of our soule with God, by any other meanes then by mortification. These vvordes are hard, vvee must dye: but they are seconded vvith great svveetnes, that is, to the end vvee may bee vnited to God by this death. Yon knovv that no vvise man putteth nevv vvine into an old vessell, the liquour of diuine Loue cannot enter, vvhere the old Adam raigneth: hee must of necessitie bee destroyed: but how, you will say to mee, vvill hee bee destroyed? hovv? my deare daughters, by punctuall obedience to your Rules: I assure you on the part of God, that if you bee faythfull to doe that they teach you, you shall attayne vvithout doubt to the end you ought to pretend, vvhich is to vnite your selues vvith God. Marke that I say, to doe: for vvee cannot purchase perfection by crossing our armes, wee must labour in good sadnes euen from the hart, to tame and reclame our selues, and to liue according to reason, our Rule, and obedience, and not according to the inclinations vvee haue brought from the vvorld. Religion tolerateth vs to bring our euill habits, passiõs, and inclinations, but not to liue according to them; it giueth vs Rules to serue vs, to presse and straine out of our harts, vvhatsoener is contrarie to God: therefore liue couragcouslye according to them.

§. 4. But some one vvill say. Good God! hovv shall I doe, I haue not the spirit of Religiõ? Truelie, my deare Daughter, I easilie beleeue you, it is a thing the vvorld bringeth not to Religion. The spiritt of the Rule is gayned in practiceing the Rule faythfully. I say the same of holie humilitie, and mildnesse, the foundation of this congregatiõ, God vvill infallibly giue it vs, prouided that vve haue a good hart, and doe our endeauour to gett it; vve shalbe verie happie if one quarter of an hovver before vvee dye, vvee find our selues reuested vvith this garment, all our life vvil be vvell impoyed, if vvee labour to vvorke thereon, somtimes one peece, somtimes another; for this holy habitt is not made vvith one onelie peece, it is requisite there bee many. You thinke peraduenture, that perfectiõ is to bee found alreadye made, and that there is no other thing necessarie to bee done, but to put it ouer your head as a garment: No no, my Deare Daughters it is not so. Mother, you tell mee, our sisters the Nouices are of good vvill: but that abillitie is vvanting to put their desires in execution, and that they feele their passions so strong, that they almost fearre to begin to goe on; Courage, my Deare Daughters, I haue tould you many times that Religion is a schoole vvhere vve learne our lesson: the Maister requireth not allvvaies, that vvithout faile the Scholers knovve their lesson, it sufficeth that they haue attention to doe their endeauour to learne it: Lett vs also doe vvhat vve can, God vvil be contented, and our superiours also.

Doe

Doe you not see euerie day those vvho learne to beare armes fall often ? in like manner doe those vvho learne to ride a horse vvell, but they are not therefore held for vanquished: for it is one thing to bee cast sõtimes to the ground, and another to be absolutelie ouercome.

Your passiõs at times make head against you, and therefore you say, I am not fit for Religion, because I haue passion: No, my Deare Daughters, you are deceaued, the matter goeth not so: Religion accounteth no great tryumph to frame a spiritt allreadye made, a svveete soule, and peacefull in its selfe: but she exceedinglie esteemeth to reduce to a vertuous course soules that are strong in their inclinations; for these soules if they are faythfull vvil surpass the others, getting by the point of the spiritt, vvhich others haue vvithout payne. VVe doe not require of you, that you should not haue passions (it is not in your povver, and God vvill [illegible] your greater meritt) nor likvvise that they bee but of little strength, for this should bee as much as to say, that a soule ill habituated could not bee fit to serue God: the vvorld is deceaued in this thought, God reiecteth nothing, vvhere malice doth not intrude it selfe; For tell mee, I pray you, if a person be of such or such a temper, subiect to such or such a passion, hovv can hee help it? therefore all cõsisteth in the acts that vvee make by the motions vvhich depend of our vvill: sinne being so voluntarie that vvithout our consent there is no sinne. Putthe case that I bee ouertaken vvith choler; I vvould say to it; Turne and returne, riue in sunder if thou vvilt, I vvill doe nothing for thy respect, no not so much as to pronounce a vvord, according to thy suggestion: God hath left this in our povver, otherwise in requireing perfection of vs, it should bee to oblige vs to a thing impossible and consequently iniustice, which cannot bee in God.

§. 5. To this purpose there commeth into my mind, a historie vvhich is proper for our purpose: vvhen Moyses descended from the mountayne vvhere hee did speake vvith God, hee savv the people, vvho hauing made a golden calfe did adore it: touched vvith iust choler for zeale of the Glorie of God, hee sayed: (turning himselfe tovvards the Leuites;) If there be any one for our Lord, let him take his svvord in hand, to kill all those that shall present themselues before him, not sparing any, neither father nor mother, sister nor brother, but put all to death: The Leuites thẽ takeing the svvord in hand, hee vvas the most famous vvho killed most: In like manner, my deare daughters, take the svvord of mortification into yonr hand, for to kill and annihilate your passions; and she vvho shall haue the most to kill shalbe the most valiant, if she vvill cooperate vvith grace. Behould these tvvo young soules (vvhereof the one is a little past six yeares old, the other about fiue) they haue fevv to kill, also their spirit is not almost borne: but these great soules vvho haue experienced many things, and haue tasted the svveetnesses of heauen, it is to them to vvhom it appertayneth to kill and annihilate their passions vvell. Deare mother, for those, who, you say, haue so great desire of their perfection, that they vvould passe all others in vertue, they doe vvell to comfort their selfe loue a little, but they should doe well to follovv the communitie in keeping their rules vvell: for that is the right vvay to arriue to God. You are verie happie, my deare daughters, in respect of vs in the vvorld, when vvee aske the vvay, one sayeth it is on the right hand,

hand, another on the left, and for the most part they deceaue vs: but you, you haue nothing to doe, but to permitt your selues to bee carried: you are like to those that saile vpon the sea, the barque carrieth them, and they remayne within it without care, and in reposeing they goe forvvarde, and haue nothing to doe to enquire if they are in their vvay, vvhich is the dutie of the marriners, vvho allvvaies see the fayre starre, the guide of the shipp knoweth that they are in a good vvay, and sayeth to the others, vvho are in the barque, courage you are in a good vvay, follovv on vvithout feare. This diuine Pilote is our Lord, the barque is your Rules, those vvho guide it are the Snperious, vvho ordinarilie call vppon you, goe forvvard sisters by the punctuall obseruance of your Rules, you shall happilie arriue to Almigtye God, hee vvill guide you surelie.

§. 6. But marke vvhat I tell you, vvalke by the punctuall and faythfull obseruãce of them; for who contemneth his vvay shal be killed, sayeth Salomon. Mother, you say that our sisters say it is good to vvalke by the rules, but it is the generall vvay, God dravveth vs by particular attracts, euerie one to her spetiall, vvee are not all dravvne by one and the same vvay; they haue reason to say so, and it is true: but it is also true, that if this tract come from God, it vvill lead thẽ to obedience vvithout doubt: it appertayneth not vnto vs vvho are inferiours to iudg of our particular attracts, this is the duetie of superiours, and therefore particular direction is ordayned; be you verie faythfull therein, and you shall reap the fruit of benediction, my deare daughters, if you doe this vvhich is taught you, you shalbe verie happie, you shall liue content and you shall experience in this vvorld the fauours of heauen at least in some small quantity. But take heede that if some interiour gust come to you and cherishings from our Lord, not to tye your selfe vnto them; it is a fevv Anniscōfitts that the Apothecarie strevv-eth vpon a bitter potion for a sicke person: the sicke must svvallovv the bitter medicine for his health: and allthough hee take from the hand of the Apothecarie these sugred graines, yet must hee of necessitie feele aftervvards the bitternes of the purgation. Therefore you see clearly vvhat the pretention is that you ought to haue, to bee vvorthy spouses of our Lord, and to make your selues capable to bee vvedded to him vpon the mount of Caluarie. Therefore all your life liue and frame all your actiōs according to it, and God vvill blesse you; All our happines consisteth in perseuerance. I exhorte you therevnto (my Deare Daughters) vvith all my hart, and pray his diuine goodnes, that hee vvill fill you vvith grace, and vvith his diuine loue in this vvorld, and make vs all enioy his Glorie in the other life. Farevvell, my Deare Daughters, I beare you all in my hart: to commend my selfe to your prayers vvould bee superfluous, for I beleeue of your pietie you vvill not bee vvanting. I vvill send you euerie day from the Altar my benediction; and in the meane time receaue it: In the name of the father, the Sonne, and the Holie Ghost.

LIVE JESUS.

THE

THE ONE AND TVVENTY ENTERTAINEMENT.

TOVCHING, THE DOCVMENT OF demaunding nothing, nor refusing any thing.

§. 1. MOther, I spake one day vvith an excellent Religious vvoman vvho did aske of mee, if hauing a desire to communicate oftner then the communitie, one might desire it of the Superiour; I sayed to her; that if I vvere a Religious man I thinke I should doe thus: I vvould not aske to cōmunicate more often thē the cōmunitie did, I vvould not aske to vveare haircloth, to make extraordinarie fasts, to take disciplines, nor doe any other thing; I vvould content my selfe to follovv in all and through all the communitie; if I vveare strong, I vvould not eate four times a day, but if my Superiour made mee eate four times a day, I vvould doe it and say nothing; if I vvere vveake, and hee did not offer mee to eate but once a day, I vvould eate but once a day vvithout thinking vvhether I should bee vveake or not. I desire fevv things, and that vvhich I desire, I desire it verie little, I haue almost no desires; but if I vvere to bee nevv borne, I vvould haue none at all, if God came to mee, I vvould also goe to him: and if hee vvould not come to mee, I vvould keepe mee there and not goe to him: I say then, vve must nether aske nor refuse any thing, but leaue our selues vvholye in the hands of the diuine prouidence, vvithout museing

museing vpon any desire, but to vvil that which God would haue of vs. Sainct Paul did excellently practice this abnegation, in the verie instant of his conuersion, when our Lord had made him blinde, presentlie hee sayed: Lord, what wilt thou haue me to doe? and from thenceforth, hee did allwaies remayne in an absolute dependance of that which God should ordayne for, and of him; all our perfection consisteth in the practice of this point: and the same Sainct Paul writeing to one of his disciples forbiddeth him among other things to permitt his hart to bee preoccupated by any desire; so great knowledg had hee of this defect.

§. 2. You say, if wee must not desire vertues, wherefore hath our Lord sayed, aske and it shalbe giuen you. O my daughter? when I say that vvee must not aske nor desire any thing, I intend terestriall things: as for vertues wee mey aske them, and demaunding the loue of God, wee comprehēd them all therein; for it contayneth them all. But for the exteriour imployment, should wee not (say you) desire base offices, because they are more paynfull, and there is more to bee donne, and to humble ones selfe the more for God. My daughter, Dauid sayeth that hee did loue better to bee abiect in the house of our Lord, then to bee great among sinners: And it is good, Lord, (sayeth hee) that thou hast humbled mee, to the end I may learne thy iustifications: notvvithstandinh this desire is verie suspitious, and perhapps a humayne cogitation: what knovve you haueing desired abiect offices, whether you shall haue the courage to accept the abiections which you shall meete withall in them? it may bee there vvill happen many disgusts, and bitternesses; although that now you feele the courage to suffer mortification, and humiliation, what knovv you, if you shall allvvaies haue it? In breife wee must hold the desire of offices, whatsoeuer they bee, base or honorable, for a tentation, it is allwaies better to desire nothing, but to prepare our selues to receaue those, obedience shall impose vpon vs, and bee they honourable or abiect, I would take and receaue them humbly, without speaking one onelie word, vnlesse my superiour did questiō mee, and then I would simply aunsweere the truth, as I should thinke it.

§. 3. You aske me hovv wee may practice this document of holie indifferency, in sicknes, I find in the holy Gospell a perfect modele in Sainct Peters wiues mother: this good woman lyeing sicke in her bed in a great feuer did practice many vertues: but that which I most admire is the great neglect she had of her selfe, relying on the diuine prouidence, and the care of her Superiours, remayning in her feuer trāquille and without any vnquietnesse, nor giueing any to those who were about her: notvvithstanding euerie one knovveth hovv much those vvho are in feuers are molested, which hindreth them from repose, and giueth them a thousand other vexations. Novv this great resignation that our sicke made of her selfe into the hands of her superiours, caused her that she vvas not vnquiett, nor did she take care for her health or her cure, she vvas content to suffer her sicknes vvith mildenesse and patience: O God! hovv happie was this good vvoman! Truelie she did deserue that they should take care of her, as also the Apostles did, vvho prouided for her cure, not being solicited by her; but by charitie and commiseration of vvhat she suffered. Happie shall those Religious persons bee, who shall make this great and absolute referring of themselues into the hands of their superiours: vvho by the motion of Charitie shall serue them, and shall carefullie prouide for all their

wants

vvants and necessities: for Charitie is more strong and presseth more neere then nature. This good sicke vvoman did knovv that our Lord vvas in Capharnaum, that hee cured the sicke: and yet she vvas not vnquiet, nor troubled nother selfe to send to tell him vvhat shee suffered, but that vvhich is more admirable, is this: That she seeing him in the house, vvhere hee beheld her, and she also beheld him, yet she did not speake one vvord to him of her infirmitie, to excite him to haue pitty vpon her, nor pressehim to touch her for to bee healed. Novv this vnquietnes of mind that vvee haue in sufferance, and sicknesses (to the vvhich are subiect not onelie vvordly persons, but also verie often the Religious) springeth from the disorderlie loue of our selues.

Our sicke sister maketh not any account of her sicknes, she is not forvvard to recount it, she suffereth it without careing whether they bemoane her, or procure her health, or no; she is content that our Lord knovveth it, and her superiours vvho gouerne her, she seeth our Lord in the house as a soueraygne Phisition; but regardeth him not as such (so little thinketh she of her recouerie) she rather considereth him as her God, to vvhom she appertayneth asvvell sicke as in health: being asmuch content to bee sicke as to possesse perfect health.

O hovv many vvould haue vsed sleights to bee cured by our Lord, and vvould haue sayed, that they asked health the better to serue him, fearing something should bee vvanting to him.

But this good vvoman thought of nothing lesse then this, making her resignation to appeere in that she did not require her health: notvvihstanding I vville not say, but that vve

may

may aske it of our Lord as of him vvho can giue it, vvith this condition if such be his vvill: for vve ought alvvaies to say *Fiat voluntas tua:* it is not sufficient to bee sicke and to haue afflictions, beccause God vvould haue it so; but it must bee as hee vvill, and as long a time as hee vvill, and in the manner it pleaseth him that it should bee, not making any choise of any sicknes or affliction vvhatsoeuer, hovv abiect or dishonorable it may seeme to bee: for sicknes and affliction vvithout abiection verie often svvelleth the hart in stead of humbling it: but vvhen vve haue sicknes vvithout honour, or vvith dishonour it selfe, disestimation and abiection are our malady; hovv many occasions are there then to exercise patience, humilitie, modesty and svveetnesse of mind and hart.

Lett vs therefore haue a great care, as this good vvomā had, to keepe our hart in mildnesse, making profitt as she did of our sicknesses: for she did rise so soone as our Lord had chaced avvaye the feuer, and serued him at the table, vvherein certaynlie she demonstrated great vertue, and the profitt she had made of her sicknes, of the vvhich being quitted, she vvould not vse her health but for the seruice of our Lord; imploying herselfe therein in the same instant that she had receaued it.

Besides; she vvas not like persons of the vvorld, vvho hauing a sicknes of some dayes, must haue vveekes and monthes to restore themselues.

Our Lord vppon the Crosse, maketh vs to see very vvell, hovv vvee ought to mortifie these delicacies: for haueing extreame thirst, hee did not aske to drinke, but simply manifested his necessitie, saying, I am thirsty: after vvhich hee perfomed an act of verie great submission, for some one hauing offered him on the point of a launce, a peece of sponge moistned in vineger to quēch his thirst, hee sucked

sucked it with his blessed lipps: a strang thing! he vvas not ignorant that this vvas a draught vvhich should augment his payne: neuerthelesse hee tooke it simply, not makeing shew that it did trouble him: that hee had not found it good, to teach vs vvith vvhat submission vvee ought to take the remedies and meates presented vs vvhen vvee are sicke, not so much as makeing shevve that vvee are disgusted and greeued, yea allso vvhen vvee shal be in doubt that this vvill increase our disease. Alas! haueing neuer so little incommodity wee doe quite contrarie to that vvhich our svveete Maister hath taught vs: for vvee cease not to lament, and find not persones sufficient, as it seemeth, to bemoane our case, and to recount our greefes by parcells vnto vs, our payne vvhatsoeuer it bee is incomparable, and those that others suffer are nothing in respect; vvee are more melancholy and impatient then can bee declared, vvee find nothing that goeth as it ought, to content vs. In fine it is great pitty to see hovv little vve are the true imitatours of our Sauiour, vvho did forgett his greefes, and endeauoured not to haue them marked by men, contenting himselfe that his eternall father by vvhose obedience he suffered did consider them, and vvould cease his anger tovvardes humayne nature, for the vvhich hee did suffer.

§. 4. You aske vvhat I desire should remayne most ingrauen in your mind, the better to put it in practice: Ah! vvhat shall I say to you, my most deare daughters, but these tvvo deare vvordes, that I haue allreadie so much recommended vnto you? desire nothing, refuse nothing, in these tvvo wordes I say all: for this document comprehendeth the perfect practice of indifferencie. Behould the poore little Iesus in the crib, hee receaued pouertie, nakednes, the companie of beastes, all the iniuries of the of the time, colde, and all that his father permitted to arriue vnto him : it is not vvritten that hee euer put forth his hāds to haue the breast of his mother, hee left himselfe wholie to her care and prouidence nether did hee refuse those little comforts that she offered him, hee receaued the seruices of Sainct Ioseph, the Adoration of the three Kinges, and of the shepheards, with equall indifferency : euen so vvee ought neither to desire nor refuse any thing, but to suffer and receaue equallie all that the prouidence of God shall permitt to happen vnto vs: God giue vs his grace so to doe. Amen.

GOD BEE BLESSED.

Out of the same Authour.

AN exercise for the morneing, vvhich being breife, simple, and tending immediatly to the loueing vnion of our vvill vvith the will of God, may bee practiced by persons who are in drinesse, sterilitie, and corporall weaknes, or ouerwhelmed with businesses.

The first point : prostrate on your knees, and profoundlie humbled before the incomprehensible Maiesty of God, doe you adore his soueraygne goodnes, vvho from all eternitie hath named you by your name, ād determined to saue you, ordayning among other things this present day, to the end that there-in you should come to exercise the workes of life and saluation, according to that which is sayed by the Prophet. I haue loued thee vvith perpetuall charitie, therefore I haue dravvne the haueing pittie of thee.

The second Point: vppon this veritable thought, you shall

you shal vnite your vvill to that of the most benigne and most mercifull celestiall father, by these or the like words cordially offerred. O most svveete vvill of my God, be thou euer fulfilled in mee. O eternall designes of the vvill of my God, I adore you, consecrat and dedicate my vvill, for to vvill eternally that which thou hast willed! O that I could doe therefore this day, and allvvaies, and in all things thy diuine will! O my sweete creatour! yea celestiall father, for such was thy good pleasure from all eternitie, So be it. O most delectable goodnes, bee it as thou hast willed! O eternall will, liue and raigne in all my wills, and ouer all my wills now & for euer Amen. The third Point. After inuocate the diuine helpe and assistance with these or the like deuoute acclamations, interiourlie notwithstanding, and from the depth of the hart. O God intēd vnto my helpe! Let thy helping hand bee vpon this poore and weake heart of mine. Behould O Lord this poore and miserable heart vvhich through thy goodnes hath conceaued many holie affectiōs: but Alas! it is to feeble and vvretched to effectuate the good it desireth vvithout thy helpe. I inuocate the most sacred virgin Marie, my good Angell and all the court of heauen, that their fauour may novv bee propitious vnto mee, if thou pleasest. The fourth Point. Make then a liuelie and povverfull Louing vnion of your vvill vvith Gods holie vvill, and then among all the actions of that day asvvell spirituall as corporall, make frequent revnions there-of; that is to say, renevv and confirme agayne the vniō made in the morning, casting a simple interiour looke vppon the diuine goodnes and saying by vvay of yealding (or) agreemēt. Yeas, Lord, I vvill, yeas my father: yeas allvvaies, yea. Also if you vvill you may make the signe of the Crosse, or kisse that vvhich you beare about you, or so-

or ſome Image; for all this ſignifieth that ſoueraynelie you deſire the prouidence of God, that you accept it, that you adore it, and loue it vvith all your hart, and that inſeparably you vnite your will to that ſupreme vvill, notvviſtāding all trouble and repugnance. The fift point. But theſe tracts of the hart, theſe interiour vvordes ought to bee pronounced ſvveetely, quietly, and cōſtantly; but peaceably, and by way of ſpeech, they ought to bee diſtilled, and ſpun as it vvere gently from the top of the ſpiritt, as vve pronunce a vvorde in the eare of a freind, that we vvould caſt deepe into his heart, that noe bodie may heare or perceaue it; for ſo theſe ſacred vvordes drayvne ſliding, and diſtilling from the intimate depth of our ſoule vvill penetrate and moiſten it more intimately, and ſtrongly then they vvould doe if they vvere ſayed by vvay of iaculatorie prayers and ſallies of the ſpiritt, experience vvill make you knovv this, prouided you bee humble and ſimple. so bee it.

GOD BEE BLESSED
FOR EVER.

A TA-

A TABLE OF THE INTERTAINMENTS.

THE FIRST ENTERTAYNMENT.

OF CONSTITVTIONS.

IN the vvhich is declared the obligation of the Constitutiōs of the Visitation of Saincte Marie, & the qualities of the deuotiō that the Religious vvomē of the said Order ought to haue.

THE SECOND ENTERTAYNEMENT.

OF CONFIDENCE.

VVHerein is demaunded if vve may approch to God vvith great confidence: namely hauing the feeling of our miserie: & hovv; and of the perfect forsakeing of ones selfe.

THE THIRD ENTERTAYNEMENT.

OF CONSTANCIE.

VPon the flight of our Lord into Egipt, vvherin is treated of the constancie vvhich

THE FOVRTH ENTERTAYNEMENT.

OF CORDIALITIE.

THE FIFT ENTERTAYNEMENT.

OF GENEROSITIE.

THE SIXT ENTERTAYNEMENT.

OF HOPE.

THE SEAVENTH ENTERTAYNEMENT.

OF THREE SPIRITVALL LAVVES.

THE EIGHT ENTERTAYNEMENT.

OF DISAPPROPRIATION.

Of Disappropriation & depriuation of all things.

THE NINTH ENTERTAINEMENT.

OF MODESTIE.

In the which is treated of the modestie & manner of receauing corrections: & of the meanes so to establish his state in God, that nothing may be able to diuert it

THE TENTH ENTERTAINEMENT.

OF OBEDIENCE.

THE ELEAVENTH ENTERTAINEMENT.

OF THE VERTUE OF Obedience.

Vpon the same subiect of the vertue of Obedience.

THE TVVELVETH ENTERTAINEMENT.

Of Simplicitie, and Religious prudence.

THE THIRTENTH ENTERTAINEMENT.

OF THE SPIRIT OF RULES.

Of Rules: and of the spiritt of the Visitation.

THE

THE FOVVRETENTH ENTERTAINEMENT.

OF PROPER JUDGEMENT.

AGainst proper Iudgment, and the delicacie vvee haue tovvards our selues.

THE FIFTENTH ENTERTAINEMENT.

OF THE VVILL OF GOD.

IN the vvhich is demaunded, vvhere-in the perfect determination of regarding, & follovving the vvill of God in all things consisteth, & vvhether vvee may bee able to find it, and follovv it in the vvills of our superiours, equalls, or inferiours, vvhich vve see to proceede of their naturall inclinations, or habitudes, and of certaine notable pointes, touching Confessours and Preachers.

THE SIXTEENTH ENTERTAINEMENT.

OF AVERSIONS.

TOuching auersions: hovv bookes ought to be receaued: and that vve ought not to be astonished in beholding imperfections in Religious persones, nor in Superiours themselues.

THE SEAVENTEENTH ENTERTAINEMENT.

OF VOICES.

VVHeerin is demaunded hovv, and vpon vvhat motiue voices are to be giuen asvvell to those they vvill admitt to profession,

as to

For Product Safety Concerns and Information please contact our EU representative GPSR@taylorandfrancis.com Taylor & Francis Verlag GmbH, Kaufingerstraße 24, 80331 München, Germany

T - #0035 - 270225 - C0 - 216/138/20 [22] - CB - 9780754604433 - Gloss Lamination